HIGHER

MODERN STUDIES
SOCIAL ISSUES IN THE UK

Frank Cooney, Gary Hughes,
and David Sheerin

HODDER
GIBSON
AN HACHETTE UK COMPANY

The Publishers would like to thank the following for permission to reproduce copyright material:

Photo credits: p.6 © Matt West/BPI/REX Features; **p.10** © Copyright photo by Murdo MacLeod. All Rights Reserved; **p.12** © Jeffrey Blackler / Alamy; **p.15** (top) © Mark Thomas/REX Features, (bottom) © Mellimage – Fotolia; **p.16** © Jeff J Mitchell/Getty Images; **p.17** © Tom Kidd / Alamy; **p.22** © Policy Echange/ https://www.flickr.com/photos/policyexchange/7929568108/sizes/l/https://creativecommons.org/licenses/by/2.0/; **p.23** © byrdyak – Fotolia; **p.26** ©Mirrorpix/ George Whitelaw published in the Daily Mirror on the 2nd December 1942/British Cartoon Archive, University of Kent, www.cartoons.ac.uk; **p.30** (top) © 67photo / Alamy, (bottom) © say_cheddar/https://www.flickr.com/photos/29271559/https://creativecommons.org/licenses/by/2.0/deed.en_GB; **p.38** © Sean Gladwell - Fotolia.com; **p.39** © Agence DER – Fotolia; **p.41** © geogphotos / Alamy; **p.47** (top) © Alan Wilson / Alamy, (bottom) © Shirokazan/https:// www.flickr.com/photos/shirokazan/5998972614/https://creativecommons.org/licenses/by/2.0/(21Aug2014); **p.50** (left to right) © Epicscotland / Alamy, © Christopher Furlong/Getty Images, © PHIL NOBLE/Reuters/Corbis; **p.53** © PhotoEd – Fotolia; **p.61** Report of the Ministerial Task Force on Health Inequalities, Crown Copyright. Public sector information licensed under the Open Government Licence v1.0. /http://www.nationalarchives.gov.uk/doc/ open-government-licence/; **p.64** (left) © Crown Copyright/http://commons.wikimedia.org/wiki/File:Nicola_Sturgeon_2.jpg/ Open Government Licence v1.0, (right) ©JJAVA – Fotolia; **p.66** © NHS Greater Glasgow and Clyde; **p.70** ©Leon Neal/AFP/Getty Images; **p.71** © Geraint Lewis / Alamy; **p.86** © Steve Back/REX features; **p.88** ©PA Archive/Press Association Images; **p.90** © Per Andersen / Alamy; **p.101** ©Monkey Business – Fotolia; **p.104** ©Leon Neal/AFP/ Getty Images; **p.105** ©2003 Graeme Hunter / TopFoto; **p.108** © BWP Media via Getty Images; **p.115** © Arto – Fotolia; **p.117** © Daily Record/Mirrorpix; **p.120** © Dan Kitwood/Getty Images; **p.125** ©PA Wire/Press Association Images; **p.127** © Scottish Government and YouthLink; **p.128** © Demotix/Press Association Images; **p.130** © Rex Features; **p.131** ©PA Archive/Press Association Images; **p.134** © Christopher Furlong/Getty Images; **p.135** © Findlay / Alamy; **p.136** The Sun 11/09/2011 © News Syndication; **p.139** © Scottish Prison Service; **p.142** ©PA Archive/Press Association Images; **p.145** © Andrew Fox / Alamy; **p.146** ©Lucy Young/REX Features; **p.151** © Crown Copyright/http://commons.wikimedia.org/wiki/File:Kenny_MacAskill,_Cabinet_Secretary_for_ Justice_%281%29.jpg/Open Government Licence v1.0; **p.155** © David Sheerin; **p.157** © David Sheerin.

Chapter opener image reproduced on pages 1, 13, 25, 45, 69, 87, 97, 111, 123, 138 and 155 © Claudio Divizia – Fotolia.

Acknowledgements: Extract from 'Celtic chief executive Peter Lawwell defends decision not to pay staff a living wage at the club's Annual General Meeting' published on www.dailyrecord.co.uk, 15th November 2013, reproduced with the permission of Mirrorpix; Extract from 'Five Stories: The harsh realities of the Government's 'bedroom tax' by Frances Ryan, copyright *The New Statesman*, 12th February 2013; Extract from 'Anxiety over Atos fit-for-work test brings on father's heart attack' by David Taylor, published in *The Daily Record*, 25th March 2013, reproduced with the permission of Mirrorpix; Extract from 'SWA should drop challenge' reproduced with the permission of *The Herald* and *Sunday Herald* © Newsquest (Herald and Times) Ltd; Extract from 'Doctors warn austerity is damaging patients' health' by Stephen Naysmith, reproduced with the permission of *The Herald* and *Sunday Herald* © Newsquest (Herald and Times) Ltd; Extract from 'Report reveals huge level of racial inequality in Scottish public sector workplace' by Martin Williams, reproduced with the permission of *The Herald* and *Sunday Herald* © Newsquest (Herald and Times) Ltd; Extract from 'Crown loses appeal against "lenient" sentence given to motorist who killed two cyclists' by Catriona Webster, reproduced with the permission of *The Herald* and *Sunday Herald* © Newsquest (Herald and Times) Ltd; Extract from 'World's End pub murders: Angus Sinclair could face retrial over 1977 deaths of teenagers Christine Eadie and Helen Scott' published on www.dailyrecord.co.uk, 16th April 2014, reproduced with the permission of Mirrorpix; Extract from 'Glasgow gang violence: David's story' by Jon Henley, copyright Guardian News & Media Ltd 2011; Extract from 'Elderly hit by new telephone scam' by Kyle Caldwell and Jessica Winch © Telegraph Media Group Limited 2013; Extract from 'Identity theft costs the UK £2.7 billion' by Lois Avery reproduced by permission of Confused.com; *Extract from 'Hundreds of police carry weapons in Scotland' by Chris Marchall reproduced by permission of The Scotsman Publications Limited*; Extract from 'Let us have sex equality in our policy on prisons' by Iain Macwhirter, reproduced with the permission of *The Herald* and *Sunday Herald* © Newsquest (Herald and Times) Ltd; The table on qualitative and quantitative research is reproduced with permission from Snap Surveys Ltd, www.snapsurveys.com; Extract from the Prescription Charges Coalition's 2013 report: *Paying the Price: Prescription Charges and People with Long-term conditions* is reproduced with the permission of the Prescription Charges Coalition, www.prescriptionchargescoalition.org.uk.

Every effort has been made to trace all copyright holders, but if any have been inadvertently overlooked the Publishers will be pleased to make the necessary arrangements at the first opportunity.

Although every effort has been made to ensure that website addresses are correct at time of going to press, Hodder Gibson cannot be held responsible for the content of any website mentioned in this book. It is sometimes possible to find a relocated web page by typing in the address of the home page for a website in the URL window of your browser.

Hachette UK's policy is to use papers that are natural, renewable and recyclable products and made from wood grown in sustainable forests. The logging and manufacturing processes are expected to conform to the environmental regulations of the country of origin.

Orders: please contact Bookpoint Ltd, 130 Park Drive, Abingdon, Oxon OX14 4SE. Telephone: (44) 01235 827720. Fax: (44) 01235 400454. Lines are open 9.00–5.00, Monday to Saturday, with a 24-hour message answering service. Visit our website at www.hoddereducation.co.uk. Hodder Gibson can be contacted direct on: Tel: 0141 848 1609; Fax: 0141 889 6315; email: hoddergibson@hodder.co.uk.

Impression number   5 4 3

Year   2018 2017 2016

Cover photo © Jonathan Stutz

Typeset in Minion Pro 12/15 by Integra Software Servises Pvt. Ltd., Pondicherry, India

Printed in Italy

A catalogue record for this title is available from the British Library

ISBN: 978 1471 835841

Contents

Section 2   Crime and the law in the UK

Section 3   Assessment

Evidence and causes of social inequality

Groups in society experience different life outcomes due to the complexities of the twenty-first century. Opportunities for access to areas such as occupation, wealth, income and health, vary between different groups based on social class, age, gender and race. The reasons for these inequalities are complex, and tackling these differences is a priority for all governments in the UK.

Poverty

Poverty is difficult to accurately define. It varies from society to society and may not be as obvious as looking simply at someone's income. Poverty is dynamic and it varies depending on a number of factors. For example, many workers in the UK gain employment on a cyclical basis and at some stages in the year they are relatively well off, but at other points in the year they may experience great hardship. Material deprivation refers to an individual's or a group's low chances of gaining assets or purchasing material goods. As a society we sometimes have a narrow visual awareness of poverty. For example, the latest gadgets, clothes and goods are often seen as a measurement of wealth, but these products may have been gained using high interest loans and so would not be an accurate way of assessing someone's wealth. The UK and Scottish Governments, therefore, define poverty with regards to a household's income.

Absolute poverty

Absolute poverty refers to individuals not having the things they need to survive, such as food, clothing, shelter and energy. This level of poverty is traditionally much more prevalent in developing countries, but it is still present in developed countries such as the UK.

Case study: Barnardo's – the reality of living in poverty

The children's charity Barnardo's claims that in order to remain above absolute poverty a family must be able to afford £12 per day per person. This needs to cover:

- all of their day-to-day expenditure, including necessities such as food and transport
- occasional items such as new shoes and clothes, school trips and activities for children, and replacing broken household items such as washing machines and kitchen equipment
- all household bills such as electricity, gas and water, telephone bills, and television licences.

Relative poverty

It is clear that within Britain poverty is not at the levels of squalor and starvation that are seen in less developed countries. Therefore, a distinction is made between absolute poverty and relative poverty in Britain. People who are in relative poverty may just be able to afford basic things such as food, energy and rent, but they are in poverty relative to someone on a higher income. This can affect households in a number of ways, such as not being able to take part in social activities like attending weddings or birthday parties. People in relative poverty may also not be able to afford to pay for goods that are seen to improve our daily lives, such as a car or a holiday.

Each household's income, adjusted for a family's individual circumstances, is compared to the UK's median income (the 'median' is the halfway point – half of households in the UK are below the median, half above). The UK and Scottish Governments agree that households with less than 60 per cent of the median income are classified as being in relative income poverty. This 'poverty line' stood at £251 per week in 2013 for a household of two adults with no children, although this figure varies depending on who lives in the household. In a household with two adults and two children under 13, the threshold rises to £317 per week. However, although this definition is agreed across the European Union (EU), there are some issues with using a measure of poverty based on a median of national income. For example, one problem of using this definition is that if a country gets poorer on the whole, the number of people categorised as poor can actually go down. Also, in today's society with the gap between rich and poor increasing, the official poverty line may not truly reflect the level at which households suffer hardship.

Living standards, poverty and inequality in the UK

The Joseph Rowntree Foundation and the Institute for Fiscal Studies (IFS) carried out a long-term review of the changing living standards of the UK and published their report in 2012. The key findings were:

- Recent forecasts by IFS researchers have suggested that the poverty line will continue to fall until 2015–16. This will represent the biggest drop since the early 1960s.
- There is evidence of a growing gap between rich and poor. Since the global recession started in 2008, the share of the UK's wealth belonging to the 'super rich' has increased, with less wealth to share among others.

Show your understanding

1 Describe, in detail, what difficulties there are when defining poverty.
2 Explain, with examples, the key differences between absolute and relative poverty.
3 Why could the poverty line be seen as an unreliable measure of poverty?
4 According to the Joseph Rowntree Foundation and the IFS, what are the key trends with regards to poverty in the UK?

Classifications of poverty

The reasons for poverty vary and it is difficult to measure over short periods of time. Typically, those in poverty are classified as follows:

- Persistent poverty – where someone experiences long periods of poverty possibly due to long-term unemployment.
- Recurrent poverty – many occupations are cyclical in nature. Those working in outdoor

activities such as skiing may find that during the summer months they may experience poverty.

- Transient poverty – some people, because of personal circumstances, may find themselves in poverty only briefly.

When measuring poverty, the UK and Scottish Governments gain only a snapshot of poverty in a short time frame. This causes difficulties when comparing poverty over long periods of time. However, from the statistics on poverty both governments and social scientists have targeted long-term poverty when producing policy and recommendations. A number of key theories have emerged over time as explanations for the causes of poverty.

Causes of poverty

With regards to those in persistent or recurring poverty, a well-known theory on why some people cannot escape poverty is the cycle of poverty or the poverty trap (Figure 1.1).

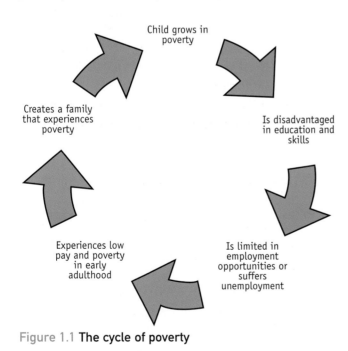

Figure 1.1 **The cycle of poverty**

Figure 1.1 explains why, once trapped in poverty, families can spend generations within poverty. Families in poverty often do not have the resources to get out of their situation, such as financial capital or the skills or education needed to raise their earnings. This cycle was highlighted in 2012 at the Conservative Party Conference when the Work and Pensions Secretary Iain Duncan Smith cited the example that three generations of the same family have never worked and so he made changes to the benefits system to 'make work pay' in order to try to break the cycle of poverty.

One major factor in creating the poverty trap is unemployment. This is sometimes referred to as 'worklessness' and it is seen as a major problem, with 3.7 million working-age (childless) households having no one in employment – 18 per cent of total households. However, when looking at households that have workless parents and unemployed grown-up children, this figure drops to 0.9 per cent, so cross-generational worklessness is perhaps overstated by some commentators in the media and in politics. This does not underestimate the issue of worklessness and its relationship with the poverty trap.

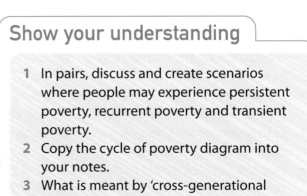

Show your understanding

1 In pairs, discuss and create scenarios where people may experience persistent poverty, recurrent poverty and transient poverty.
2 Copy the cycle of poverty diagram into your notes.
3 What is meant by 'cross-generational worklessness'?

Social exclusion

Social exclusion is a term used to explain the impact of poverty on individuals and groups. It relates to the extent to which people are unable to participate in aspects of society because they are in poverty. This impacts on a variety of experiences including education, health and housing.

According to the World Health Organization (WHO), social exclusion leads to 'a continuum of inclusion/exclusion characterised by unequal access to resources, capabilities and rights which leads to health inequalities and reduced life chances'.

The reality of social exclusion is that those in poverty experience a level of exclusion in participating fully in society. This limits their access to fundamental human rights, which has a knock-on effect and contributes to the poverty cycle as social exclusion prevents people from achieving their full potential. Young people being brought up in low income households are more likely to suffer poor physical and mental health, struggle at school and have a higher chance of experiencing unemployment and poverty in later life.

Social exclusion, therefore, is a key consequence of poverty and reveals the huge inequalities that exist in society. For more on the impact of poverty on key groups, see Chapter 2. For an analysis of how the UK Government has attempted to address the barriers and difficulties that contribute to inequality, see Chapter 3. For analysis of gender and ethnic minority inequalities, see Chapter 5.

Fact file

Groups at risk of social exclusion

- Lower levels of skills through poor education attainment lead to a greater risk of unemployment and low paid employment.
- Unemployment or low paid work results in some people not being able to participate in social networks such as being members of exercise clubs or activity groups.
- The size and type of family can create a situation of social exclusion. For example, lone parents may find themselves less likely to gain well-paid employment because of their childcare needs. Also, large families may find themselves with higher costs and so have less disposable income.
- Children from lower income backgrounds may not be able to participate in many activities such as school trips or after-school clubs. This can affect their self-esteem and contribute towards the cycle of poverty.
- Disability and long-term ill-health are also more likely to result in social exclusion. There will be less access to employment and increased living costs.
- Elderly people are often on fixed incomes through the state pension and so rising living costs can push many into poverty.
- Women are generally at higher risk of social exclusion as they are usually more involved in unpaid care work (such as for their children or elderly parents). They are also more likely to be in lower paid employment or part-time work and tend to have lower pensions.
- Those from ethnic minority groups frequently experience more social exclusion because of discrimination and racism. This impacts on their access to high paid work and contributes to the cycle of poverty.

The impact of social exclusion

The Joseph Rowntree Foundation has published several recent reports looking at the impact of social exclusion. It looked in detail at the lack of socially perceived 'necessities' experienced by those in poverty. Some of their key findings at the beginning were:

- Around 8 million people in the UK cannot afford one or more essential household goods.
- Almost 7.5 million people are too poor to engage in common social activities considered necessary by most of the population.
- 2 million British children go without at least two things they need.
- About 6.5 million adults go without essential clothing.
- 4 million people are not properly fed by today's standards.
- Over 10.5 million suffer financial insecurity.

In 2012 the think-tank Demos revealed the full extent of social exclusion and the difficulties faced by those in poverty across Scotland. The report called *A Wider Lens* found that Glasgow is the worst affected area, with more than one in ten families facing severe disadvantages. Families in Glasgow often find themselves experiencing disadvantages such as low income, unemployment, no educational qualifications, ill health, poor mental health and life in poor neighbourhoods. This means that Glasgow has proportionately more families living in severely excluded and disadvantaged situations than any other city in the UK. The report also identified lone parents in large urban areas in social rented housing as the group most likely to suffer severe social exclusion. The Chief Executive of Scottish charity Quarriers said: 'This report paints a truly bleak picture of what life is like for thousands of families across Scotland who experience social exclusion and inequality every day.'

Show your understanding

1 Limiting your answer to 140 characters, create a tweet defining 'social exclusion' in your own words.
2 Look at the Fact File on groups at risk of social exclusion. Rank the eight groups in order of which you feel are most likely to suffer social exclusion. Give reasons for choosing each of your top three groups.
3 Using the information about the impact of social exclusion, create a mind map using illustrations to show your understanding.

Social class

Social class can be defined as a large category of similarly ranked people according to their occupation, education, lifestyle, income and/or wealth. Historically in Britain, social class had a huge impact on the future prosperity of individuals and there were clear lines between the upper, middle and lower classes. This is perhaps best illustrated in the hugely popular television series *Downtown Abbey* in which the lives of both the wealthy upper classes and their lower class servants are characterised in a drama series. These different groups rarely mixed and lived completely different lives. In more recent times, the issue of class is less prevalent but many social commentators insist that a class system still exists, albeit in a more complex way. The UK and Scottish Governments recognise social class when they analyse data relating to a variety of statistics. Since the beginning of the twentieth century, the UK and Scottish Governments have broadly classified people into the Registrar-General's Social Class (RGSC) model. This relates to the occupation of people and makes distinctions between the social standing of occupations in the community:

A	Professional occupations
B	Managerial and technical occupations
C1	Non-manual skilled occupations
C2	Manual skilled occupations
D	Partly skilled occupations
E	Unskilled occupations

This model, which sometimes expresses the six categories in roman numerals from I to VI, is useful as it is easy to understand. It is still used today when sociologists and political scientists analyse statistics relating to society, such as crime and health statistics. Election data is also analysed this way to compare the voting habits of different social groups. However, there are many problems by simplifying class in this way. For example, the RGSC model does not take into account the huge variations in income for certain occupations. For example, most plumbers make a decent wage, but if they expand and make a large business out of their skills then they could earn a very comfortable living. The model also does not take into account other people in society who do not fit into the occupational categories such as those who are retired or unemployed.

Since the beginning of the twenty-first century the UK and Scottish Governments have used more detailed models of measuring social class as the occupational profile of society has grown ever more complex. Various models are now used by government departments to analyse changes in society. Since 2001, the Office for National Statistics (ONS) has used the National Statistics Socio-Economic Classification (NS-SEC) (Table 1.1). This model further breaks down various occupations into classifications and takes into account sections of society such as people who are long-term unemployed. This allows the government to target resources and help develop policy. However, in the 2011 Census further sub-division was needed so that reliable and accurate information could be gathered. In total, 42 classifications of occupations were used. All government departments use this data to shape policy and track changes to society.

It is widely recognised by sociologists that the issue of social class extends far beyond occupation and wealth. Indeed, in modern society there are many examples of well-known people from working-class backgrounds who have become very successful.

Wayne Rooney

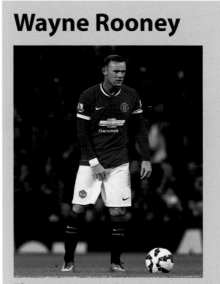

Figure 1.3 Wayne Rooney

The professional footballer Wayne Rooney was born in Croxteth, Liverpool, and went to a state comprehensive school. He was raised in a traditional working-class area and with working-class values. He is now a world-class footballer and a multi-millionaire, but his close family and friends maintain that he is still 'working class'.

Table 1.1 **National Statistics Socio-Economic Classification**

	Classification		Description/examples
1	Higher managerial, administrative and professional occupations		
	1.1	Large employers and higher managerial and administrative occupations	Company directors, senior managers, senior civil servants, senior police officers
	1.2	Higher professional occupations	Doctors, lawyers, teachers and social workers
2	Lower managerial, administrative and professional occupations		Nurses, journalists, actors, musicians, lower ranks in the police and armed forces
3	Intermediate occupations		Clerks, secretaries, driving instructors, telephone fitters
4	Small employers and own account workers		Publicans, farmers, window cleaners, painters and decorators
5	Lower supervisory and technical occupations		Printers, plumbers, television engineers, butchers
6	Semi-routine occupations		Shop assistants, hairdressers, bus drivers, cooks
7	Routine occupations		Couriers, labourers, waiters, refuse collectors
8	Never worked and long-term unemployed		Non-working spouses, unemployed for various reasons
	'Not classified' is added to cover students and other groups		

Source: Office for National Statistics

Changes to social class

Radical changes in modern society took place during the twentieth century. Perhaps the greatest driver in these changes was the movement from an industrial economy to a service economy. Britain was once known as the 'workshop of the world', but we have seen most manufacturing move on to developing economies. According to the 1911 Census, only 15 per cent of the workforce belonged to AB occupations (professional and management), but by 2011 this figure increased to nearly 40 per cent. There have also been huge increases in C1 occupations (civil servants and office workers). This reflects the growing number of people entering the middle classes as Britain has lost its traditional heavy industries such as mining and shipbuilding. This movement is referred to as 'class dealignment'

and it means that as people have moved from traditional working class into lower middle class they have changed many of their cultures and traditions.

As a result of the changes to occupations as well as many cultural changes, we have seen huge variations in the gender patterns of the workplace. In the early twentieth century, men dominated the jobs market, with most women almost exclusively consigned to jobs involving domestic service such as maids. Some women were also expected to give up employment once married. With the huge social changes that have taken place, we now see women equalling men with regards to the number in jobs – around 12.5 million. However, there remain huge inequalities between the types of occupations undertaken by women, with many in part-time and service industries (see Chapter 5).

Socio-economic status

A variety of other measurements aim to take into consideration additional factors that may determine someone's social class. Indeed, some sociologists have come to see classification by occupation as too simplistic and argue that social class actually has three dimensions: economic, social and cultural. The wider socio-economic attributes of individuals are perhaps a better measurement of position in society. In the twenty-first century we should perhaps look to measure an individual's 'resources' in each of the following areas, which can collectively be referred to as 'capital':

- Economic capital – this relates to someone's wealth in the form of money or assets such as properties. The global financial crisis of 2008 and its recession have largely made class divisions more defined rather than less so.
- Cultural capital – this goes beyond wealth and looks into someone's lifestyle. This term relates to the types of people and activities you may be associated with, such as whether you are a member of a political party or a pressure group.
- Social capital – this looks at someone's interests, and could relate to your education, your participation in social activities and what you do in your spare time.

Social class is therefore not as obvious as it once was. In the early twenty-first century, class boundaries have become blurred as attitudes play a bigger role than income in defining social groups. However, although not as clear as previous generations, there are still divisions in society based on a person's socio-economic status. This has a huge potential impact on an individual's health, living standards and life chances, and is known as social inequality.

Show your understanding

1 Explain, in detail, the ways in which the idea of social class is defined.
2 In groups, come up with three individuals in society who challenge the traditional view of social class and explain why.
3 Explain what is meant by the term 'class dealignment'.
4 In your own words, explain why it may be more useful to look at an individual's socio-economic status rather than occupation. Give examples in your answer.

Social inequality

Following the financial crisis of 2008 and the resulting recession, we have seen the gap between the rich and poor within the UK grow. According to the Joseph Rowntree Foundation, average incomes of the lowest social groups D and E have fallen by 8 per cent. As a result, around 2 million people in the UK live in households whose income is below the poverty line level given in 2008. In addition, the number of people in low paid occupations has risen to 5 million people who earn less than the living wage (see page 31). In contrast, according to the Organisation for Economic Co-operation and Development (OECD) social groups A and B have seen much bigger proportional rises in their incomes than any other group. These changes have opened up the debate of class in today's society and have questioned how socially mobile the UK actually is – that is, the ability of people from lower classes to work their way up the class ladder.

A child born in one of the poorest areas in Scotland is three times more likely to be born into a home in which no one has a job and they are twice as likely to leave school with few qualifications. According to Save the Children, a child born in Lenzie, a more affluent area of

Glasgow, can expect to live 28 years longer than a child born in Calton, a more deprived area of the same city. The effects on health are stark, with children from households with incomes below £10,000 up to 2.5 times more likely to suffer chronic illness than households with incomes above £52,000. In terms of education, by three years old, children from deprived areas are already nine months behind the average developmental level for that age. Children entering secondary school from deprived backgrounds can expect to be 22 per cent behind their peers in reading and writing levels and 17 per cent behind in maths. Therefore, it is clear that social class still exists and impacts on our life chances. For more on the Lenzie and Calton areas of Glasgow, see page 47.

In fact, the debate on social class and social mobility has taken on more relevance in recent times in the age of austerity. Since 2010, the Coalition Government has tried to address the UK's national debt by making severe cuts to the Welfare State. There has been much scrutiny put on this Government as their slogan behind their election campaign was that they wanted to promote a Big Society where 'we're all in this together'. However, many commentators have pointed to the irony of this approach as many members of the Government are very wealthy and come from high class backgrounds. In May 2012, the *Telegraph* printed the headline 'Cabinet is worth £70 million' as it reported that, according to a consultancy firm, 19 out of the 29 Cabinet ministers had a personal wealth of over £1 million. Top of the list was the then Defence Secretary Philip Hammond, who is estimated to have a wealth of over £8.2 million. Prime Minister David Cameron came in at £3.8 million; however, both he and his wife stand to inherit over £23 million. The report described Mr Cameron as a 'Berkshire native, born into a wealthy family with distant ancestral links to the British monarchy'. In addition to this, 53 per cent of the Cabinet and one-third of the Shadow Cabinet attended private

educational institutions such as Eton, where annual fees can reach well above £30,000. This fact was criticised by former Cabinet Minister Baroness Warsi, who commented in 2014 that 'It can't be right that the 7 per cent of kids who go to independent school end up at the top tables, not just of politics, but banking, and law, and every other profession.' It is estimated that 75 per cent of judges, 70 per cent of finance directors, 45 per cent of top civil servants and 34 per cent of MPs were independently schooled. In contrast, the Scottish Parliament is far less elitist (Figure 1.4).

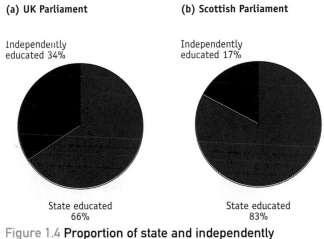

(a) **UK Parliament**

Independently educated 34%

State educated 66%

(b) **Scottish Parliament**

Independently educated 17%

State educated 83%

Figure 1.4 **Proportion of state and independently educated MPs and MSPs**

Social class, therefore, still has a huge impact on society. Many groups could be defined as 'disadvantaged' because the area you are from, the income of your household and the living standards you experience can have an affect on your whole life. Social mobility, although improving for some, still remains unachievable for many in the twenty-first century.

Poverty and social class in the age of austerity

Since the economic difficulties that began in 2008, Scotland and the UK's poverty profile has experienced some dramatic changes. A huge programme of UK Government cuts to the welfare bill, together with rising poverty, has pushed the problems of poverty and the ways of tackling it to the top of the political agenda. It has become one of the most talked-about aspects of society in the mass media and political discussions. Popular television programmes such as *The Scheme, Benefits Street* and *Famous, Rich and Hungry* focused on the experience of those in poverty and the trials and tribulations of their attempts to escape the cycle of poverty. The programme *Skint* aired in November 2013 and was a huge ratings winner for Channel 4, with an estimated 4 million viewers. The documentary centred on the experiences of those in low paid employment or on state benefits and the decisions they had to make in order to budget and juggle household bills on a limited income.

Figure 1.5 **Channel 4's *Skint* looked at how people survive without work**

In April 2014 Oxfam published a report called *A Tale of Two Britains: Inequality in the UK*, which showed the growing inequalities within Scotland and the UK. It focused on the gap between the richest in society and the poorest. Its key findings were outlined in a report by the *Guardian* newspaper with the headline 'Britain's five richest families worth more than poorest 20 per cent'. Oxfam said the poorest 20 per cent in the UK had wealth totalling £28.1 billion. This equates to an average of £2,230 per person.

This was compared to the 2014 *Forbes* magazine rich list, which showed that the five top UK entries – the family of the Duke of Westminster, David and Simon Reuben, the Hinduja brothers, the Cadogan family and Sports Direct retail boss Mike Ashley – between them had property, savings and other assets worth £28.2 billion.

The most affluent family in Britain, headed by Major General Gerald Grosvenor, owns prime real estate in Belgravia in London and has been a beneficiary of the foreign money flooding in to the capital's soaring property market in recent years. Oxfam said Grosvenor and his family had more wealth (£7.9 billion) than the poorest 10 per cent of the UK population (£7.8 billion).

According to Oxfam's Ben Phillips, 'Britain is becoming a deeply divided nation, with a wealthy elite who are seeing their incomes spiral up, while millions of families are struggling to make ends meet. It's deeply worrying that these extreme levels of wealth inequality exist in Britain today, where just a handful of people have more money than millions struggling to survive on the breadline.'

The report also showed that changes in income had been made even more adverse by increases in the cost of living over the past decade. 'Since 2005 the majority of the British public (95 per cent) have seen a 12 per cent real terms drop in their disposable income after housing costs, while the richest 5 per cent of the population have seen their disposable income increase.' The report goes on to say that for the first time more working households were in poverty than non-working ones, and predicted that the number of children living below the poverty line could increase by 800,000 by 2020. It said cuts to social security and public services together with falling real incomes and a rising cost of living are creating a 'deeply damaging situation' in which millions were struggling to get by. For more details on the Welfare Revolution, see page 36.

Case study: The rise of food banks

Following the economic crisis of 2008 and the cuts to the welfare budget, many of those in poverty are turning to local food banks in order to provide emergency groceries and supplies. This indicates a growth in absolute poverty within the UK. A report by the UK's largest food bank network the Trussell Trust reported that over 900,000 adults and children have received three days' emergency food and support from their food banks in the last 12 months, a 163 per cent rise on numbers helped in the previous financial year. Despite signs of economic recovery, the poorest have seen incomes squeezed even more than last year reports. More people are being referred to food banks than ever before.

The reasons for the rise in the use of food banks vary, but many commentators claim static incomes, rising living costs, low pay, underemployment and problems with welfare, especially sanctioning, are significant drivers of increased demand. Some 83 per cent of Trussell Trust food banks surveyed recently reported that benefits sanctions, which have become increasingly harsh, have caused more people to be referred to them for emergency food. Half of referrals to food banks in 2013–14 were as a result of benefit delays or changes.

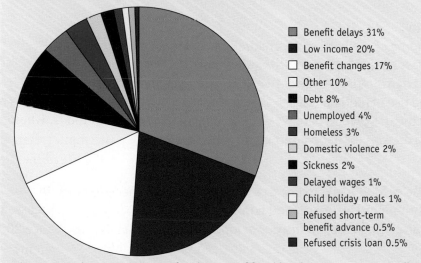

- Benefit delays 31%
- Low income 20%
- Benefit changes 17%
- Other 10%
- Debt 8%
- Unemployed 4%
- Homeless 3%
- Domestic violence 2%
- Sickness 2%
- Delayed wages 1%
- Child holiday meals 1%
- Refused short-term benefit advance 0.5%
- Refused crisis loan 0.5%

Figure 1.6 The main reasons for the use of food banks, 2013–14, Trussell Trust

Oxfam's Head of UK Poverty Programme, Rachael Orr, said: 'The fact that the number of people forced to turn to food banks has doubled in the last year and the situation is worsening for people in poverty is deeply worrying. Food banks and the thousands of people who support them are doing an impressive job in helping stop people from going hungry, but the truth is that in a country as rich as the UK there should not be food poverty at all. The Government needs to provide adequate support to the poorest in society and urgently tackle the low incomes and rising bills that are leaving people hungry.'

In March 2014 many Church leaders in England and Wales collectively called on the Government to tackle the emerging national crisis of food poverty and hunger in the UK. This has led to Frank Field, MP for Birkenhead, and Laura Sandys, MP for South Thanet, to launch an All-Party Parliamentary Group to investigate the root causes behind hunger, food poverty and the huge increase in demand for food banks across Britain. The group is looking into a variety of complex issues such as delays to benefit payments, benefit sanctions, stagnant wages and high food prices.

Figure 1.7 **A typical food bank**

Show your understanding

1 Explain the term 'social mobility'.
2 Create a mind map showing some of the barriers for children from deprived backgrounds.
3 Describe some of the social class issues that have surrounded the 2010 Coalition Government.
4 Outline the main findings of Oxfam's report *A Tale of Two Britains: Inequality in the UK*.
5 Look at the case study into the rise of food banks.
   a) What are the key trends in the use of food banks?
   b) What are some of the main reasons for people turning to food banks?

Develop your skills

6 Using the case study on the rise of food banks, come to a conclusion about the following:
   a) the impact of the benefit system on the use of food banks
   b) the impact of low income and rising costs on the use of food banks.

ICT task

Go to **http://foodpovertyinquiry.org** and provide a 150-word summary detailing the progress of the All-Party Parliamentary Group into the use of food banks.

2 The impact of social inequality

This chapter looks at the impact of social inequality on specific low income groups in society, including the elderly, children, low income families in work and the unemployed. Read Chapter 5 for the causes and impact of social inequality on gender and ethnic minorities.

The elderly

The proportion of pensioners living in poverty (after housing costs are deducted) has fallen sharply from 26 per cent of all pensioners in 2001–02 to 14 per cent in 2011–12 (Figure 2.1). It is still the case that single pensioners are more likely to live in poverty than pensioner couples.

The number of pensioners who live in poverty in the UK is of grave concern. Someone who has contributed their life to working hard, paying taxes and furthering Britain as a nation should be able to live their final years in comfort and dignity. However, for many pensioners this is not the case, with income inequality evident around the country. In 2013 it was estimated that 1.8 million elderly people were living below the official poverty line. Of that figure, 1 million lived in severe poverty (below 50 per cent of average income after housing costs). In addition to this, it is more likely that pensioners who are over the age of 75 will be living in poverty compared to younger pensioners. Around 9 per cent of pensioners aged over 65 (about 800,000

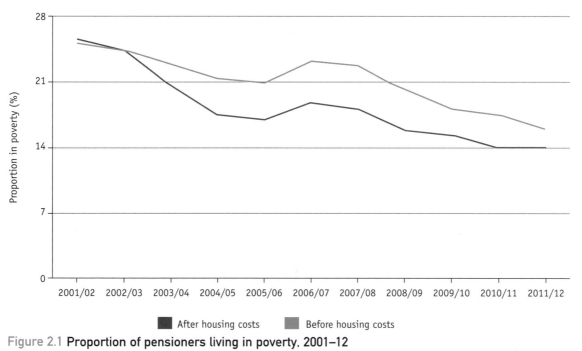

Figure 2.1 **Proportion of pensioners living in poverty, 2001–12**
Source: Department for Work and Pensions

people) in the UK are materially deprived – that is, they do not have certain basic goods, services or experiences because of financial barriers.

Analysing the number of people in receipt of guaranteed pension credit is the best indicator available for the geographic distribution of low income among pensioners. More than twice as many people are in receipt of this in Glasgow than in most of the rest of Scotland. In Scotland around 140,000 pensioners have no income other than the state pension and other state benefits. This amounts to about one in four single pensioners and one in thirteen pensioner couples. In the UK about one-third of all pensioner households entitled to pension credit are not claiming it (1.3 million households). It is estimated that if all means-tested benefit entitlements had been taken up in 2013, pensioner poverty would have been 9 per cent, rather than 14 per cent. Many pensioners are not aware that they are entitled to extra benefits and many who are aware are unsure of how to make a claim or are confused by the bureaucratic claims process.

On the other hand, there are many elderly people in the UK who live a comfortable lifestyle and are well off. Many older people have paid into a private pension throughout their working lives and have put away money into savings and investments. Further to this, many older people own their homes outright and so have low housing costs: many bought their homes under the Right to Buy policy in the 1980s. In some cases, a pensioner may be 'asset rich and income poor', meaning that much of their wealth is tied up in their home. This often leads to older people downsizing their house, usually a family home, to a modest-sized house or flat, which in turn makes a cash sum available for retirement. However, housing inequality is an issue in the UK with around 23 per cent of people over 65 renting their house from a local authority. As many older people live on their own, housing costs can push those renting into poverty.

Women are more likely to live alone, especially at older ages as they have a higher life expectancy. In 2014, 60 per cent of women over 75 and 29 per cent of men over 75 live alone. Another potential issue is, as people become older, factors such as decreasing mobility and illnesses relating to old age sometimes mean that their accommodation is no longer suitable without some support or adaptation. Some people decide to stay in their current home whereas others move into specialist accommodation. Adapting the home or moving to specialised sheltered accommodation can be expensive, but there are payments to support those in need.

Fuel poverty

One of the problems facing many pensioners is fuel poverty. This term has been used more and more in recent years as energy prices rise. This has left many households unable to afford to heat their homes to a comfortable level. It is pensioners who have felt the brunt of this. This is partly because of their typically lower incomes than other, younger households, but it is also because older people are more likely to spend more time at home. Older people also require the room temperature to be slightly warmer in their homes.

The official definition of fuel poverty is when a household must pay more than 10 per cent of its disposable income to heat the home to an adequate level. Fuel poverty is determined by three key factors: income poverty, home energy efficiency and energy prices. Since 2010 it is estimated that energy prices have increased by 37 per cent and this has led to dramatic increases in fuel poverty.

In the UK, fuel poverty for single-pensioner households stands at about 58 per cent. Research in 2013 by charity Age UK found that more than 90 per cent of those aged over 60 were worried about rising fuel costs and that half of all pensioners have turned their heating down when they were not warm enough in an attempt to save money. These statistics are worrying for both the UK and the Scottish Governments, which have a statutory obligation to eradicate fuel poverty by 2016.

Fuel poverty can damage the quality of people's lives and health. The likelihood of ill health increases in cold homes with illnesses such as flu, heart disease and strokes all exacerbated by the cold. The need to spend a large part of income on fuel means that fuel-poor households may have difficulty buying other household essentials and this can lead to poor diet and/or withdrawal from the community. With many older people unaware of the potentially fatal consequences of living in poorly heated housing, every winter approximately 24,000 people die due to cold weather.

Figure 2.2 **Fuel poverty is particularly prevalent in rural areas, where household energy bills are 27 per cent higher than in urban areas**

Show your understanding

1 Using Figure 2.1, describe the trend of pensioner poverty over the last ten years.
2 Why could it be stated that pensioner poverty is of 'grave concern' to society?
3 Why is housing inequality an issue for the elderly in the UK?
4 What is fuel poverty?
5 What are the effects of fuel poverty on pensioners?
6 Read the case study about Brian Hughes. In what ways is Brian struggling to live a comfortable life?

Case study: Brian's story

At the age of 78, Brian Hughes, a pensioner from Glasgow, is struggling to make ends meet, having stopped work at 63 after an accident. He used to have plenty to live on, but now he must survive on his state pension and pension credit. In poor health, he has the extra expense of relying on his car as the only means of getting around. Brian is anxious about his financial situation, but knows that there is nothing he can do about it because he cannot work. His strategy is to give absolute priority to paying household bills. He economises on food by buying 'own brands' at the supermarket and tries to look for the best deals in pound and charity shops. He aims to have a small amount of money left over and is able to afford a meal out – for example a £3.99 'senior citizen special' lunch – about once a month. Brian anticipates not being able to heat his home adequately next winter because of rising fuel costs and is already trying to put extra money away to cover winter fuel bills.

Figure 2.3

Child poverty

Figure 2.4 **It is estimated that absolute child poverty in the UK will remain at the same level in 2020 as it was in 2010 – the first decade it will have failed to drop**

For children, the poverty trap that their families find themselves in can have a huge influence on their progression throughout life and this in turn creates the cycle of poverty (Figure 1.1, page 3). Poverty has a devastating impact on children growing up. It affects their whole life, from health and well-being to educational attainment and aspirations.

There were 3.5 million children living in poverty in the UK in 2014 – that is 27 per cent of children, or more than one in four. At a local level, statistics are even more concerning in some areas. In the Calton area of Glasgow, for example, 49 per cent of children live in poverty. In Manchester, Liverpool and Glasgow overall, approximately one-third of all children live below the poverty line.

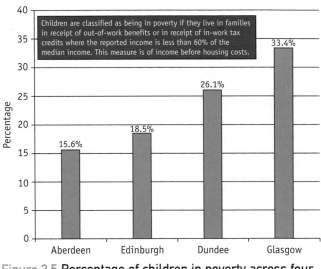

Figure 2.5 **Percentage of children in poverty across four major Scottish cities, 2012**
Source: Child Poverty Map of the UK 2013, End Child Poverty

Fact file

Child poverty in the UK

- 3.5 million (27 per cent) children live in poverty in the UK.
- Child poverty is projected to rise, with an expected 600,000 more children living in poverty by 2016. This upward trend is expected to continue with 4.7 million children projected to be living in poverty by 2020.
- Work does not provide a guaranteed route out of poverty in the UK. Two-thirds (66 per cent) of children growing up in poverty live in a family where at least one member works.
- Child poverty imposes costs on broader society, estimated to be at least £29 billion a year.
- By 3 years old, children from low-income households are nearly three times more likely to suffer mental health problems than children from more affluent homes.
- Children living in poverty are almost twice as likely to live in bad housing. This has significant effects on both their physical and mental health as well as educational achievement.
- Children from low income families often forgo events and social trips that most of us would take for granted.

Source: Child Poverty Action Group

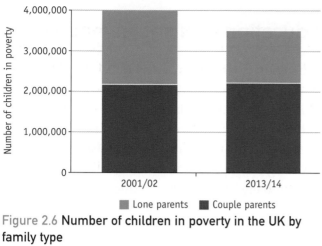

Figure 2.6 **Number of children in poverty in the UK by family type**
Source: Department for Work and Pensions

Health and housing

Poverty adversely affects health and shortens lives (the impact of poverty on health is discussed in Chapter 4). Children from poor families are at ten times the risk of sudden infant death as children from better-off homes. Babies from disadvantaged families are more likely to be born underweight – an average of 200g less than children from the richest families. Comparing the UK with Sweden, the country with the lowest mortality rate for children and young people, we find that in the UK every day five more children under the age of 14 die than in Sweden. Furthermore, poorer children are 2.5 times more likely to suffer chronic illnesses such as asthma and diabetes. One of the main reasons for such vast health inequalities among children is that parents living in poverty face the grim reality of debt and impossible choices between heating homes or cooking nutritious meals for their children. The vast majority of children who come from these homes go without a balanced diet and the recommended five portions of fresh fruit and vegetables a day. Indeed, children who are from socially deprived

backgrounds are more likely to be obese because of a poor diet of junk food and cheap ready meals. Children may also be living in sub-standard housing. In major cities around the UK, there are high-rise flats that accommodate hundreds of poorer families (Figure 2.7).

Figure 2.7 **Some of the Red Road high-rise flats in Glasgow**

Within these tower blocks, flats are often affected by damp, which can lead to conditions such as asthma and respiratory problems in younger children. In addition, the housing and surroundings of a socially deprived area can have a harmful impact on the mental well-being of children as these areas are usually materially deprived, run down, lacking amenities and have higher rates of drug, alcohol and associated social issues. Research has highlighted that psychiatrically diagnosed conditions such as attention deficit hyperactivity disorder (ADHD) have shown an association with deprivation. One of the more distressing consequences of mental health in young people is self-harming and suicide, which are most common among young males, with boys from the lowest social gradient 2.5 times more likely to self-harm than those from the highest.

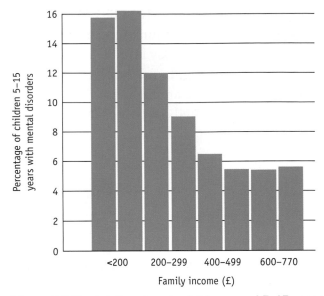

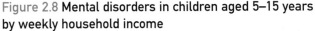
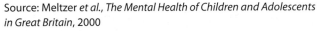

Figure 2.8 Mental disorders in children aged 5–15 years by weekly household income
Source: Meltzer *et al., The Mental Health of Children and Adolescents in Great Britain*, 2000

'Poverty is now one of the greatest dangers faced by our children. If poverty were an infection, we would be in the midst of a full-scale epidemic. It is one of society's greatest inequalities that poor health in children is so dramatically linked to poverty.' (*Professor Nick Spencer, University of Warwick*)

Education and social mobility

Education is vital in breaking the cycle of poverty and it should be a route out of poverty for many children. It gives children a chance to gain valuable knowledge and skills, and to improve their lives. It is well known that children growing up in poorer families leave school with substantially lower levels of educational attainment. Such achievement gaps are a major factor in explaining patterns of social mobility and poverty. In Table 2.1 you can see that the percentage of pupils achieving three Higher As is much lower in poor households. In 2013, in Scotland as a whole, just 2.5 per cent of the 8872 fifth-year students who came from the bottom 20 per cent of households achieved three As or more. This becomes a problem when a young person is thinking about a future career and the prospect of higher education. Universities are looking for pupils who have a strong set of Higher results. For example, Oxford's entry requirements are extremely tough: it needs a minimum of four As and one B at Higher. In 2013 only 50 pupils from the poorest areas got five As at one sitting, with another 70 getting four As. This situation is the

Case study: Response of the Scottish Government to child poverty

In March 2014 the Scottish Government revised its child poverty strategy and set a three-year approach from 2014 to 2017. The strategy is built around three outcomes – 'pockets', 'prospects' and 'places':

- Pockets – the first aim is to reduce income poverty and material deprivation by maximising financial entitlements and reducing pressure on household budgets among low income families, as well as by maximising the potential for parents to increase family incomes through good quality, sustained employment, and promoting greater financial inclusion and capability.
- Prospects – the second aim is to improve children's well-being and life chances by breaking inter-generational cycles of poverty, inequality and deprivation. This requires a focus on tackling the underlying social and economic determinants of poverty and improving the circumstances in which children grow up – recognising the particular importance of improving children's outcomes in the early years.
- Places – the last aim is to address area-based factors which currently exacerbate the effects of individual poverty for many families by continuing to improve the physical, social and economic environments in local areas, particularly in those areas of multiple deprivation in which child poverty is more prevalent.

Table 2.1 **Percentage of pupils achieving three or more As in Scottish Highers in 2013, by income quintile**

Local authority	Income					
	Bottom 20%	20%–40%	40%–60%	60%–80%	Top 20%	All
East Renfrewshire	5.6	7.2	17.6	18.1	32.2	23.8
Fife	2.1	3.8	7.6	14.0	14.5	8.8
Glasgow City	2.4	4.3	6.5	10.7	11.5	4.6
North Ayrshire	3.8	3.0	9.8	13.8	19.4	8.1
West Lothian	1.8	3.0	5.9	9.3	15.4	7.3

same when looking at entry into competitive courses such as law or medicine, which often require four or five As at first sitting. Looking at Figure 2.9, which shows the various types of leaver destinations by deprivation decile, we can see clearly that over 60 per cent of pupils from the least deprived areas go to university whereas only 18 per cent attend from the most deprived areas.

The educational gap between children from richer and poorer backgrounds widens especially quickly during primary school. This is mainly down to parental aspirations and attitudes towards their child while at school and material resources such as a computer and access to the internet at home. Reading charity Booktrust commissioned research into the reading habits of children and found that those from lower socio-economic backgrounds read much less. The study indicated that there are clear links between deprivation and not reading books, with parents from poorer households less likely to read with their children. It is estimated that five-year-olds from poorer families are about a year behind in problem solving and vocabulary.

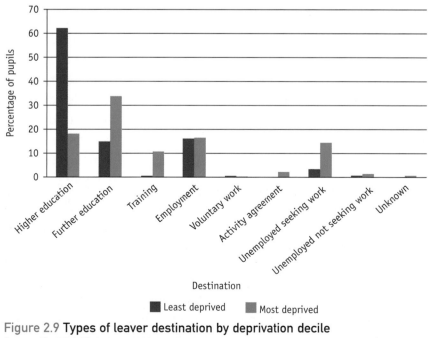

Figure 2.9 **Types of leaver destination by deprivation decile**
Source: Scottish Government

19

Furthermore, the general effects of poverty on the well-being of a child can harm their education. Many pupils living in poverty go to school hungry, tired and in worn-out clothes. Free school meals and clothing grants assist pupils, but home life for some can be detrimental.

> 'Children who grow up in poverty tend to do less well in education because of factors in their home background, for example having parents who are more stressed, less able to afford educational activities and resources and less well-placed to help them with their school work.'
> (*Joseph Rowntree Foundation*)

University education

To achieve a fair, just and equal society it is vitally important to try to promote access to university for the poorest in society. Education is one of the most significant political issues, so reducing educational inequality is a top priority of any government. In 2012 in England, the Coalition Government increased the amount that universities are allowed to charge their students for tuition. Annual fees of £9000 are now permitted and over half of universities in England charge this maximum fee. Many others charge around £6000 a year, depending on the course and level. The maximum annual fee a university could charge before 2012 was £3290. By contrast, university education in Scotland is free to all Scottish students and fees are paid for by the Scottish Government. The Scottish Government states that access to higher education should be based on the 'ability to learn, not on the ability to pay'.

There has been strong criticism of the UK Government's decision to increase fees, but the UK Government cut university funding as part of its deficit reduction programme and hence decided that a fee increase was necessary. Critics argue that such high fees will damage participation and social mobility, as those from poorer and working-class backgrounds simply will not be able to afford to go to university. A better-off student will enjoy financial assistance from their family to help with the burden of fees, accommodation and living expenses whereas poorer students may finish university with debts of approximately £36,000.

As much as Scotland may seem like a student's utopia with no tuition fees, Scottish universities are still coming under severe criticism for not admitting enough students from poorer backgrounds. At St Andrews, one of Scotland's top universities, only 14 pupils from the poorest 20 per cent of Scottish neighbourhoods gained entry to the university in 2012 – a low 2.7 per cent of its overall intake. However, universities argue that the issue is not that they do not have an interest in attracting pupils from deprived backgrounds; the problem is actually that so few pupils from deprived backgrounds meet the standard entry requirements. St Andrews University said it believed the greatest barrier for children from deprived areas getting into top universities was long-term poverty, and a lack of educational and social support from a very early age. The Scottish Government has responded to the worrying statistics of low admittance of the poor by increasing funding to universities that admit pupils from poorer backgrounds. Through 'outcome agreements' made with universities, they will have to admit more pupils from poorer backgrounds to receive the additional funding. For example, by 2016 Edinburgh will increase its intake of students from the poorest areas by 50 per cent, or an extra 45 places, and Glasgow, the university in the region with the greatest poverty levels, is promising a 1 per cent increase of its total intake (around 35 students).

Show your understanding

1 Describe the levels of child poverty with reference to specific cities in the UK.
2 In what ways does poverty affect a child's health?
3 Explain the harmful effects of poor housing on a child.
4 Outline the achievement gap between richer and poor children.
5 What action is the Scottish Government taking to improve access to higher education?
6 What is the Scottish Government doing to tackle child poverty (see the Case Study on page 18)?

12-mark question

Analyse the impact poverty has on a child.

Added Value idea

The impact of poverty on children is highly controversial. This could be a good opportunity for your Added Value unit assignment as you could investigate options to create equality (e.g. set university quotas for poorer pupils) knowing that children from wealthier backgrounds are usually more successful than children from poorer backgrounds. You will need to research and develop your own sources and present your findings in the form of a report. Discuss this with your teacher.

'Working poor' families

Income inequality has become a significant focus in the UK as people struggle to make ends meet after the recession. It is widely reported that the rich in our society are getting richer and the poor are getting poorer. The average annual income of the top 10 per cent of earners is £79,196, with the remaining 90 per cent earning on average only £12,969. Low paid and part-time working is a serious concern as families are falling below the poverty line even although there is a family member at work. Over half of those living in poverty are from working families. Most children who live in poverty live in 'working poor' households. The UK Government stresses that 'work is the best route out of poverty', but without action to tackle low pay, improve job quality and help parents progress in work, it is difficult to make progress on tackling poverty. The Joseph Rowntree Foundation suggests that the gap between the national minimum wage (NMW) and the income needed to pay for a basic household budget has widened. An adult working a 40-hour week on the NMW earns £1027 a month, which translates annually to £12,334 in pre-tax income. According to the Foundation, however, a single person now needs to earn at least £14,400 a year in order to reach a minimum income standard and afford a socially acceptable standard of living. This has led to calls for the NMW to be increased and for a living wage to be adopted. Chapter 3 looks at the NMW and the living wage campaign in more detail.

The impact of low income as well as worklessness can be distressing on a family. Families below the poverty line have to live on a tight financial budget and balance paying household bills, rent, debt repayment and food costs. Very little money is left over to spend on material goods or social outings. This in turn leads to social exclusion where families struggle to participate in the goings-on of modern society.

Figure 2.10 Rachel Reeves

'It's not right that millions of people are going out to work, working harder and harder, and can't afford to bring up their families.' (*Rachel Reeves, Shadow Work and Pensions Secretary*)

Unemployed young adults

The unemployment rate for 16- to 24-year-olds is now more than four times the rate for older workers. In 2014 the Office for National Statistics (ONS) reported that young people in Britain have borne the brunt of the financial crisis, with a larger proportion of 16- to 24-year-olds now out of work than any other age group. The unemployment rate among 16- and 17-year-olds is 36 per cent, and 18 per cent among 18- to 24-year-olds. This compares to 4.7 per cent among 35- to 49-year-olds, and 4.4 per cent among 50- to 64-year-olds. Averaging across 2013, the unemployment rate was higher for young women than for young men. To ascertain a more accurate picture of youth unemployment, it is better to analyse youths who are 'Not in Education, Employment or Training' (NEETs). Figure 2.11 compares the statistics for young males and females, but together there are nearly 1 million 16- to 24-year-olds regarded as NEET in the UK.

Unemployment of young people, especially in cities, can lead to a host of major societal issues, such as poverty, social exclusion, physical and mental well-being of the individual through to drug abuse and related crime. The Government has many challenges in this area: in-work poverty, the number of young adults with few or no qualifications, young adult unemployment, health inequalities and low income households' lack of access to essential services. The London Riots of summer 2011 epitomised a youth who feel they have no place in society and no prospects to aim for. Former Prime Minister Tony Blair stated 'a big cause of the riots in England was an alienated, disaffected youth … outside the social mainstream'.

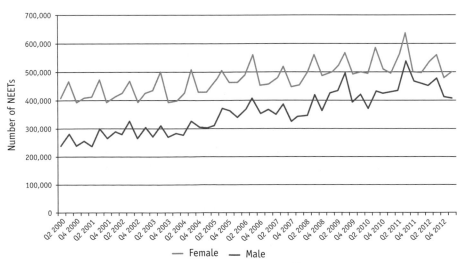

Figure 2.11 **Number of 16- to 24-year-old NEETs, 2000–12**

Case study: Barry's story

Barry Gallagher is 20 and lives in Hackney in north-east London. He is currently unemployed and feeling very despondent about his employment prospects. He would like to be a mechanic as he has learnt a great deal about car maintenance from his cousin and has a keen interest in motorsport. He enjoyed school as 'it was a laugh' and he could 'see his mates', but missed all his exams as he frequently truanted. Barry said he did not mind at the time, but now regrets having no qualifications and 'ending up with nothing and being bored and depressed'. He said he received advice from his local Job Centre, but

Figure 2.12

felt that a lot of the courses did not suit his interests. Barry often uses the internet to look for jobs and courses, but argues that there are simply too few or no jobs around at the moment. He states that his mum wants him to get a job as soon as possible and earn some money to help with household bills, and she gets annoyed when he drinks with his friends during the week. He did hold down a job at a local supermarket for nearly a year, but says 'that kind of fizzled out … when you do something for a long time, it gets boring'. He admitted that he had not been laid off because of the economic situation or because the supermarket was cutting back on staff, and acknowledged he actually lost his job for being an unreliable employee. However, Barry sees this as an opportunity to now finally become a mechanic but is lacking the skills, motivation and confidence to get on the path to his dream career.

Fact file

The general challenges of poverty across the UK

- Poverty levels vary across the UK. Generally, there is a 'north–south divide', with poverty greater in the north than in the south.
- Poverty is generally concentrated in inner-city areas and areas where heavy industry was once located.
- In areas such as West Dunbartonshire, there are 40 people claiming Job Seekers' Allowance (JSA) per job advertised.
- In Scotland, 200,000 young people who left school between 2009 and 2012 have never held regular work since.
- In one in four families in Scotland no one works. In the UK as a whole, the figure is one in five.
- In 2013 the *Scotsman* ran the headline 'Glasgow: Jobless Capital of the UK'.
- Glasgow is the lowest performing local authority in education – the city where poverty is at its most rife.

Show your understanding

1 Explain the issues surrounding low pay and why this causes families to fall into poverty.
2 Describe the impact of low pay and worklessness on a family.
3 Outline to what extent young adults are more likely to be unemployed than older people.
4 What are the consequences of unemployment among young adults?
5 Read the case study about Barry Gallagher. Do you feel sympathy for his situation? Justify your answer.

20-mark question

To what extent is there a poverty crisis in the UK?

Use this chapter to assist you in writing this essay. Include balance throughout, arguing that there is a problem with poverty (refer to specific groups) but that progress has been made by the Government (refer to specific policies) to reduce poverty to some extent. Chapter 1 will also help you. Make an essay plan with your teacher before you start.

Government responses to social inequality

For almost 70 years the UK public have supported the principle of the Welfare State – that the government has the responsibility to protect the well-being of its citizens, to strive to reduce social inequality and to ensure that everyone has a minimum standard of living. However, the banking crisis and global recession from 2008, which led to a massive increase in UK debt, has necessitated cuts to government spending and to a review of social security spending. Between 2010 and 2015 spending cuts of £81 billion have been made and further cuts will continue after the 2015 General Election, regardless of which party is in government. As Table 3.1 indicates, the annual repayment of debt interest in the fiscal year 2014–15 is £53 billion, up from £44 billion in 2010–11. It should be noted that four years of inflation will reduce the spending power of the 2014–15 figures, so an estimated increase of 14 per cent would in real terms be a modest increase.

The Welfare State

The government aims to meet everyone's basic needs by providing services so that we have the opportunity to live long and prosper. This idea was born out of the chaos of the Second World War in which millions of Britons had their homes destroyed and many had to endure the horrors of total war. In 1942 a government report was published in which it made recommendations to tackle the Five Giants of Want, Ignorance, Disease, Squalor and Idleness, which were seen as the 'evils' holding back progress in society. This report was written by William Beveridge, who argued that in order to effectively tackle Want, a government would have to also address the underlying issues associated with the other giants. At the end of the war, a Labour Government was elected on the promise of revolutionising the country's public services and creating a safety net for all citizens, especially the old, disabled and unemployed.

Table 3.1 **Selected government spending, 2010–15**

Sector	2010–11 (£ billion)	2014–15 (£ billion)
Education	89	98
Transport	22	23
Defence	40	38
Public order and safety	26	30
Health	122	140
Social protection	197	222

Source: UK budgets, 2010 and 2014

Fact file

Beveridge's Five Giants

Want – a reformed social security system to provide every citizen with their basic financial needs.

Ignorance – education to be reformed so that every child would gain a worthwhile level of education.

Disease – the creation of a new national health service that would be free at the point of entry for everyone's health needs.

Squalor – a massive rebuilding of safer and progressive housing to ensure better living standards for all.

Figure 3.1 Beveridge's Five Giants

Idleness – reformed economic policy to ensure low unemployment and provide stable occupations.

Show your understanding

1 What is the main idea behind the Welfare State?
2 What was the main motivation for introducing the Welfare State?
3 What were the five areas that Beveridge identified as being key to the creation of a Welfare State?

Develop your skills

4 Referring to Table 3.1, what conclusions can be made about the following?
   a) The sectors that have best protected their budget.
   b) The sectors that have least protected their budget.

Founding principles

Following the reforms carried out after the Second World War, the state became responsible for providing:

● financial support for those without a suitable level of income
● everyone's health care needs
● a basic level of education
● decent housing
● help in finding employment.

The Welfare State would therefore provide a service 'from the cradle to the grave'. It was founded on the following four principles: that it is comprehensive, universal, based on equality and collectivist.

Comprehensive

The state undertakes to provide for all aspects of need. For example, the creation of the National Health Service (NHS) meant a commitment to provide 'a comprehensive health service for the improvement of the physical and mental health of the people … for the prevention, diagnosis and treatment of illness'. The NHS therefore is responsible for all aspects of the nation's health care.

Universal

The Welfare State was intended to be free for all regardless of individual circumstances. However, from the beginning the universal principle was not applied across all provisions. Although universal health care has remained and is still largely free at the point of need, charges are made for dental care and eye treatment. Free prescriptions are in place in Scotland as health care is a devolved power, but most people in England have to pay for prescriptions. Across Britain, free compulsory education up to the age of 16 remains a universal provision.

Even from the beginning, the idea of basing entitlements on National Insurance contributions meant that many people – mainly women – were excluded and had to depend on means-tested benefits. The Labour Government (1997–2010) had a policy approach that it called 'progressive universalism', which was an extension of means-testing. Therefore, benefits they introduced, such as pension credit and working tax credit (see page 34), were means-tested. Labour retained Child Benefit as a universal benefit as a recognition of the extra cost of bringing up children. However, in 2013 the Coalition Government introduced means-testing to Child Benefit and placed caps on other benefits.

Based on equality

The aim of the Welfare State was for equal provision for all people in all regions and areas. Another factor that has challenged the equality of the Welfare State is the devolution of some services to the Scottish Parliament. Within Scotland young people have access to free higher education, whereas young people in England and Wales have to pay up to £9000 a year. Also, in Scotland there is free personal care for the elderly, benefiting more than 77,000 people, whereas in the rest of Britain this would come at a cost to many individuals. In recent years there have been large government cuts to various areas of the Welfare State. One of the areas seeing the largest cuts has been the central funding of local authorities, which has seen a 3 per cent year-on-year reduction for councils across the UK, impacting on important local services such as education.

Collectivist

Society collectively supports the view that those in need should be supported and protected by the state. The UK Government decides on the amount of funding to be given to pensions, benefits and other services, such as health and education. The Government pays for these services through National Insurance contributions and general taxation.

However, with many of the services provided by the state there have been continuing increased costs because of factors out of government control, such as population increases and an ageing population. Successive governments have had to review the way the Welfare State has been funded. People on the right of the political spectrum argue that welfare reduces incentives to encourage individuals to find their own solutions to problems. For example, it is argued that some people over-rely on benefits and as such are disincentivised into finding paid employment, and in some instances they may not find themselves any better off financially. On the other hand, those on the left criticise the Welfare State for not doing enough help some groups in our society such as women and ethnic minorities (see Chapter 5).

Since 2010 there has been a Welfare Revolution, which has seen a further erosion of the collectivist principles of the Welfare State towards more individualist principles (see page 36).

Success in tackling the Five Giants

Want

Today, Want is known as poverty. There are a huge range of benefits available to the unemployed, the elderly, children and people with a disability. From 1997 to 2010, the Labour Governments significantly increased in real terms welfare spending.

Ignorance

Education remains universal for every child up to the age of 16 and as a result the UK has one of the highest literacy rates in the world. In education there has been an increase in privately funded schools and the development of free schools in England and Wales, which are free from local authority control. In England and Wales higher education students have to pay annual tuition fees of up to £9000. In Scotland, university tuition remains free for Scottish students, but there are fees for students from other parts of Britain and the EU.

Disease

In the NHS there has always been inequality. From the beginning, private health care provided more opportunities for those who were wealthy. To a great extent, the NHS has provided an increasing level of prevention and treatment. Life expectancy continues to increase year on year, with an extra ten years being added to life expectancy between 1970 and 2010. However, as specialist consultants vary from area to area and some drugs are available in some areas and not in others (the 'postcode lottery'), not everyone has access to all treatments in all areas of the UK. Also, there are huge variations in life expectancy across all areas of the UK and, indeed, within cities themselves (see Chapter 4).

Squalor

There has been a gradual change in government priorities on housing, with a massive reduction in local government provision of council housing. For example, the Conservative Government in the 1980s sold off large numbers of council (social) housing in their Right to Buy scheme. Of the social housing that remains, we have seen more and more being handed over from local authority control. For example, Glasgow City Council has, in recent years, handed over the management of its social housing to housing associations such as the Glasgow Housing Association and since then they have embarked on one of the largest reforms to social housing in Europe with the demolition of the Red Roads flats.

Idleness

Various governments have met with varying degrees of success depending on the economy of the country. In the last three years, with the economy having problems, both poverty and unemployment are increasing despite a variety of programmes to tackle them. Programmes such as the Work Programme and Jobcentre

Plus (see page 35) are provided by the state to tackle 'idleness' and the Coalition Government has looked to eradicate the 'something for nothing' culture. In addition, the state also provides a wide range of public sector jobs through education, health and services.

Government action on wealth inequalities

The proportion of pensioners and children living in poverty declined between 1991 and 2011, according to the Joseph Rowntree Foundation (Figure 3.2). Pensioners' incomes have been protected by the Government's promise in 2010 to guarantee to increase the state pension every year by inflation, or by the rise in average earnings, or by a minimum of 2.5 per cent, whichever is the highest. Further analysis of the Joseph Rowntree Foundation's *Annual Poverty Report 2012* highlights that in Scotland child poverty fell by 9.9 per cent in the decade to 2011, compared with 5.7 per cent in England. However, the report adds that changes to benefits are likely to increase poverty for children, especially in workless families. This was confirmed in 2014 in a report by the leading charity Oxfam Scotland. It estimated that 82,000 families had been affected by the welfare reforms. The worst-hit families are losing out by £18 per person per week, or £864 per year.

The new policies introduced by the Coalition Government of 2010–15 to get people back into work and to tackle a 'dependency culture' in the Welfare State are:

- removing the spare room subsidy ('bedroom tax')
- lowering of the limit on local housing allowance to people renting private homes rather than living in social housing
- introduction of a £500 per week benefit cap
- job-seeker sanctions
- the annual increase for most welfare benefits to be capped at 1 per cent.

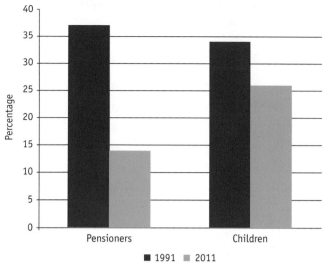

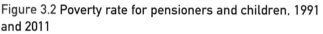

Figure 3.2 Poverty rate for pensioners and children, 1991 and 2011
Source: Joseph Rowntree Foundation

Show your understanding

1 a) In your own words, explain the terms 'comprehensive', 'universal', 'based on equality' and 'collectivist'.
   b) For each term, explain some of the difficulties encountered by the government in maintaining the Welfare State.
2 What evidence suggests that poverty had declined in the UK in the ten years to 2011?
3 What evidence suggests that families on low incomes are being badly affected by welfare cuts?

12-mark question

Analyse whether the Welfare State has met its aims.

Strategies to increase levels of employment

The Labour Government from 1997 to 2010 designed its social policy around programmes and strategies that would get the unemployed off welfare and into work. From 1997, successive governments tried to do this through a number of strategies, as discussed below.

National minimum wage

The long-term aim of the national minimum wage (NMW) is to remove the problem of 'poverty pay' that exists when earnings from paid work do not adequately cover living expenses and fail to push people out of poverty. It was introduced because of increasing:

- income inequality
- child poverty
- burden on the state to provide in-work benefits.

The NMW was introduced in April 1999. Since then, it is estimated that around 1 million people a year benefit from the annual rise in the NMW (Table 3.2).

Figure 3.3 **The national minimum wage sets minimum hourly rates that employers must pay their workers**

Table 3.2 **National minimum wage, 2010–14**

Year	21 and over	18–20	Under 18	Apprentice*
2010	£5.93	£4.92	£3.64	£2.50
2011	£6.08	£4.98	£3.68	£2.60
2012	£6.19	£4.98	£3.68	£2.65
2013	£6.31	£5.03	£3.72	£2.68
2014	£6.50	£5.13	£3.79	£2.73

This rate is for apprentices aged 16–18 and those aged 19 or over who are in their first year.

Impact of the NMW

Members of the Political Studies Association recently voted the NMW the single most successful government policy of the last 30 years. In October 2014 the NMW rose for all age groups, with those 21 and over seeing the largest rise from £6.31 to £6.50.

The impact of the NMW varies considerably across sectors. One in ten women benefits from a

NMW compared to just 4 per cent of men. One in five under-25s have had their wages boosted by NMW. However, one-third of those benefiting from NMW are not heads of households but young people living at home or married women living with employed husbands.

Figure **3.4** Vince Cable

'The recommendations [a rise in NMW from October 2014] mean that low paid workers will enjoy the biggest cash increase in their take-home pay since 2008. This will benefit over 1 million workers on the NMW and marks a welcoming new phase in minimum wage policy.' (*Vince Cable, Secretary of State for Business, Innovation and Skills*)

The 2013 *Low Pay Commission Report* claimed that the NMW applies to over 1.3 million workers and it has reduced the gender inequality gap as women account for 59 per cent of low paid jobs, which means the NMW plays an important role and has a greater impact on raising women's earnings in comparison to those of men. The report also claims that the gap between ethnic minority workers and white workers has been significantly reduced.

'The national minimum wage has helped outlaw blatant exploitation and the tax credit system has helped boost the pay of thousands of low paid workers. But despite this, the Scottish Low Pay Unit estimates that over 350,000 full-time workers are low paid. The existence of so many low paid jobs traps individuals and families in poverty, denying the opportunities and choices that should be for everyone in a country as wealthy as Scotland.' (*Public sector union UNISON*)

Table 3.3 **Arguments in favour of and against the national minimum wage**

In favour of the NMW	Against the NMW
Wealth inequality is reduced and income is redistributed	Staffing costs are increased for businesses, which may reduce employment
The unemployed may be encouraged to get jobs because the higher wage is an incentive for individuals to work, thereby reducing poverty overall	Increased wages for those at the bottom may lead to demands for wage increases at all levels to maintain wage differentials
As it is illegal to pay below the national rates, most employers will be dissuaded from exploiting individuals	NMW only helps those employed. Many of the most impoverished in Britain are in that situation on account of long-term unemployment
If workers are paid more, they will make a bigger contribution to the economy, boosting business and increasing employment	It may encourage some employers to pay workers casually through cash-in-hand and informal work contracts, which reduce workers' rights

Case study: NMW versus the living wage

Since 2001 London Citizens, a community alliance made up of faith groups, businesses and campaigners, has promoted the London Living Wage Campaign. The alliance was appalled at the living conditions of many of London's low paid workers. Since then, this campaign has evolved into a national movement promoted by the Living Wage Foundation. During this time, there has been a growing acceptance that the NMW does not adequately provide an amount needed to let workers lead a decent life – a living wage.

The Living Wage Foundation campaigns tirelessly to encourage employers to offer a living wage rather than the basic NMW. The NMW is compulsory by law and moving to a living wage would be on a voluntary basis. It is estimated that nearly 600 employers across Scotland and the UK have now signed a commitment to providing a living wage of £8.80 per hour for those living in London and £7.65 per hour for the rest of the UK. By comparison, the NMW is significantly lower.

Case study continued...

Many well-known companies provide a living wage such as Aviva, KPMG and Nationwide. However, according to a report by KPMG, one in five workers in the UK is paid less than what is required for a basic standard of living. The report states that nearly 5 million people failed to command a living wage. It also claims that Northern Ireland has the highest proportion of below-living-wage workers, at 24 per cent. It is estimated that around 780,000 sales and retail staff are paid below the living wage and this represents the highest figure of all occupations. Other occupations in which employees are most likely to be paid below the living wage are bar staff, waiters and waitresses, where an estimated 85–90 per cent of employees are paid below living wage levels.

In support of a living wage

'It is shocking that in this day and age one in five workers is still earning less than is needed to maintain a decent standard of living. The living wage is not a luxury, and means low paid workers do not have to make tough choices over whether they can afford the everyday things that most of us take for granted, such as their fuel bill or a winter coat for their children. Many more employers could afford to adopt the living wage, and we hope that many more decide to pay it in the coming months. Now more than ever is the time for employers to put an end to poverty pay.' (*Frances O'Grady, General Secretary of the TUC*)

Against a living wage

'Every employer would want to be as reasonable as they possibly can, but in the current economic climate it is not going to be possible for those sectors that have traditionally struggled to even pay the national minimum wage. Rent and rates are becoming more expensive and so are energy costs, so the living wage is an aspiration but not affordable for some employers. Pay should be determined by the market and reflect what is affordable for employers.' (*Mike Cherry, Policy Chairman, Federation of Small Businesses*)

Celtic chief executive Peter Lawwell defends decision not to pay staff a living wage at the club's Annual General Meeting

Celtic chief executive Peter Lawwell has defended the Parkhead board after their rejection of a proposal to make the club a living wage employer was denounced as shameful by one shareholder at the club's AGM on Friday.

Jeanette Findlay of the Celtic Trust launched a measured but scathing attack, describing their decision not to back Proposal 11, which would cost Celtic £500,000 per year, as 'the grubbiest' ever made by a Parkhead board which 'shames you and shames us'.

Celtic reported pre-tax profits of £9.74 million for the year to 30 June on a 47.7 per cent rise in turnover to £75.8 million. The living wage rate is set to rise to £7.65 per hour next year.

Findlay was given a standing ovation by the majority of shareholders who also backed the proposal on a show of hands, after two other shareholders also spoke passionately in support. Chairman Ian Bankier confirmed that the board recommended that shareholders vote against the resolution and a poll was called for which, with the proxy votes held by him, means it is almost certain to be rebuffed.

⇨

Speaking in the boardroom afterwards, Lawwell said: 'It was very emotional and you have to respect the points of view but it is a very complicated issue. What I can say is this club is a first-class employer. We look after our people and their well-being, I don't think there would be any club or company in Britain that would look after them better. They are satisfied, we had a staff survey last year which showed that. The majority of staff who fall into that [living wage] category are on match-day, so it is second incomes for people, who top-up in stewarding and catering on a Saturday. It is an established payment structure which is independent to anybody, government or companies, and we have to be in control of our business.'

Source: Adapted from the Daily Record, *15 November 2013*

Show your understanding

1 What were the original aims of the NMW?
2 Outline how the NMW has impacted on various groups in society.
3 Summarise the main arguments for and against the NMW.

Develop your skills

4 Read the case study about the NMW versus the living wage and the article from the *Daily Record*. Imagine you are a government adviser and you have been asked to prepare a report accepting or rejecting a proposal to increase the NMW to living wage levels.
   a) In your report you must clearly state your recommendation.
   b) Give two detailed reasons for this recommendation.
   c) Explain why you did not choose the other option.

Added Value idea

The debate over pay rates for low earners is hugely topical. This could be a good opportunity for your Added Value unit assignment. You will need to research and develop your own sources and present your findings in the form of a report. Discuss this with your teacher.

The New Deal

The New Deal (renamed the Flexible New Deal from October 2009) was a programme introduced by the Labour Government in 1998 to reduce unemployment by providing training, subsidised employment and voluntary work to the unemployed. The scheme had the power to withdraw benefits from those who refused 'reasonable employment'.

Although originally targeting the young unemployed only, the New Deal programmes subsequently targeted other groups, including:

- The New Deal for Young People (NDYP), which targeted unemployed youth (aged 18–24) who had been out of work for six months or longer.
- New Deal 25+, which was targeted at those aged over 25 who had been unemployed for 18 months or more.
- New Deal for Lone Parents (NDLP), which was aimed at single parents with school-age children. Since NDLP came into effect, lone parents have increasingly moved into employment, and relative poverty among this group has substantially declined. There is also the belief that parents' employment has positive effects for their children in terms of health gains, and improved behavioural and educational outcomes.

- New Deal for the Disabled, which targeted those with disabilities in receipt of Incapacity and similar benefits.
- New Deal 50+, for those aged over 50.
- New Deal for Musicians was a little-known element aimed at unemployed musicians.

The New Deal ended in 2011.

Tax credits

The Labour Government of 1997–2010 had a long-term goal to halve child poverty by 2010 and abolish it within a generation. Tax credits, which are payments from the government, were central to this strategy. The Budget of 2000 confirmed that the Labour Government would reform the way families with children and those in work on low incomes would be supported through the tax and benefit system. The reforms created two new tax credits: child tax credit and working tax credit.

Fact file

Child tax credit and working tax credit

- Child tax credit (CTC) is paid to families with children and a low income. It is available in addition to child benefit. You do not have to be working to claim CTC. The lower the family's income, the more CTC payable. All taxable income is tested for CTC, so a couple who both work and have children will have both salaries taken into account.
- Working tax credit (WTC) is based on the hours you work and get paid for, or expect to be paid for. You can claim whether you are an employee or self-employed, but unpaid work does not count for WTC. This is a means-tested benefit that can be claimed by individuals, childless couples or working families with dependent children.

Tax credits are designed to tackle child poverty and help to ensure that work pays more than welfare, and that people have incentives to move up the earnings ladder. The WTC aims at tackling persistent poverty among working people.

Tax credits are considered to be a success for the following reasons:

- more money for those in need
- less form-filling and faster payments
- simpler administration and more responsive system
- fairer system: less scope for people to 'play the system'
- better incentives for dual-earner couples
- better incentives to save
- support for children paid to the main carer.

According to the Institute for Fiscal Studies, the Labour Government's main taxation and welfare benefit changes managed to halt rising inequalities but failed to significantly reverse the growing gap in incomes between rich and poor that opened up during the Conservative Government of 1979–97.

In 2010 the Coalition Government announced that the working tax credit will, by 2017, be integrated into and replaced by the new universal credit (see page 38).

Show your understanding

1 What was the impact of the New Deal?
2 Explain the differences between CTC and WTC.
3 In what ways could the tax credit system be deemed to have been successful?

Jobseeker's Allowance

The Jobseeker's Allowance (JSA) was introduced in 1996 to replace Unemployment Benefit or, as it was affectionately known, 'the brew'. JSA is part of the UK's social security benefits system. It is meant to cover the cost of living expenses when the claimant is out of work and therefore provide a safety net against absolute poverty. According to the Department for Work and Pensions website, in order to receive JSA you must:

- be available and actively seeking work (you have to visit the Jobcentre every two weeks to prove this)
- not be in full-time education
- be aged 18 or over but under state pension age
- work fewer than 16 hours a week.

The amount someone receives varies depending on their status, but on average the amount (in April 2014) is:

- aged 16–24: £57.35 per week
- aged 25+: £72.40 per week.

A claim can begin online or by visiting a Jobcentre, where the claimant has to attend an interview. Here, a Claimant Commitment (see page 41) agreement is drawn up, in which the claimant agrees what steps they need to take in order to claim JSA, such as improving their skills, writing a CV, preparing for interviews and registering with employment agencies. Claimants then have to attend a Jobcentre interview every two weeks ('sign on') to show how they have been searching for a job in order to keep getting JSA. If a claimant fails to carry out the details in the agreement, their benefits can be stopped.

In May 2014 the Government announced that all new claimants for JSA or Employment and Support Allowance (ESA) would have to wait seven days instead of the previous three days before they would be eligible for financial help. (ESA replaced Incapacity Benefit and Income Support in 2008 and is paid on the grounds of ill-health or disability.) The TUC stated: 'Forcing people to wait for job support will not help anyone find work. Instead it will make them easy prey for loan sharks.'

Criticism had already been made of the new sanctions introduced to encourage people to stay in a job or accept any offer of work. Anyone who leaves their employment voluntarily will not be

entitled to benefits for 13 weeks. Failure to attend an interview will lead to claimants losing all of their allowance for a fixed period of four weeks for the first failure and 13 weeks for subsequent failures.

Jobcentre Plus

Jobcentre Plus is a government agency supporting people of working age from welfare to work and helping employers to fill their vacancies. Its primary role is to help people who are unemployed get back in to work by providing a market for job vacancies and assistance with managing the day-to-day costs of looking for work through out-of-work benefits. In addition, it also helps to provide opportunities for people to retrain and gain more skills to increase the likelihood of them entering employment. However, it also provides a wide range of other services such as help in claiming financial assistance because of ill-health or disability.

Jobcentre Plus provides the resources to enable job-seekers to find work through Jobpoints (touch-screen computer terminals), Jobseeker Direct (telephone service) and the Jobcentre Plus website. The Jobpoints are linked to a government website called Universal Jobmatch. This website is the busiest recruitment website in the UK, with up to 6 million hits a day. The website also allows the Department for Work and Pensions to track users' attempts at getting work and those seeking JSA can have their payments stopped if they are not active enough users.

Traditionally Jobcentre Plus would administer claims for benefits such as Income Support, Incapacity Benefit and JSA, in addition to providing assistance to those who seek work. However, many of these roles are now being offered by outside agencies and many of the services are processed centrally by call centres and via online systems. In 2012 the Coalition Government announced a major shake-up of the role of Jobcentre Plus and since then more and more the services are being provided online.

Pension credit and other benefits

Pension credit is money for some people aged 60 and over. It has two parts: guarantee credit and savings credit. Guarantee credit tops up your weekly income to a guaranteed level. Savings credit is an extra payment for those who have saved some money towards their retirement. Pension credit is means-tested and depends on how much income and savings you have. In a recent survey of pensioners, nine out of ten of them knew that pension credit existed, but only two out of ten claimed it.

All elderly people regardless of income receive the winter fuel payment of £200 per household, but the cold weather payment is means-tested.

A new state pension system will be introduced in 2016.

Show your understanding

1. What steps do claimants need to go through in order to claim JSA?
2. 'The JSA is adequate.' Is this statement correct? Justify your answer.
3. Explain the main purpose of Jobcentre Plus.
4. In what ways does the UK Government provide extra assistance to the elderly who may find themselves in poverty?

The Welfare Revolution

Since the 2010 election, the Coalition Government has embarked on the most radical reform to social welfare since the emergence of the Welfare State in 1948. The 2008 economic crisis has resulted in the Government aiming to find £81 billion in public spending savings before 2015. The Government was concerned about the ever-growing costs of welfare in the new age of austerity – overall spending on benefits was now three times higher in real terms than it was in the late 1970s. The Government was also aware that the working public suffering from wage constraints and rising fuel bills supported a tough policy on welfare. According to *The Economist*, 'In 1993 only one-fifth believed that a less generous system would encourage people to stand on their own feet. By 2012 more than half did so.' The Conservative slogan that the system should reward strivers not skivers met with general approval.

According to the Government, a policy to reduce the dependency culture and to encourage a work ethos would at the same time stop the increased growth in welfare spending. Those out of work represent a drain on public finances and so getting people into work and contributing to the economy is the best solution to reducing the public deficit. This policy represents a radical change in outlook. According to Work and Pensions Secretary Iain Duncan Smith, too many people are trapped on benefits and his aim is to 'make work pay' by encouraging an individualist approach to the benefits system. More emphasis has been placed on an individual's responsibility to find work, and the reforms include many financial sanctions for those who do not show enough effort to find employment. The Coalition Government also aims to simplify the system by amalgamating a number of working-age benefits and tax credits into one single monthly payment, called universal credit.

Many of the changes to the welfare system came about through the Welfare Reform Act 2012. The Government claims the changes will be cheaper to administer, improve the incentives to work, reduce fraud and encourage those on benefit to display greater financial responsibility – for example, housing benefit will no longer be directly paid to the landlord but direct to the claimants as part of their universal credit monthly payment. Claimants will be expected to manage their budgets and

pay direct to the landlord. However, given the lifestyle of some individuals on welfare, there is a danger that payments will not be managed wisely.

Summary of the reforms

The following five policy features (pages 37–41) summarise the reforms.

Ending the spare room subsidy

Details

Commonly dubbed the 'bedroom tax', although it is not a tax at all, this policy was introduced to address some of the problems with shortages in social housing. Its aim is to encourage those living in large houses to downsize and so reduce waiting times for larger families in finding suitable accommodation. Introduced in April 2013, all current and future working-age tenants renting from a local authority, housing association or other registered social landlord no longer receive help towards the costs of a spare room. The new rules allow for one bedroom for each person or couple living as part of the household, with the following exceptions:

- Children aged under 16 of the same gender are expected to share.
- Children aged under 10 are expected to share regardless of gender.
- A disabled tenant or partner who needs a non-resident overnight carer is allowed an extra room.
- Children who cannot share a bedroom because of a disability or medical condition may be entitled to an extra room. Claimants will be asked for medical evidence to support their claim.

This policy is implemented through a reduction in housing benefit of 14 per cent for those with one spare bedroom and 25 per cent for those with two or more spare bedrooms.

Issues

From the outset, this policy has received widespread criticism. In June 2013, less than a month after the policy was introduced nationally, the *Guardian* ran an article under the headline 'The bedroom tax has made huge problems even worse' and claimed that the policy was deeply flawed. In May 2014 it was announced that the bedroom tax would be scrapped in Scotland after the Coalition Government agreed to give Scottish ministers full powers to compensate the 70,000 Scottish households affected by this policy.

Some of the main issues that have arisen include:

- Some of Britain's hardest-pressed, low-income households such as single-parent households and families with disabled persons are being forced to find, on average, an extra £720 a year or face losing their home.
- There have been huge difficulties for families in trying to persuade the Government that their children with disabilities require their own room.
- There are difficulties with temporary under-occupancy such as children who are students or who serve in the armed forces.
- Most tenants are not moving to smaller housing. Instead, they are falling in to rent arrears or being forced to cut back on other necessities such as energy or food to survive.
- Many vulnerable people with complex needs are feeling pressured into considering moving to other accommodation, sometimes moving to different towns. (See also page 42.)

Universal credit and Help to Work

Figure 3.5 People's universal credit payments will reduce gradually as earnings rise

Details

Universal credit is the Government's flagship benefit scheme. It is on a national rollout and will eventually replace all working-age benefits by 2017. It is a new single payment for people who are looking for work or on a low income. The aim of universal credit is to help claimants and their families to become more independent, simplifying the benefits system by bringing together a range of working-age benefits into a single payment. Claimants who have been unemployed for more than two years and who have been unsuccessful in the Work Programme will be enrolled in the Help to Work scheme and offered casual contracted work, also known as zero hours contracts. The jobs do not offer any long-term workers' rights and can be withdrawn at any time. Should a claimant refuse these offers of work without any good reason, they could lose payments for more than three months.

By 2017 universal credit will replace the following separate payments:

- income-based Jobseeker's Allowance
- income-related Employment and Support Allowance
- Income Support
- child tax credits
- working tax credits
- housing benefit.

Issues

Since the rollout began, there have been a number of issues with the implementation of universal credit. The Joseph Rowntree Foundation claims that, unless major changes are made to the implementation of the policy, it could act as a trap for people in poverty. The main issues identified include:

- Switching to monthly single payments is a significant challenge for low income families as they manage their shoestring budgets.
- Universal credit relies on claimants applying initially online, but this excludes many people in poverty or those lacking ICT skills.
- The computer system to process universal credit is due to cost the Government £2.4 billion to create. It is a particularly complicated system to implement, which may delay the 2017 date.
- By April 2014 the Government had only managed to set up 20 per cent of its expected claimants on the new scheme, with many complaining of difficulties with navigating through the process of setting up a claim.

There is growing pressure on the Government to delay the implementation of the system while technical problems are resolved. Former Labour welfare minister Frank Field said: 'Universal Credit staggers on a life support machine which costs taxpayers increasingly dear. Worse still, these problems are cropping up amongst the claims that are meant to be the easiest ones to process.'

Personal Independence Payment and Work Capability Assessment

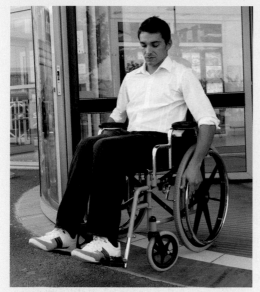

Figure 3.6 Personal Independence Payments help with some of the extra costs caused by long-term ill-health or disability if you're aged 16 to 64

Details

Previously known as Disability Living Allowance (DLA), the Personal Independence Payment (PIP) is a payment given to people with long-term illnesses or disability. PIP is based on an assessment of individual need whereas the DLA would have relied on a list of conditions to assess need. PIP considers how someone's impairment affects their life, taking into account their ability to carry out a range of everyday activities. Most people will be asked to attend a face-to-face consultation with an independent health professional as part of the assessment process. PIP will be rolled out to the whole of the UK by 2017.

The Work Capability Assessment (WCA) is applicable to anyone receiving Incapacity Benefit, Severe Disablement Allowance and Income Support paid on the grounds of illness or disability. Claimants will now be assessed individually whereas previously claimants would require only a doctor's certificate. The assessments were carried out by Atos, a specialised private organisation that considered:

- an individual's physical and mental capabilities and concentrated on the functional effects of an individual's condition rather than the condition itself
- an individual's ability to work, taking into account the modern workplace and developments in health care
- evidence which shows that work can benefit individuals with health conditions and disabilities and may even help recovery.

Issues

There has been widespread criticism of these policies as some commentators believe the Government is unfairly targeting vulnerable members of society. The use of a private firm to assess WCAs has drawn widespread criticism, with claims that the assessment puts undue pressure on the applicants. There have also been high profile cases of misdiagnosis and the resulting loss of benefit from some in society. In February 2014 it was reported that, between August 2010 and June 2013, 158,300 people with disabilities or a serious illness were wrongly assessed as fit for work. However, following appeals the Department for Work on Pensions overturned these decisions and re-categorised those applicants as not yet ready to return to the job market. This has led to the Government seeking to end the contract with Atos and instead tender the contract to another firm. (See also page 42.)

Individual benefits cap

Details

From April 2013 the Coalition Government introduced a cap on the total amount of benefits that working-age people can receive. Households on working-age benefits can no longer receive more in benefits than the average wage for working families. The Government claims this is fair for the whole society, but another aim of this cap is to increase the incentive for people on out-of-work benefits to find jobs because once they are receiving working tax credit their benefits will no longer be capped. According to Work and Pensions Secretary Iain Duncan Smith, the Government 'had to fix the broken welfare system. The benefit cap means claimants no longer receive more in benefits than hard-working households' average earnings and universal credit ensures being in work pays; making the welfare system fair for claimants and the taxpayer that funds it.'

The cap is £2167 a month for joint claimants and single claimants with children, and £1517 a month for single claimants with no dependent children. This roughly equates to no more than £26,000 a year being claimed in benefits. Eventually this cap will only be applied through universal credit once the rollout is complete.

Issues

Since the policy was introduced in July 2013, there have been trials in parts of London with the eventual rollout taking until 2017. A total of 28,500 households had their benefits capped by October 2013, according to the Department for Work and Pensions (see Figure 3.7). About 3.5 per cent of capped claimants were in Scotland. There have been a number of criticisms of this policy:

- Many households are losing a large sum of money and some have to apply for crisis loans in order to survive. In a study of London households, over half of households affected were losing between £50 and £200 a week.
- It unfairly punished those with large families. In London, some 2383 children are in families affected by the cap, while a third of capped households have more than four children.
- Some critics have highlighted the disruption caused by the policy in which some schools have reported pupils leaving because of families moving away to cheaper housing. Increased stress on households has led to illness and increases in domestic violence.
- Critics say the cap fails to tackle underlying issues, such as the difficulty of finding work, the cost of housing and regional differences.

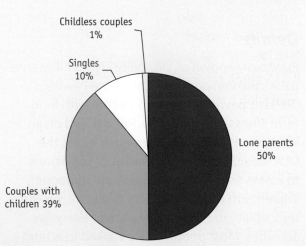

Figure 3.7 Types of household affected by the benefits cap, 2013–14, Department for Work and Pensions

The Claimant Commitment and Work Programme

Figure 3.8

Details

The Claimant Commitment replaces the previous Jobseeker's Agreement. An interview with an adviser takes place, in which a personal plan is agreed outlining what the claimant must do as part of their Claimant Commitment to give themselves the best chance of finding work. This could include regular specific tasks and training opportunities. The adviser explains the penalties claimants could face for failing to meet their responsibilities to get into work and the plan is reviewed regularly.

According to the Department for Work and Pensions, 'The Claimant Commitment strengthens the ability of Jobcentre Plus staff to support claimants back into work at the earliest opportunity and redefines the relationship between the Welfare State and claimants. In return for state support, we expect claimants to do all they can to meet their responsibilities to return to work.'

In addition, in 2011 the Government introduced the Work Programme in which those who have been unemployed for a longer period of time (usually more than 12 months) will be entered on to a special programme in which private and voluntary companies, together with the Jobcentre Plus advisers, work to get claimants into long-term and sustained employment. Providers of the Work Programme are paid in instalments over a period of up to 27 months, which would give them an incentive not only to get people into work, but also to keep them there. This scheme replaced the New Deal and Pathways to Employment. Serco and G4S are two of the private firms involved, whereas in the voluntary sector the Citizens Advice Bureau, the Prince's Trust and Action for Blind People are among the organisations that have signed up.

Issues

Since the Work Programme began in June 2011, there have been several issues. First, its cost: the Work Programme is being delivered at a cost of between £3 billion and £5 billion over the first five years. Also, because of the pay-on-results nature of the scheme, there are accusations that private companies are concentrating on people more likely to generate a payment for the company and not helping jobless people who require more time and investment. Another issue is the success of giving people long-term employment. The Public Accounts Committee claims that during the first 14 months of the programme, only 3.6 per cent of claimants were moved into reliable and sustained employment.

Anxiety over Atos fit-for-work test brings on father's heart attack

A dad who started feeling seriously unwell during his interview with Atos assessors – and suffered a massive heart attack the next day – has been deemed fit to work. Jim Elliott says he was struggling to breathe, sweating and had chest pains during his 20-minute work capability assessment earlier this month. 'All they seemed to care about was getting through the ridiculous list of questions they have, which is supposed to determine whether someone is fit to work or not. I could have dropped down dead in front of them but all they are interested in is getting people off benefits.'

Former welder Jim, who had worked all his adult life until he suffered a heart attack 18 months ago, said: 'It was very clear that I wasn't 100 per cent. I was sweating profusely, my breath was very laboured and I had been confused during the interview. I wasn't able to concentrate on a lot of what they were saying. They gave me a glass of water but that was it. They were more concerned with asking me questions such as, "Can you walk 200 metres and can you raise your arm up in the air?"'

The very next day, he had a heart attack as he was walking down a street in Glasgow's west end. Jim was rushed to hospital by ambulance and ended up spending days in the Golden Jubilee Hospital in Clydebank, which has a specialist cardiac unit. But while he was still lying helpless in his hospital bed, a letter from the Department for Work and Pensions dropped through the door of his home telling him he had been assessed as being fit to go back to work. Jim first started claiming benefits after he had a heart attack 18 months ago. But in November, he was taken off the benefits he was on and put on Jobseeker's Allowance instead – meaning he has to be actively looking for a job or his payments will be cut completely. Jim said: 'My GP told me she has no doubt it was the stress of

the appeal and the anxiety that brought on the heart attack. She said I was definitely having a preliminary attack while in that office.'

A spokeswoman for the DWP said: 'A decision on whether someone is well enough to work is taken following a thorough face-to-face assessment and after consideration of all the supporting medical evidence provided by the claimant at the time. If someone disagrees with the outcome of their assessment, they have the right to submit new evidence and appeal.

Source: Adapted from the Daily Record, *25 March 2013*

The harsh realities of the Government's 'bedroom tax'

Fred Williams understands what it is to be reliant on your home. He has cerebral palsy and his two-bedroom council house in south London has been heavily adapted to meet his needs. Williams, 59, had shared the house with his wife and step-children since 1991 but after the break-up of his marriage, now lives alone. Under the housing benefit changes, he will be classified as 'under-occupying' what was his family home and is now being told to look for somewhere smaller to live.

'We're talking about disabled people who can't just be picked up and dumped anywhere,' he tells me. His house has over twenty years' worth of adaptations to it. There's an existing stairlift and the council added ramps to the front and back doors. It also now has an extended kitchen and an accessible shower.

Any property he moved to would have to be similarly adapted, he stresses. It's an example of the cold economic thinking behind the bedroom tax: moving people from adapted homes, on the justification of savings for the public purse, only to have to pay for identical changes to whatever property they move to.

Source: By Frances Ryan, adapted from the New Statesman, *13 February 2013*

Show your understanding

Read the articles about Fred Williams and Jim Elliott.

1 Explain what Iain Duncan Smith meant when he said that he aims to 'make work pay'.
2 Explain the main aims *and* potential impact of the following government policies:
   a) ending of the spare room subsidy
   b) universal credit
   c) Work Capability Assessment
   d) individual benefits cap
   e) Work Programme.
3 What arguments does Fred have against the bedroom tax?
4 In what ways does Jim call into question the ability of Atos to assess his health condition correctly?

20-mark question

'Recent government policies are successful in tackling income inequalities.' Discuss.

Use this chapter to assist you in writing this essay. Include balance throughout, arguing the ways in which government policies have reduced inequality as well addressing some of the reasons why they have not been successful in tackling inequality. Chapter 2 will also help you. Make an essay plan with your teacher before you start.

Benefits: universal or means-tested?

Another key debate surrounding the Welfare State is whether benefits such as child benefit and state pension should be universal and given to all citizens regardless of income or whether they should be means-tested and given only to those most in need. Optical and dentistry services were once universal benefits and free to all, but now they are means-tested. Similarly, prescriptions – once a universal benefit – are still free in Scotland but means-tested in England. Government cuts have led to difficult decisions being made regarding some universal benefits.

The Scottish dimension

The SNP Government has reintroduced free prescriptions as it supports the concept of universal benefits (free eye tests also apply in Scotland but not England). However, Johann Lamont, Scottish Labour leader, has questioned the affordability of these benefits in addition to no university fees for Scottish students. With £3.3 billion of cuts to be imposed on the Scottish budget, she has argued for the end of a 'something-for-nothing culture' and for a review of all universal benefits.

Case study: Child benefit – from universal to means-tested benefit

In January 2013 the Government changed the child benefit system so that instead of being a universal benefit paid to all families regardless of how much they earn, it is now mean-tested. HMRC has said about 1.1 million families have been affected, 70 per cent of which will lose all of their child benefit. Any household in which someone earns more than £50,000 will no longer be entitled to the full payment and those that include someone earning more than £60,000 will not be entitled to any child benefit at all.

However, rather than just paying parents less, the Government will continue to pay the full amount and claw back overpayments through the self-assessment tax return system – unless the family opt not to receive the payments.

The tax charge has been set so the more you earn in excess of £50,000 the more you need to pay back. It is set at 1 per cent of the amount of child benefit for each £100 of income you receive beyond £50,000. If, for example, you earn £55,000 and have two children, you will need to repay 50 per cent of the benefit you have received over the tax year: £876 of the £1752 received.

Critics of this move argue that it penalises mothers who stay at home to bring up their children and is unfair. A one-income family with four children and a salary of £60,000 receives no child benefit, yet the next-door neighbour with one child and both parents working on incomes of £49,500 each (£99,000 combined) still receives full child benefit.

The current rate of child benefit is £20.30 a week for the oldest child and £13.40 a week for each subsequent child. Iain Duncan Smith plans to absorb child benefit into the universal credit system by 2017, thus making it truly means-tested.

Added Value idea

The issue over universal versus means-tested benefits is one that has received a lot of coverage in the media and in parliament in recent times. The elderly still receive the following universal benefits: state pension, winter fuel payment and free bus travel. On the other hand, the cold weather payment and other benefits such as pension credits are means-tested. Many argue that the winter fuel payment should be targeted more to those elderly people in poverty whereas some argue that there could still be a group of people who would suffer due to means-testing and others argue that given many elderly people have been paying into the Welfare State all of their life they are entitled to the payments.

One of the fundamental principles on which the NHS was based in 1948 was a commitment to remove inequalities in the provision of health care. Yet despite the achievements of the NHS, there is clear evidence that someone's social position, gender, ethnic origin and the area in which they live can affect their chances of achieving good health.

For this reason, care must be taken before concluding that poverty or social class, or other factors, are the key to explaining differences in mortality (death) or morbidity (illness) among individuals or groups. This explains the heated debate in the UK over the causes of health inequalities. One school of thought argues that poverty is the most crucial factor and cites numerous reports to support this viewpoint. The solution is a collectivist approach to tackle the social and economic impact of social exclusion. In contrast, the individualist approach states that all citizens have access to the NHS and must take responsibility for their own

health. The explosion in alcohol consumption and a rising tide of obesity are clear evidence of poor individual health choices.

Geographic inequalities

There is a clear north–south divide in the health of the British public. According to government statistics, death rates are highest in Scotland followed by the North and North West regions of England. UK health statistics highlight the wide disparities in cancer care and death rates across the UK. Scotland has almost twice the death rate in the South West of England. Life expectancy for men is lower in Scotland compared to England and Wales (Figure 4.2).

These differences cannot be explained through a disparity in health care expenditure and health service employees: annually more than £200

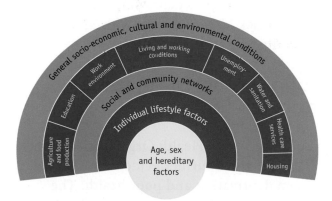

Figure 4.1 **Factors influencing health**

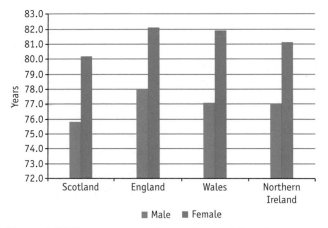

Figure 4.2 **Life expectancy for males and females born in 2010**

extra per person is spent on health care in Scotland, yet people who live in Scotland experience more ill health. Staffing levels in health care are also about 30 per cent higher than those in England. Scotland suffers greater social deprivation and has a lower percentage covered by private health care. For geographical reasons, it costs more to supply the same level and quality of service in Scotland than in England. Scotland has less than 10 per cent of the UK population, but about 33 per cent of its land area. In addition, Scotland has numerous island communities that need to be provided with adequate health care services.

Local differences

Although there are geographic inequalities, the explanation is not really one of geography but of wealth and poverty. There are areas in Scotland and northern England that compare favourably with the healthiest areas in the South East of England, whereas some deprived areas in London have poor health compared to more affluent areas.

It is clear that social class and lifestyle play a crucial role. This is highlighted in the findings of numerous government and health reports such as the examples outlined below.

Official reports on health inequalities

The Black Report, 1980

This was the report of the expert committee into health inequality chaired by Sir Douglas Black. The document demonstrated that, although overall health had improved since the introduction of the Welfare State, there were widespread health inequalities. It also found that

the main cause of these inequalities was economic inequality. The report had a huge impact on political thought in the UK and overseas. It led to an assessment by the Office for Economic Co-Operation and Development and the World Health Organization of health inequalities in 13 countries, though not of UK Government policy.

The Acheson Report, 1998

In 1997 the Labour Government set up a commission under the chairmanship of Sir Donald Acheson to investigate health inequalities in the UK. The document provided a comprehensive survey of the condition of the disadvantaged and its conclusion echoed the Black Report – poverty had to be tackled through concerted government action and a policy of social inclusion in education, housing, employment, social services and health provision.

Wealth of the Nation Report, 2006

This report highlighted the north–south health divide and confirmed the shockingly unhealthy lifestyles of a significant number of Scots. The document found that Scots are more likely to suffer long-term illness, take less exercise, be more overweight and spend more on cigarettes and alcohol than other Britons. A headline in the *Herald* summed up its depressing statistics: 'Scotland: Sick Man of the UK with 22 of the Top 25 Illness Areas'.

World Health Organization Report, 2008

In 2008 the World Health Organization (WHO) provided further evidence of the link between deprivation and poor health. The *Herald* in its article on the report had as its headline 'Poverty Takes 30 Years Off Your Life'. The WHO report had carried out a three-year analysis of the 'social determinants of health'. The report concludes 'social injustice is killing people on a grand scale'. For example, a boy in the Calton district of Glasgow's east end is likely to live to 54, but just a few miles away in the prosperous suburb of Lenzie average male life expectancy rises to 82. The report admits that there has been an improvement in people's health over the last decade, but the benefits to the worst off have not been as significant as those seen among the best off.

Figure 4.3 **Calton in Glasgow's east end**

Figure 4.4 **Lenzie, a prosperous suburb of Glasgow**

Scottish Health Survey, 2012

This report states boys and girls born in the most affluent areas of Scotland in 2011–12 can hope to reach the age of 70 and 72 respectively before suffering poor health. In contrast, boys in the poorest areas will only reach 46. Minister for Public Health Michael Matheson stated that income inequality was an important factor and the Scottish Government needed to develop a welfare system to support those who needed it.

Health and Social Care, 2014

This report from the Office for National Statistics (ONS) has revealed that only three-quarters of boys and 85 per cent of girls born in Glasgow will reach their 65th birthday. The average life expectancy of babies born in the city in 2010 to 2012 was 72.6 years for boys and 78.5 years for girls – eight to ten years behind the best performing areas in the UK. Boys born in East Dorset, the best performing area for males, can expect to live until they reach 83 and baby girls born in Purbeck can expect to reach 86.6 years (Table 4.1). Of Scotland's 32 local authorities, 72 per cent lie in the lowest league for life expectancy in the UK. In contrast, only 14 per cent of local areas in England are in this category.

'The problem cannot be solved with health solutions alone as other factors such as entrenched problems of poverty, educational under-attainment, unemployment and poor mental well-being also play a significant role in health inequalities.' (*Scottish Government*)

Table 4.1 **Bottom and top five ranked local areas by life expectancy at birth, 2000–02 to 2010–12**

Male (lowest)	Region	Age	Female (lowest)	Region	Age
Glasgow City	Scotland	72.6	Glasgow City	Scotland	78.5
Inverclyde	Scotland	73.7	West Dunbartonshire	Scotland	78.7
Blackpool	North West	74.0	North Lanarkshire	Scotland	79.1
West Dunbartonshire	Scotland	74.1	Dundee City	Scotland	79.3
Dundee City	Scotland	74.3	Manchester	North West	79.5
Male (highest)	**Region**	**Age**	**Female (highest)**	**Region**	**Age**
East Dorset	South West	82.9	Purbeck	South West	86.6
Hart	South East	82.9	East Dorset	South West	86.5
South Cambridgeshire	East	82.9	Richmond-upon-Thames	London	85.9
South Northamptonshire	East Midlands	82.2	Winchester	South East	85.9
Guildford	South East	82.1	South Cambridgeshire	East	85.9

Source: Office for National Statistics

The 'biology of poverty'

Recent research from the Centre for Population Studies indicates that the cycle and extent of poverty has a biological effect, which means that generations of families who live in areas of deprivation are more likely to succumb to illness. Harry Burns, the former chief medical officer of Scotland, referred to the West of Scotland experiencing a 'biology of poverty' and stated that conventional explanations for Scotland's appalling health record are no longer adequate. He argues that the collapse of heavy industry from 1950s onwards, which led to unemployment for skilled and manual workers and a breakdown in family and community relationships, has affected generations of children and created a cycle of entrapment.

The most significant finding is the variation across the UK in health for social class V (the group most likely to suffer poverty). The social class V figure for heart disease is almost double in Scotland compared to that in England, and the Scottish figure is significantly greater for all cancers. A key question is why, coming from a similar poor socio-economic background, is the health of the Scots so much worse?

Three Cities Report, 2010

Further evidence of the complexity of the causes of health inequalities appeared in the *Journal of Public Health* in March 2010. The research examined the health and death rates of the citizens of Glasgow, Manchester and Liverpool between 2003 and 2007, cities with broadly similar deprivation figures but with different health outcomes. The headline in the *Herald* – 'Blame Glasgow Effect for City's Chronic Ill Health – Not Deprivation' – clearly indicated that lifestyle, not just poverty, was to blame. The *Herald* concludes: 'We cannot casually blame it on our genetic inheritance or the climate and this research shows we can no longer put it down to poverty, so we must change our behaviour.'

These findings confirm the research by Professor Phil Hanlon of the University of Glasgow Centre for Population Health. This points to a Glasgow/West of Scotland effect in which the combination of decades of unemployment with factors including poverty, chronic stress, relationship issues, attitudes and behaviour, and damage to physical and mental health, results in early deaths for adults in these areas.

Fact file

The 'Glasgow effect'

- In Glasgow about one-quarter of the population are classed as deprived. Manchester and Liverpool have similar profiles. However, there are 900 extra deaths a year in Glasgow compared to Manchester and Liverpool.
- Deaths among the most wealthy were 15 per cent higher in Glasgow than in the other two cities and 18 per cent higher among the most deprived.
- Glasgow's cancer and heart disease deaths are well above those of Manchester and Liverpool (Figure 4.5).
- More disturbing are the alcohol- and drugs-related deaths in Glasgow – more than double the figures of the other two cities.

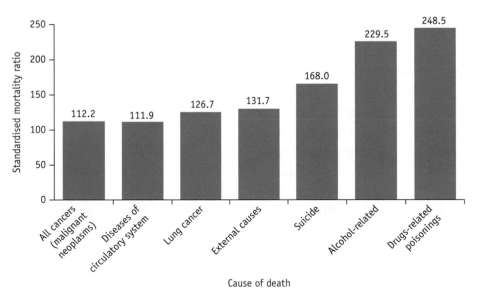

Figure 4.5 **Standardised mortality ratios 2003–07 for Glasgow relative to Manchester and Liverpool (combined) for seven causes/groups of causes**
Source: *Journal of Public Health*, 2010

Figure 4.6 Deprivation in (from left to right) Glasgow, Manchester and Liverpool

Show your understanding

1 To what extent is there a north–south divide in the health of the UK public and is finance to blame?
2 Outline the evidence that supports the view that social class/poverty is a crucial factor in health inequalities.
3 What conclusions does the Three Cities Report make?

Lifestyle issues

Poverty is a major factor in explaining health inequalities. However, this cannot explain why the health of Scots in areas of deprivation is worse than that of their counterparts in England. As indicated in the Three Cities Report, lifestyle is also an important factor. Unhealthy diets and obesity, cigarette smoking and drugs and alcohol – all lifestyle choices – play a crucial role in someone's health. Figures published in November 2013 highlight the obesity crisis facing Scotland and the UK. Around 64 per cent of Scots are overweight or obese, with a staggering 27 per cent falling into the latter category. Obesity figures have increased from 17 per cent in 1996 to 27 per cent in 2013. The rise in the number of overweight children is a phenomenon common in the western world and is based on a diet of high fat junk food and a dramatic reduction in physical activity. About 31 per cent of children aged 2 to 15 were overweight or obese with 17 per cent at risk of obesity. Children with two obese parents run a 70 per cent risk of becoming obese themselves, compared with a risk of less than 20 per cent among children with two lean parents. In 1996, 10 per cent of children in the UK were obese, with the figure rising to 18 per cent by 2010.

Social class and obesity

A careful examination of socio-economic distribution of people in Britain who are overweight or obese confirms that fat is also a class issue. The lowest social class has levels of obesity that matches American levels whereas the highest social classes have the lowest obesity levels.

A 2014 report on the body mass index (BMI) of Primary 1 children who started school in 2012–13 highlighted the disparity between those in the richest and poorest areas of Scotland. Although 81 per cent of children in the most affluent areas were at a healthy weight, the figure fell to about 70 per cent in the most deprived areas. Significantly, the children classified as obese were twice as likely to be from an area of deprivation

Obesity

- 7000 adults in the UK cannot work because they are registered as obese. The cost to the taxpayer is nearly £30 million a year in welfare payments.
- The Department for Work and Pensions reveals that welfare payments for those registered as obese have doubled in five years.
- Up to 74 children were taken into care in the UK between 2008 and 2013 because they were morbidly obese.
- 183 children under 12 years old have been recorded as weighing more than 101 kg (16 stones) between 2010 and 2013. Eight were more than 127 kg (20 stones) and the heaviest weighed 146 kg (23 stones).
- A study of Scottish babies indicates that children born to obese mothers are more likely to die before they reach the age of 55.
- Between 2008 and 2013, fire crews in Scotland were called out more than 200 times to rescue people too overweight to move.
- In March 2014, Liam Johnson, Scotland's heaviest man, died of a suspected heart attack. Liam was only 22 but he weighed an estimated 420 kg (66 stones).
- The number of people with diabetes in the UK is now more than 3.2 million, up from 1.4 million in 1996. Type 2 diabetes is linked to obesity and unhealthy lifestyles.

than from an affluent area. Chris Mantle, a member of the Association for Nutrition, stated: 'The data shows us that sadly as deprivation increases, healthy weight declines. In this, as in many other areas of health, we see that social inequalities often result in health inequalities.'

It is estimated that obesity costs the NHS in Scotland £457 million every year. The drug bill alone is over £5 million, with some 12,000 Scots taking obesity drugs. At present, an estimated 3400 people die in Scotland as a direct result of obesity every year. The scale of the problem is reflected in hospitals spending tens of thousands of pounds on specialist beds that can take patients who are obese.

Smoking

Smoking is a crucial factor in the ill health of people who live in deprived areas, and it is a class issue. In 1960 there were no significant differences in the smoking habits of all social classes in the UK. The award-winning TV series *Mad Men*, set in 1960s affluent America, depicts all the top executives as smokers. However, by the 1990s the professional classes had listened to health advice and the number of smokers in social class A had fallen by 75 per cent. In contrast, the number of smokers in social class V had dropped by only 30 per cent.

It is clear that smoking is one factor that explains the different mortality rates between the social classes. For women booking into antenatal clinics, 36 per cent of those from the most deprived 20 per cent of the population were smokers, compared to 6 per cent who were in the least deprived 20 per cent.

In 2010, 47 per cent of adults in deprived areas of Scotland were smokers, a higher proportion than in deprived areas of England and Wales where the figure was 41 per cent. This geographic difference can be explained by poverty and lifestyle. This explains why the Scottish Government banned smoking in public places in 2006 (see page 56). Every year there are more than 13,000 smoking-related deaths in Scotland alone.

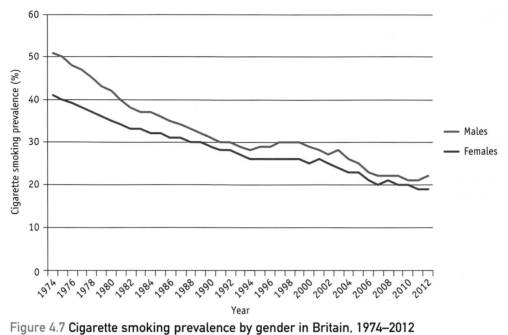

Figure 4.7 Cigarette smoking prevalence by gender in Britain, 1974–2012
Source: Cancer Research UK, June 2014

Unfortunately the number of women experiencing lung cancer has significantly increased, as shown by the 2014 Cancer Research report. Although Scottish lung cancer rates for men have fallen 40 per cent since 1974, they have increased 97 per cent for women. Figure 4.8 illustrates the dramatic change in lung cancer rates.

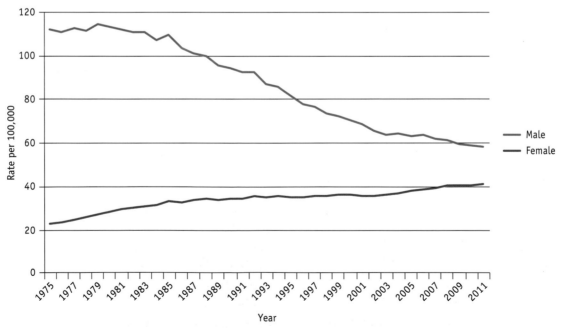

Figure 4.8 Lung cancer rates per 100,000 of population by gender in Britain, 1974–2011
Source: Cancer Research UK, June 2014

Figure 4.9 **The combination of smoking, poor diet, lack of exercise and drinking too much increases the risk of death**

Alcohol and drug abuse

Excessive consumption of alcohol leads to ill health with increased likelihood of illnesses such as cirrhosis of the liver and high blood pressure. Parts of Scotland are blighted by a 'booze culture' which, according to the NHS, kills 40 Scots a week.

Total recorded alcohol consumption doubled in the UK between 1964 and 2010. The 2010 Scottish Health Survey indicated that Scots are more likely than drinkers elsewhere in Britain to binge on alcohol and to exceed the recommended daily intake. Daily alcohol consumption in Scotland for both men and women is 25 per cent higher than in England. Average weekly consumption for men is 43 units, which is more than double the official recommended intake.

A further major concern is the increase in the number of young people who drink to excess. Ian Gilmore of the Royal College of Physicians stated that it had once been unusual to see serious alcohol-related liver damage before the age of 40. Now people in their 30s or even 20s are showing signs of such damage. The youngest person found to have alcohol-related liver damage was a 17-year-old who started drinking at the age of 12.

Unfortunately there is a clear link between alcohol-related deaths and deprivation, with some of the most deprived parts of Glasgow and its surrounding areas having an alcohol death rate more than three or four times the UK average (Table 4.2).

Table 4.2 **Glasgow: alcohol-related deaths per 100,000 of population, 2013**

Area	Number of deaths
Glasgow Shettleston	76
Glasgow Maryhill	56
Greenock and Inverclyde	49
Dundee East	46
Glasgow Springburn	44
Dumbarton	41
Eastwood Glasgow	11
Tweeddale, Etterick and Lauderdale	4
Paisley South	38
UK average	13

Source: Scottish Government

The minority SNP Government failed in November 2010 to have its proposals to tackle alcohol abuse approved by the Scottish Parliament. However, after the 2011 election, the majority SNP Government passed a minimum pricing bill (see page 59).

Scotland also faces a serious drugs problem. According to a 2009 United Nations report, Scotland is ranked second out of 47 European countries for heroin, cannabis and ecstasy use. The same report shows that 3.8 per cent of people in Scotland consume cocaine, compared with 2.3 per cent in England and Wales.

Gender inequalities

The gender gap in health, summarised by Agnes Miles in her 1991 book *Women, Health and Medicine*, is still relevant: 'Women live longer but suffer from more health problems in their lifetime.' The causes of death, moreover, vary between men and women for different age groups. In the 1–14 age group, for example, nearly twice as many boys as girls die from accidents and violence, while in middle age, deaths from lung cancer, heart disease, accidents and suicide are the major reasons for males' higher mortality rates. In Scotland, the major cause of death in women is lung cancer rather than breast cancer. Although breast cancer is still common, the recovery rate is far higher than for lung cancer. The smoking habits of women over the last 25 years are causing concern and there is clear evidence that the number of females who die from lung cancer is increasing (see Figure 4.8).

Mortality

Life expectancy is a commonly used indicator of health, and women live longer than men across all social classes. The life expectancy of women in the most deprived social class is lower than for males in the least deprived. Differences in life expectancy reflect biological and social differences. Men are more likely than women to die prematurely from heart disease and have higher death rates from lung cancer, injuries, poisoning and suicide.

In the UK, the most common causes of death in both men and women are cancer and circulatory diseases. However, women are more likely than men to die from strokes when they are much older, and men suffer heart attacks at an earlier age. Pressures on men from social expectations and norms mean that they are more likely to suffer from health problems and deaths related to smoking, alcohol and fast driving. The number of male

deaths from chronic liver disease and cirrhosis is nearly twice the number of female deaths.

Morbidity

Although women live longer, they also suffer from more ill health than men. Figures in the General Household Survey suggest that women in the lowest social class group report more than twice the rate of illness of women in the highest group. Women's traditional domestic responsibilities lead them to suffer higher levels of anxiety and depression compared to males, particularly if they are poor and lone parents. Women are two to three times more likely than men to be affected by depression or anxiety. They are however more likely to report illness at an earlier stage and so are more likely to make use of their doctor and be admitted to hospital.

Ethnicity and health

Poverty

Just as in the general population, poverty has an important impact on health in ethnic groups. Those groups that have incomes closest to the white population average, such as Africans, Asians and Chinese, record health levels close to those of the white population. Those groups that are poorest record significantly poorer levels of health. For example, Pakistanis and Bangladeshis record health levels that are 50 per cent worse than white people, and Caribbeans are 30 per cent worse.

Reported ill health

Asians report greater levels of ill health than other groups in the population. Chinese are less likely than the general population to report poor health. However, it is only in the over-50 age group that there is any significant difference in long-term limiting illness between ethnic minorities and the majority population.

Ethnic minorities differ in their risk of suffering from certain diseases. Diabetes is a particular problem for Pakistanis and Bangladeshis, who are more than five times more likely to suffer from it than the white population. Indians of both genders are three times more at risk. Pakistani and Bangladeshi men and women, and black Caribbean women, face a higher risk of heart disease than average, whereas Chinese face a lower than average risk.

Smoking and alcohol consumption

Culture has a significant impact on lifestyle choice. For example, Islam does not permit the consumption of alcohol. Social customs among some groups do not approve of women smoking.

The 2010 Health Survey for England found that members of all minority ethnic groups were less likely to drink alcohol than the general population, and those who did consumed smaller amounts. Only 6 per cent of men in the general population were non-drinkers, compared to 43 per cent of black Caribbean men, 29 per cent of Chinese men, 32 per cent of Indian men and 90 per cent of Pakistani men. Overall, ethnic minorities suffer fewer diseases linked to alcohol over-consumption such as cirrhosis of the liver.

Bangladeshi men are more likely to smoke than any other group, followed by black Caribbean men. However, Indian, Pakistani and in particular Chinese men are less likely to smoke compared to the general population. Obviously, smoking has a significant impact on health, particularly in the rates for cancer and respiratory problems.

Barriers to accessing health care

Many members of the minority ethnic community fail to access health care because of poor English language skills. Often without interpreters, minorities have difficulty knowing what is available or explaining what the problem is, so do not seek medical care. There are also cultural barriers. Different groups in the minority ethnic community have different ways of dealing with ill health and these might not be understood by health care professionals in the UK. For example, research has shown that the diagnosis of chronic illness may not be discussed in the South Asian community so they may find it difficult to accept care from someone outside their community.

Show your understanding

1 What problems do obesity, alcohol and cigarettes create for an individual's health?
2 What evidence supports the view that lifestyle is a social class/poverty issue?
3 Compare the differences in both mortality and morbidity for men and women.
4 Higher levels of ill health among British minority ethnic groups can be linked to a number of factors. Provide evidence for each of the following: poverty, lifestyle, access to health care.

Government responses to health inequalities

The UK Labour Government of 1997–2010 and the Scottish Government of 1999–2011 identified poverty and its links with lifestyle as being a major cause of health inequalities. Health is a devolved issue and the Scottish Labour/Liberal Democrat Coalition Governments (1999–2007) and the SNP Government (2007 onwards) have done much to improve the health of the Scottish public. Labour and the Liberal Democrats can point to their Working Together for a Healthier Scotland strategy, which is reflected in the banning of smoking in public places in 2006, and the SNP to its Equally Well strategy (see page 61), which is reflected in the introduction of free prescriptions in 2011, as key initiatives in tackling health inequalities.

The UK Labour Government, through its welfare changes (see Chapter 3), did much to reduce child poverty. However, the banking crisis of 2008 and the recent economic recession followed by the massive Coalition Government cuts in public spending 2010–15 will make it difficult to maintain progress in the reduction of health and wealth inequalities.

This chapter considers measures taken by the Scottish Government to improve the health of the Scottish people and to reduce health inequalities. Although health is a devolved issue, the UK Government, in its economic measures, impacts on health spending in Scotland. In the period 2003–08, NHS spending in the UK significantly increased to bring UK health spending as a percentage of GDP in line with European levels. In England health spending rose from £34 billion in 1998 to £90 billion and in Scotland from £4.6 million to £10.3 million over the same period. Both the Coalition Government and the Scottish Government have protected health spending. However, a modest increase in health spending is actually a significant cut as the NHS has a much higher rate of inflation than the economy as a whole. It offers a 24-hour service and the demands placed on it continue to increase – with an ageing population, new medical technology, the introduction of new drugs and an obesity crisis.

Vigorous and controversial measures have been taken against smoking and tackling obesity, especially in the young, and tackling binge drinking is a high priority. The decision to restrict smoking has led some health specialists to advocate greater government intervention in controlling the drinking and eating habits of the Scottish public (see page 59).

What has been achieved?

Smoking ban

It was hoped that the smoking ban in enclosed public places (pubs, restaurants and other public places) introduced in Scotland on 26 March 2006 would dramatically reduce health inequalities in Scotland. England followed Scotland's example in 2007. Recent health statistics clearly indicate that Scots are living longer and that the death rates for cancer and heart disease are declining. One would assume that the ban has contributed to this improvement, as evidence from researchers at Edinburgh University supports the above assertion. The researchers have been tracking changes in the lifestyle choices of school pupils aged between 11 and 15 every four years since 1990. The latest analysis, published in March 2011, found that between 2006 and 2010 the smoking rates among boys and girls had decreased. The rate for girls had fallen from 28 per cent to 19 per cent by 2010. This suggests that there are roughly 600 fewer 15-year-old smokers across Scotland. Professor Currie, Head of the Research Unit, stated: 'The smoking ban is the most obvious explanation.' The same report also provided evidence of a decrease in drink and drug use by young people. The number of young people drinking alcohol at least once a week has fallen by more than one-third, and experimental and regular cannabis use has halved since 2002.

The Office for National Statistics' General Lifestyle Survey 2014 confirmed that smoking has more than halved in just under 40 years. In 1974, 45 per cent of adults smoked compared to 20 per cent today. It is estimated that the ban has saved 600 lives every year and saved the NHS £8 million annually. However, lung cancer rates are 49 per cent higher in Scotland than in England and Wales and it is clear that advertising campaigns against smoking have had limited impact.

NHS Scotland revealed in September 2011 that the number of Scots giving up smoking had beaten the Scottish Government targets, with 89,075 people quitting in the period 2007–11. This supports the view that the smoking ban has acted as an incentive for many to quit their smoking habit (Figure 4.10).

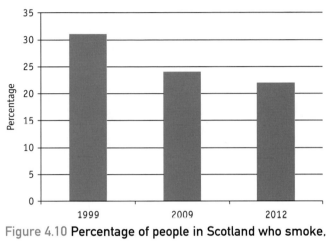

Figure 4.10 **Percentage of people in Scotland who smoke, 1999–2012**
Source: Scottish Household Survey, 2013

The Scottish Government hopes to introduce further measures to discourage smoking. Under proposed 2014–15 legislation, motorists would be banned from smoking in their cars if children are passengers. Any such motorist caught smoking by the police would be fined £60. This proposal is opposed by the smokers' group Forest. Its director, Simon Clark, stated: 'A ban on smoking in private vehicles would represent a major intrusion into people's lives. What next, a ban on smoking in the home if children are present?'

The Scottish Government is also considering a proposal that cigarettes should be sold in plain packaging. In a survey carried out by Cancer Research, only 12 per cent of Scots were against the proposal. Anti-smoking campaigners argue that such a move would help to reduce the product's 'deadly allure'.

Electronic cigarettes

Electronic cigarettes, or e-cigarettes, are battery-powered devices that simulate tobacco smoking. Their supporters argue that they are a safer alternative to cigarettes and encourage smokers to end their smoking habits. Critics argue that e-cigarettes still contain nicotine and they might encourage non-smokers, especially young people, to take up e-smoking. Safety concerns have also been raised following a woman hospital patient being engulfed in flames and seriously burned after her e-cigarette ignited oxygen. The Welsh Government is considering whether to ban e-smoking in public places.

What is certain is the growing popularity of e-cigarettes. Since 2011 the number of people using them has tripled from 700,000 to 2.1 million. Robert West, director of tobacco research at University College London, stated: 'About 85 per cent of people using cigarettes are smokers trying to quit, but many relapse and are now using e-cigarettes.'

In May 2014 a leading environmental health organisation called for a ban on the public use of e-cigarettes. The Royal Environmental Health Institute for Scotland (REHIS) stated that 'There are still serious questions to be answered on the long-term health implications of these devices.'

Added Value idea

The debate over e-cigarettes is hugely topical. This could be a good opportunity for your Added Value unit assignment. You will need to research and develop your own sources and present your findings in the form of a report. Discuss this with your teacher.

The smoking ban and the health of young children

A 2014 report by Edinburgh researchers on the effects of smoking laws in different countries provides positive evidence that the smoking ban improves the health of young children. The research, published in the *Lancet*, noted that there had been in Scotland a one-tenth fall in premature births and a similar reduction in attendance at hospital for children experiencing asthma attacks.

Daniel Sanderson wrote in the *Herald* (28 March 2014) that 'Passive smoking can cause babies to be stillborn or born prematurely and is linked to birth defects, asthma and lung infections. Studies have also suggested that being exposed to second-hand smoke during childhood may have long-term health implications, contributing to heart disease and diabetes.'

Diet and obesity

An important recommendation of the World Health Organization's 1997 report *Obesity: Preventing and Managing the Global Epidemic*, chaired by Professor Philip James, was an investigation into how to limit children eating junk food, rich in sugar, fat and salt, all of which are linked to obesity and heart disease in later life. The main proposal was to:

- introduce healthier food menus in schools
- stop the sale of sweets, salty snacks and soft drinks inside schools
- set a legal limit on the age at which children are allowed out of school during lunchtime
- prohibit food companies targeting food advertising at the young.

For adults, several health promotion campaigns have been financed by the Government to raise health awareness. Advertising on the television and radio has had some impact. Many adults are aware that they should try to eat at least five portions of fruit and vegetables a day and to reduce their salt intake. Campaigns to encourage improved physical fitness, such as Be All You Can Be, can be measured in part by the increase in the number of people out jogging and participating in special sporting events.

Television chef Jamie Oliver's high-profile campaign to improve school dinners was one factor in influencing government action in England, the cost of which was £220 million. In September 2006 the Labour Government implemented new food standards in England and Wales, following the lead set by the Scottish Government. The Schools (Health Promotion and Nutrition) Scotland Act 2007 and the Nutritional Requirement for Food and Drinks in Schools (Scotland) Regulation 2008 build on the achievement of Hungry for Success by establishing uniform standards for all food and drinks in schools.

In response to Deputy Prime Minister Nick Clegg's pledge of £600 million to fund free school meals for all Primary 1–3 children from September 2014, Alex Salmond announced that free school meals would also be provided for all Primary 1–3 Scottish pupils from January 2015. Local councils would receive £64 million to provide this new legal requirement. Free school meals are provided for every child if the parents are receiving welfare benefits. However, Labour-controlled councils have declared that the funding allocation will not meet the costs of providing a universal free school meal. They argue that it will cost £88 million, leaving a shortfall of £24 million. The Child Poverty Action Group, which campaigns for free school meals to be introduced, supports the move.

The Scottish Government can take some comfort from the findings of the September 2010 Scottish Health survey. The survey stated that the number of people classed as overweight had

Case study: Calorie tax plan recipe for tackling obesity

At a 2011 public health conference attended by the country's leading public health professionals, Dr Chandler, public health doctor for NHS Dumfries and Galloway, proposed that a minimum price per calorie should be set. This proposal would drive up the cost of fatty and sugary products such as crisps and chocolate. In Denmark, the government had already imposed tax increases of 25 per cent on ice cream, chocolate and sweets to tackle the rising tide of obesity and heart disease, although this policy was scrapped just over a year after its introduction.

Dr Chandler's view was reinforced in 2014 by the Academy of Medical Royal Colleges, which stated that obesity is the country's biggest health crisis and costs the NHS more than £5 billion a year. They argued that fizzy drinks should be heavily taxed and that fast-food outlets near schools or colleges should be banned. Television adverts for fatty foods and sugary drinks should also be banned. A 2013 investigation by the *Sunday Times* stated that the amount of sugar in some baby and toddler foods is as much as three times higher than a limit set by the Government. Dr Mars Skae, a consultant paediatrician, stated: 'I am increasingly being referred children as young as four in our specialist obesity clinics who suffer from morbid obesity.'

Glasgow University medical researchers have also concluded that fruit juice cartons contain as much sugar as some fizzy cans. They further added that if the food industry cut the amount of sugar it put into food by 30 per cent, the obesity crisis could abate. However, the Scottish Government's attempts to collaborate with the big supermarket chains over restrictions on multi-buy deals and in-store promotions in order to tackle obesity did not succeed. In December 2013 the Scottish Retail Consortium (SRC) withdrew from the voluntary scheme, stating that the scheme was 'prescriptive and unworkable'.

fallen for the first time in 15 years. The proportion of boys with a weight problem fell from 38 per cent to 31 per cent, a significant improvement. The survey also indicated that children have a healthier diet. In 2003, 54 per cent enjoyed chips at least twice a week but this has dropped to 40 per cent. However, 86 per cent of children were still failing to eat enough fruit and vegetables.

Tackling alcohol abuse

Following the SNP's success in the 2011 elections, the Scottish Parliament passed the minimum unit pricing (MUP) for alcohol. (It had failed in an earlier attempt in 2010.) This proposal was opposed by the other main parties. However, the bill was supported by Dr Harry Burns, Scotland's chief medical officer, and the British Medical Association (BMA) in Scotland and at UK level. 'Scotland has an unenviable reputation when it comes to alcohol. We are, sadly, world-class when it comes to damaging our health through heavy drinking,' Dr Burns stated.

The SNP proposed to fix a minimum price for all alcoholic drinks at 50p per unit. That would double or treble the cost of the cheapest super-strength ciders sold by major supermarkets, and raise the cost of cheap supermarket vodka by nearly £4 a bottle. Nicola Sturgeon, Deputy First Minister, argued that minimum price was essential to help tackle the high death toll and health burden from alcohol abuse in Scotland, where 25 per cent more alcohol is drunk per head of population than in the rest of the UK. The SNP Government claimed that MUP would lead to

50 fewer deaths, 1200 fewer hospital admissions and millions of pounds saved in health care every year. Nicola Sturgeon stated: 'For too long, too many Scots have been drinking themselves into an early grave. It is no coincidence that as the affordability of alcohol has plummeted in recent decades, alcohol-related deaths, crime and disorder have spiralled. It cannot be right that a man can exceed his weekly recommended alcohol limit for less than £3.50.'

The proposal was lambasted by the drinks industry, which is challenging the plan for a minimum unit of 50p on the basis that it contravenes EU trading rules. Opposition politicians at Holyrood also oppose the proposal. Jackie Baillie, Labour's Shadow Health Secretary, said the proposal was a 'tax on the poor', which would increase revenue for supermarkets by £140 million. 'The SNP has got this one badly wrong – it will make no difference to problem drinks, like Buckfast, but it will punish people on low incomes.'

However, research produced in 2014 by the University of Sheffield and published in the medical journal the *Lancet* supported the view that MUP would effectively target high-risk drinkers without affecting people on low incomes who drink in moderation. Overall, those most affected by the change would be the 5 per cent of the population whose drinking is classed as harmful, which is more than 50 units a week for men and 35 units for women.

In a powerful appeal to the Scottish whisky Industry, the *Herald* published a letter from 22 doctors and academics which called on the Scottish Whisky Association (SWA) to drop its opposition to the bill. The headline in the *Herald* of 1 April 2014 was no April's Fool.

New evidence from Canada supports the view that MUP will save lives. The chief executive of Alcohol Focus Scotland stated that in Canada a 10 per cent increase in average minimum alcohol pricing contributed towards a reduction in the number of alcohol-related deaths of almost one-third.

SWA should drop challenge

It is now one year to the day when minimum unit pricing should have been introduced in Scotland.

Yet still we wait for this vital public health policy, supported by the Scottish Parliament, to come into force. It has been delayed because the Scotch Whisky Association (SWA) is fighting its implementation every step of the way. The SWA has mirrored the tactics of the tobacco industry in delaying life-saving legislation. It opposes any measure that might affect its profits, no matter the obvious benefits to people's health. By taking this legal action, it is undermining the united view of the Scottish Parliament and costing taxpayers thousands of pounds in legal bills.

Despite recent welcome improvements, alcohol is a huge health and social problem for Scotland. Getting rid of ultra-cheap alcohol through minimum pricing is a crucial first step in turning things round and one which will make a genuine, lasting difference to health, crime and society. Minimum pricing will cut alcohol-related hospital admissions and save lives. We cannot afford to delay any longer.

This is an appeal to the Scotch Whisky Association to immediately drop its legal challenge and bow to the will of the Scottish Parliament. It's the right thing to do.

Source: Letter by 22 doctors and academics, published in the Herald, *1 April 2014*

Show your understanding

1 Outline the policies introduced to tackle smoking and obesity and assess their effectiveness.
2 Outline the arguments for and against MUP.

Equally Well report, 2008

The SNP Government was aware that the causes of health inequalities were complex and that any strategy had to include a partnership model. The *Equally Well Report of the Ministerial Task Force on Health Equalities* concentrates on poverty, lack of employment, children's lives, support for families and physical and social environments, as well as on health and well-being. Extracts from the report clearly indicate that wealth and health inequalities interact. According to the Scottish Government, 'there is a clear relationship between income inequality and health inequality'.

Delivering on the Task Force's recommendations depends on a strong joint working commitment between the NHS, local government, the third sector and others within community planning partnerships.

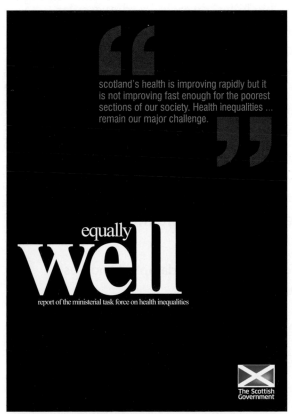

Figure 4.11 The Scottish Government's *Equally Well* report, 2008

Key points

- Health inequalities remain a significant challenge in Scotland.
- The poorest in Scottish society die earlier and have higher rates of disease, including mental illness.
- Healthy life expectancy needs to be increased across the board to achieve the Scottish Government's overall purpose of sustainable economic growth.
- Tackling health inequalities requires action from national and local government and from other agencies including the NHS, schools, employers and third sector.
- Priority areas are children, particularly in the early years, 'killer diseases' such as heart disease, mental health and the harm caused by drugs, alcohol and violence.
- Radical cross-cutting action is needed to address Scotland's health gap to benefit its citizens, communities and the country as a whole.

Decline in children's tooth decay

The *Equally Well* report placed emphasis on promoting the health of the young, especially in areas of deprivation. A December 2013 report concluded that tooth decay among young people was at its lowest ever level. The 2005 Action Plan to improve oral health in Scotland set a target for all Primary 1 and Primary 7 children to receive a basic dental inspection at school. Across Scotland, 67 per cent of Primary 1 children are decay-free. For the first time, all NHS boards have met the Scottish Government's target of 60 per cent of Primary 1s to have no obvious signs of decay. Inevitably there is still a gulf between the dental health of children from affluent families and those from poorer homes. The two health boards with the highest rates of tooth decay are Greater Glasgow and Clyde, and Lanarkshire.

Key health inequalities

The Task Force identified some significant challenges, including:

- In Scotland in 2006, healthy life expectancy at birth was 67.9 years for men and 69 years for women. In the most deprived 15 per cent of areas in Scotland in 2005–06, healthy life expectancy at birth was considerably lower at 57.3 years for men and 59 years for women.
- A higher proportion of babies born to mothers living in the most deprived fifth of the population have a low birth weight than those born to mothers living in the most affluent areas (9 per cent compared to 5 per cent in 2004–05).
- People who had a low household income, or reported finding it difficult to manage on their household income, had poorer mental well-being than those with a high household income or who reported finding it easy to manage on their income.
- There are large and increasing relative inequalities in deaths amongst young adults due to drugs, alcohol, assault and suicide.
- More than two-thirds of the total alcohol-related deaths were in the most deprived two-fifths of areas.

- Those living in the most deprived 10 per cent of areas of Scotland have a suicide risk double that of the Scottish average.
- Adult smoking rates increase with increasing deprivation. In Scotland in 2005–06, smoking rates ranged from 11 per cent in the least deprived 10 per cent of areas to 44 per cent in the most deprived 10 per cent.

Priorities

In order to reduce inequalities in healthy life expectancy, the report identified the following priorities where action is most needed:

- Children's very early years, where inequalities may first arise and influence the rest of people's lives.
- The high economic, social and health burden imposed by mental illness, and the corresponding requirement to improve mental well-being.
- The 'big killer' diseases: cardiovascular disease and cancer. Some risk factors for these, such as smoking, are strongly linked to deprivation.
- Drug and alcohol problems and links to violence that affect younger men in particular and where inequalities are widening.

Fact file

Characteristics of policies more likely to be effective in reducing inequalities in health

- Structural changes in the environment (e.g. installing affordable heating in damp cold houses).
- Legislative and regulatory controls (e.g. smoking bans in workplaces).
- Fiscal policies (e.g. increase price of tobacco and alcohol products).
- Income support (e.g. tax and benefit systems, professional welfare rights advice and health care settings).
- Reducing price barriers (e.g. free prescriptions).
- Starting young (e.g. pre- and post-natal support and interventions, home visiting in infancy, good quality pre-school day care).

Source: *Equally Well* 2008, Scottish Government

'Early intervention is a hallmark of this Government's approach to improving the lives of Scots and delivering the better Scotland that we all want to see. The early years of a child's life are a key opportunity to build resilience and reduce the impact of inequalities on health outcomes.' (*Adam Ingram, Minister for Children and Early Years*)

Free prescriptions

In April 2011 all prescriptions became free in Scotland and this flagship policy of the SNP Government was hailed as a significant strategy in improving the health of the Scottish public and in reducing health inequalities. Critics argued that in a time of economic recession it was a misguided policy that would deprive the NHS of badly needed funding and would benefit the better off. The SNP pointed out that more than 90 per cent of prescriptions (some 68 million) issued in 2010 applied to those entitled to free prescriptions. The loss of income from prescription charges is estimated to be £57 million annually.

In October 2012 Johann Lamont, Scottish Labour leader, spoke about the need to end a 'something-for-nothing culture'. She argued that with £3.3 billion of cuts to be imposed on the Scottish budget, a review was needed of universal benefits and especially free prescriptions. In March 2014 Ruth Davidson, Scottish Conservative leader, stated that Scotland should end free prescriptions. She argued that ending the policy of universal free prescriptions could free up cash to spend on more hospital staff.

The move was immediately attacked by SNP Health Secretary Alex Neil who stated: 'Thousands of people are benefiting from the abolition of prescription charges, including many with long-term conditions who otherwise might not get the treatment they need. Prescription charges were a tax on ill health, they prevent people getting the medication they need and damage their ability to work.' According to the Government, the policy has meant that around 600,000 adults with an annual income of less than £17,000 are now entitled to free prescriptions.

Since charges were scrapped in 2011, there has been an increase of more than 10,000 prescription items for those with Crohn's disease and about 237,000 items for those with asthma.

Fact file

Free prescriptions

Free prescriptions were introduced in Wales in 2007, Northern Ireland in 2010 and Scotland in 2011. In England in 2014 a prescription charge is £7.85 per item or £104 for an annual pre-payment certificate. It is free in England for all of those who are:
- claiming aspects of universal benefits
- aged 60 or over or under 16 or students under the age of 19
- pregnant or have had a baby in the last 12 months
- suffering from a medical condition that is listed on the free prescription list.

Those who oppose free prescriptions highlight that the number of prescriptions in Wales has grown by more than 50 per cent in ten years. More prescriptions are given per person in Wales, which began a gradual phasing out of prescription charges in 2004, than in any other country in the UK (Figure 4.12). However, a Welsh Government spokesperson stated: 'There is no link between the number of prescriptions per head and prescriptions charges. Wales has dispensed more prescriptions per head than England since as far back as the 1970s.' Furthermore, a comparison between the figures from England and Scotland undermine the view that free prescriptions are wasteful and extravagant as consumption per head of population is slightly higher in England.

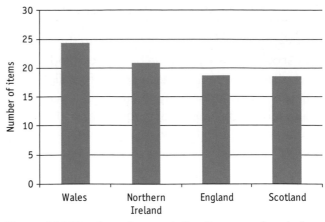

Figure 4.12 **Number of prescription items per head of population, 2013**
Source: Welsh Government

Figure 4.13 Nicola Sturgeon, Deputy First Minister

'Prescription charges are a tax on ill health, and can be a barrier to good health for too many people. This Scottish Government is committed to building a healthier nation; through tackling the health inequalities that still scar our nation and supporting people to live longer and lead healthier lives. I also want the NHS to be true to its founding principle: the principle of health care free at the point of need.' (*Nicola Sturgeon*)

'Prescription apartheid'

The British Medical Association in England and voluntary groups are unhappy that many English patients have to pay for their prescriptions while the Scots, Welsh and Irish receive them free. Here is the view of Emily Watt, an English student from Liverpool, now studying and living in Dundee. She was diagnosed with ulcerative colitis in 2010 at the age of 18 and now needs to take medication for the rest of her life.

I'm living in Dundee and enjoying studying Law at the University of Dundee. If I had to pay for my prescriptions, I would sometimes have to decide between paying my bills or paying for my medicine. I'll have this condition for the rest of my life and in my view it's a tax on ill health for the English public. Basically, it's prescription apartheid.

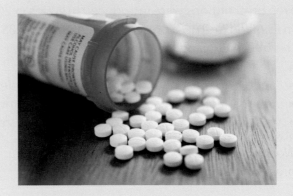

Table 4.3 Arguments in favour of and against free prescriptions

In favour of free prescriptions	Against free prescriptions
Meets the founding principles of the NHS of health care free at the point of need. Prescription charges are a tax on ill health. Wales introduced free prescriptions in 2007. The previous system was inconsistent, for example, those patients with epilepsy received free prescriptions while those with high blood pressure or Parkinson's disease had to pay.	The principles of free prescriptions were quickly abandoned in the 1950s. We have free visits to the doctor and hospital treatment is free. It will encourage people to obtain prescriptions that they do not need. Prescription charges still exist in England.
It makes a significant contribution to achieving a healthier Scotland. No longer does cost discourage the sick from consulting their doctor and picking up their prescriptions. Those working individuals just above the Income Support level are facing the present hardships of the economic recession. Many have received no or minimum wage rises in the period 2011–15 and face a reduction in their living standards.	There is no evidence that it reduces health inequalities. The elderly and those on Income Support do not pay at present. The massive cuts in public expenditure in the period 2011–15 suggest that we cannot afford free prescriptions.
In the long run it saves money. It improves people's health and places less pressure on the NHS. Free drugs to control blood pressure and heart problems reduce morbidity and mortality. Free prescriptions only reduce the income received by the NHS by £57 million annually.	Real cuts are being made in the NHS budget and we cannot afford to lose £57 million of income every year. The money is needed to employ more nurses and to provide better care.

Show your understanding

1 Outline the key points of the *Equally Well* report and its main priorities.
2 To what extent has the oral health of children improved?
3 Outline the arguments for and against free prescriptions.

Research activity

Should Scotland end free prescriptions for all? Working in pairs, investigate this issue and present your findings to the class.

The role of the private sector within the NHS

The practice of patients 'going private' and paying for the services of GPs, consultants and hospital provision is long standing within the UK. Roughly 13 per cent of the UK population is covered by private health insurance. The private sector was regarded as a factor in health inequalities with, for example, those covered by private health being able to jump the queue for operations.

The role of the private sector working in partnership with the NHS to tackle health inequalities creates great controversy. On the one hand, opponents of the private sector claim

Private finance initiatives and public–private partnerships

The 'buy now, pay later' policy of private finance initiatives (PFIs) adds further pressure to NHS spending, which faces cuts in its future spending. The NHS in Scotland faces an estimated bill of £6.7 billion in repayments over the next 30 years, a huge amount. The 27 capital projects, for example Hairmyres Hospital in East Kilbride, covered by the £6.7 billion have an estimated value of the much smaller sum of £1.28 billion.

The SNP Government is hostile to public–private partnerships (PPP) and refers to the scandal of the PPP-built Royal Infirmary of Edinburgh where,

Figure 4.14 New South Glasgow University Hospital and Royal Hospital for Sick Children

overall, £1.5 billion will be paid for the £228 million it cost to build. The SNP Government has therefore replaced public–private partnerships with the Scottish Futures Trust (SFT) and the New South Glasgow University Hospital and Royal Hospital for Sick Children has been funded by the public not private purse (Figure 4.14).

that such partnerships will destroy state-funded health care provision and this creeping privatisation will eventually create a USA-style model of a first-class private sector and a third-rate state system dealing with trauma and acute illness. Supporters of the involvement of the private sector argue that partnership models reduce waiting lists, improve efficiency and provide state-of-the-art hospitals.

The Conservative Party (1979–97) involved the private sector by allowing private finance initiatives (PFIs) to deliver NHS services, a move that was opposed by Labour. The UK Labour Government, once hostile to private health care, embraced the private sector in the period 1997–2010. In 2000 Labour redefined the core principles of the NHS to include partnership with the private sector.

The SNP Government has worked in partnership with the private sector to reduce waiting lists and in 2014 allocated £540,000 to Lothian Health Board to send NHS patients to private hospitals. This was to ensure that Lothian patients did not breach the Government's treatment time guarantee (TTG), which offers a legal right to treatment within 12 weeks for many inpatient procedures. Several health boards have struggled to meet the TTGs and in 2012–13 health boards spent £28 million in the private sector to meet waiting-time targets, or 0.8 per cent of the total budget. The SNP Government has been accused of hypocrisy by Labour as the Government has publicly urged health boards to use the private sector, but only in exceptional circumstances.

Improved health

Both the UK and Scottish Governments in the period 1997 to 2011 set out to improve the health of British citizens and to reduce health and wealth inequalities. These were for the most part the golden years of plenty but during the global recession we entered an age of austerity where cuts were being made to public services

Doctors warn austerity is damaging patients' health

GPs working in the most deprived communities in Scotland have warned of increasing levels of mental and physical health problems among patients affected by austerity.

The Deep End group of GPs, representing 360 doctors in 100 practices, said job losses, welfare reform and cuts to social services were all affecting the health of their patients. The 100 Deep End group of general practices that serves the most socio-economically deprived areas of the country was set up in 2009. It is backed financially by the Scottish Government.

In a new report, the group says austerity measures are causing increased distress and poverty among their patients, and an increased workload for family doctors. The GPs add that the growing impact of benefit cuts mean much of their time is taken up with social issues rather than patients' underlying health problems. The report says: 'GPs report less time to deal with physical problems, as these are no longer a priority for the patient.'

Benefit changes were also a concern for many GPs, because they felt patients were wrongly being declared fit to work in medical tests on behalf of the Department for Work and Pensions (DWP). The report states this causes great distress to patients, while increasing the workload of GPs, who are called upon to write letters to support appeals. 'This impacts on practice time that would otherwise have been spent on health concerns,' the report notes.

Source: By Stephen Naysmith, adapted from the Herald, *15 May 2012*

and unemployment was increasing, which has had an impact on the health of UK citizens.

The health of all citizens is improving, including those in areas of deprivation. The life expectancy of men who live in Glasgow has increased by 2.6 years, which is excellent news. The 2014 ONS report provides some further cheer. The gap in life expectancy between the best and worst parts of the UK has fallen from 10.6 years in 2000–02 to 10.3 for men and from 9.2 years to 8.1 years for women.

The headline in the *Herald* of 13 December 2013 stated: 'Health Inequalities Persist Despite £2 billion Investment'. The report by public spending watchdog Audit Scotland stated: 'Many initiatives to reduce health inequalities have lacked a clear focus from the outset on cost-effectiveness and outcome measures.'

It is clear that the ban on smoking in public places has improved the health of the nation. According to the 2012 Scottish Household Survey, more than 200,000 Scots have given up smoking over the last ten years.

Table 4.4 highlights that death rates from coronary heart disease have fallen significantly across the UK, especially for women. The Scottish rate is disappointing compared to England and Wales, so much has still to be done in the future with fewer resources to improve the health of the Scottish people and to reduce health inequalities.

Table 4.4 **Decrease in death rates from coronary heart disease in men and women under 65, 2005–11, selected countries, UK and Europe**

	Men (%)	Women (%)
Scotland	18	29
England	28	35
Wales	29	35
Finland	18	23
Netherlands	31	37

Source: Institute for Health Metrics and Evaluation, University of Washington, 2013

Table 4.5 highlights a life expectancy increase of 4.2 years but a fall in the UK's ranking between 1990 and 2010. However, the Institute for Health Metrics and Evaluation indicates that the UK's pace of decline in premature mortality has

significantly fallen behind the average of Europe, partly because of the dramatic increase in alcohol and drugs disorder. Only men older than 55 in the UK have experienced significantly faster drops in death rates compared with other nations.

Table 4.5 Life expectancy at birth (years), 1990 and 2010

	1990		2010	
	Life expectancy	Rank	Life expectancy	Rank
Austria	75.7	11	80.6	8
Australia	76.9	8	81.5	1
France	77.1	3	80.9	5
Greece	76.9	6	79.6	15
Ireland	74.8	18	79.9	13
Norway	76.8	9	80.8	6
UK	75.7	12	79.9	14
USA	75.2	15	78.2	19

Source: Institute for Health Metrics and Evaluation, University of Washington, 2013

Show your understanding

1 Describe the types of activities that would be covered by the term 'privatisation'.
2 To what extent does the private sector help to improve health?

Develop your skills

3 'The health of the Scottish public has improved over the last 20 years and we are as healthy as those who live in England and Wales.'
To what extent is this view correct?

20-mark question

'Government policies have been successful in tackling health inequalities.' Discuss.

Use this chapter to assist you in writing this essay. Include balance throughout, arguing the ways in which government policies have reduced health inequality as well as addressing some of the reasons why they have not been successful in reducing health inequality. Make an essay plan with your teacher before you start.

5 Social inequality: gender and ethnicity

There have been huge changes in society in the last century. No longer are specific jobs reserved for men or for women, and the traditional family model is increasingly redefining itself for modern life. For example, 10 per cent of fathers remain at home while their partners go out to work and 20 per cent of board members of the top 350 companies in the UK are women. However, we are still a long way off from a fair and equal society and two groups in particular face huge barriers to equality: women and those from ethnic minority backgrounds. Many face huge barriers in relation to income, education, health and the workplace due to discrimination, sexism and racism.

Women in a changing society

The traditional image of the nuclear family – a husband, wife and children – is no longer necessarily the norm in society. Around 50 per cent of men and women live as married couples and a further 10 per cent of men and women cohabit in an unmarried relationship. More than 20 per cent of women and nearly 30 per cent of men live on their own and never marry. Since 1971, the proportion of the population living in a nuclear family with married parents and children has fallen from 52 per cent to 37 per cent. Nearly 25 per cent of children live in lone-parent households, with more than 90 per cent headed by mothers. These figures are constantly evolving as society continues to move away from 'traditional' lines.

On the whole, women continue to be placed in the traditional role as carer. Many find themselves as the main carer for children, elderly, sick or disabled relatives. They are placed at a financial disadvantage on account of their commitments. Many become full-time carers, take career breaks or work part time. Many do not have the opportunity to enter into paid employment and so must live off welfare. As well as the burden on time, many women face a disproportionate financial cost in their traditional roles. However, although women do face these disadvantages, there is evidence of slow change realised through changing attitudes in society and through government legislation. However, it is clear that more needs to be done in order to reduce social inequality experienced by women.

Theories and explanations for social inequality

The glass ceiling

Recent research indicates that women have better education and experience at the outset of their careers. However, after ten years in the job market, despite working continuously full time, men overtake women's earnings as they progress through management levels. Table 5.1 shows that, despite women seemingly to be in a better position at the beginning of their careers, as they advance they fall behind men in progressing upwards through management and promotions. This unseen, unbreachable barrier that prevents women from rising to the upper rungs of the corporate ladder, regardless of their qualifications or achievements, is known as the glass ceiling.

Table 5.1 **Percentage by gender as men and women progress in businesses**

	Male (%)	Female (%)
University graduates	44	56
Professionals	54	46
Executive management	81	19
CEOs	97	3
Board directors	83	17

Source: Bain & Co

The glass ceiling is most often used to apply to barriers to senior management positions, as indicated in Table 5.1. A 2011 report, *Ambition and Gender at Work* by the Institute of Leadership and Management, found that 73 per cent of women felt that barriers still exist for women seeking senior management and board-level positions. Only half of women at the beginning of their careers expected to become mangers compared to two-thirds of men.

Perhaps the biggest reason for a lack of women in top senior positions is the culture of 'presenteeism' that exists within UK businesses. Many senior managers are expected to work long hours. Employees in the UK work longer hours than any other European country and this is especially true in management positions. There is a real lack of flexible and part-time working arrangements in senior positions. However, some companies have introduced better working practices for senior positions.

Other reasons put forward to explain the glass ceiling include:

- Male directors may be discriminatory about a woman's commitment and ambitions – in particular, having children is often seen to be incompatible with senior roles because of the required time commitments.
- Women as the main carers take career breaks, which prevent career development.

'Women prefer to be their own boss'

Figure 5.1 Karren Brady

A report conducted by the London School of Economics for cosmetic company Avon found that many women today actually see self-employment as the best path to success. It predicted that there would be a doubling in young female entrepreneurs over the next ten years. Some 72 per cent of the 16–24-year-olds questioned said that the idea of being their own boss appealed to them. Karren Brady, vice-chairwoman of West Ham United, judge on the television series *The Apprentice* and Avon mentor, said that women would 'define the next generation of entrepreneurship and rewrite the rules in this perceived male-dominated world'. The report continues with Liz Gardiner from charity Working Families saying that because of discrimination 'particularly against those who chose to be mothers and also against those who chose non-traditional patterns of work', many women are turning to self-employment as they will have more control over the hours they work.

- It is difficult for women to access male-dominated networks based on membership of 'old-boy' groups such as golf clubs.
- There is a lack of women in senior positions and this can have an effect on young women's ambitions. Table 5.1 shows that women are very much in the minority in top posts in the UK.

MSN UK (Microsoft) introduced a project to move away from long hours and presenteeism when it opened up flexible working for all staff. It began by retraining its senior managers. The business has benefited from improved morale and staff retention, and 81 per cent of employees believe they provide a better service and meet their objectives because they work flexibly.

The debate about equality for women in the workplace

Figure 5.2 Dr Catherine Hakim

Some academics are challenging the view that discrimination still exists. Dr Catherine Hakim, a university academic, argues that the pay gap is down to women's lifestyle choice – the battle for sexual equality is over. She claims that women now have the freedom to choose between raising children or entering senior posts and that the new 2010 Equality Law is pointless and based on feminist myths. She says: 'People are confusing equal opportunities with equal outcomes, and there is little support for social engineering being demanded by feminists and legislators.' She also argues that a top-flight career is not the priority for many women and that previous equality legislation has not failed. Critics of Hakim argue that these figures explain why further action is needed to break the glass ceiling. They support positive discrimination action, such as suggestions that 40 per cent of the company board should be female.

Added Value idea

The idea of introducing a minimum percentage of female boardroom members is controversial. In other countries such as South Africa there has been positive discrimination to try to balance inequalities in senior positions. What would be the main arguments for and against this move?

Show your understanding

1 In pairs, write a short list of jobs that you consider to be gender-specific. Come up with explanations of why this is the case.
2 In your own words, define the term 'glass ceiling'.
3 Explain some of the main reasons for a lack of female progress in senior positions.
4 Why is entrepreneurship a better alternative for some women seeking successful careers?
5 What is the counter-argument put forward by Dr Catherine Hakim?

Factors in women's employment patterns that create inequality

Women earn less

Since the 1990s the wage differences between men and women has remained fairly static for top earners. The best-paid women who work full time earn around 20 per cent less than the best-paid men who work full time. There is still a gap between male and female earnings for full-time employees in low paid jobs, but this gap is slowly narrowing on account of the introduction of legislation such as the national minimum wage. According to a 2013 report by the Resolution Foundation, low paid mothers increased their earnings by 26 per cent in real terms between 1997 and 2008.

The gender pay gap also varies from industry to industry, with the biggest differential being in banking and finance where men earn 44 per cent more than women. The smallest difference is in agriculture and forestry, where men earn 2 per cent more than women.

Research by the Women and Equality Unit indicated that the main reason for lower earnings was discrimination, followed by fewer women working in full-time employment, interruptions to working lives and careers caused by family care commitments, and then working in lower-paid sectors of the economy.

Women work in lower-paid sectors of the economy

Men and women work in different areas of the economy and within these in different occupations. Women are over-represented in areas of the economy that are low paid. Nearly two-thirds of women are employed in 12 occupation groups. These are sometimes described as the five Cs – caring, cashiering, catering, cleaning and clerical occupations.

Of those working in education, social work and health services, 78.3 per cent are women, and women are also well represented in offices dealing with cash, marketing and sales, and personnel. These sectors have been traditionally lower paid than equivalent skilled work in other areas of the economy.

More than twice as many men as women are in the higher and professional occupations in the UK. Therefore in occupations where women are over-represented, men tend to have the higher managerial positions.

Interrupted employment

Women are more likely than men to take time out of work to care for children or other people, so their working lives are interrupted over time. Experience is one of the factors that employers reward and it is often difficult for women to return to work at the same level or at a higher level after taking time out.

After a long period out of work, women face barriers to returning such as low confidence and outdated skills. Even after a relatively short time it can be difficult for women to find jobs that match their skills, particularly if the work they want to find is local or part time. An interrupted employment record means fewer pension contributions, so women continue to face poorer circumstances when in later life.

Part-time work

Many more women than men work part time. Women are most likely to work part time when they are caring for young children. Approximately two-thirds of women with children under the age of eleven work part time, compared to only one-third of women with no dependent children.

Women tend to work part time between the ages of 25 and 45. This is the main child-rearing age, but they are also the prime years of their career. Men, on the other hand, mostly work part time when they are students or winding down to retirement. Women who work part time earn 32 per cent less per hour than women who work full time and 41 per cent less than men who work full time. Part of the reason is that women working part time often have lower levels of education than those who work full time. However, the main reason is that part-time work is concentrated in lower-paid jobs. One in four women working part time is employed as a retail sales assistant, cleaner or care assistant; few work as managers.

In order to find work at times that suit their childcare responsibilities, many women have to change their employer and their occupation and take a pay cut. Time travelling to and from work is also an issue. Women with children often need to have shorter travel-to-work times because they also have to access childcare. This limits the range of jobs available to them.

Government public-sector cuts

One of the Coalition Government's economic policies has been to reduce the number of public-sector workers while at the same time encouraging growth in the private sector. This strategy has had a detrimental impact on female employment. More women than men work in local government and other public services, and the extensive cuts to council budgets has led to a significant reduction in staffing. The Fawcett Society and the Scottish Close the Gap project highlight that since 2010 three times as many women as men have become long-term unemployed: 103,000 women compared to 37,000 men.

Show your understanding

1 Create a mind map explaining what factors in women's employment patterns can create inequality. Your diagram should be detailed and can be supported by illustrations.
2 Why have cuts in public-sector workers had a greater impact on women than on men?

Social factors that create inequality for women

Lone parents

Perhaps the greatest reason why women face huge inequalities is the impact of being a lone parent. In the UK 25 per cent of families are lone-parent families – that is 1.7 million parents with 2.9 million dependent children. Nine out of ten lone parents are mothers. Lone-parent families are particularly vulnerable to poverty. In Scotland, 70 per cent of lone-parent families have an income of less than £10,000 per year compared to only 25 per cent of two-parent families. Figures show that 79 per cent of lone parents have no savings compared to 41 per cent of two-parent families.

Lone parents may find it more difficult to hold down a job and look after the needs of their family, so they have a higher unemployment rate. However, in Sweden 70 per cent of lone mothers work and in France the figure is 82 per cent, whereas in the UK it is only 55 per cent. This is because in France and Sweden there is far more affordable childcare available for lone parents. In the UK the Childcare Cost Survey for the Daycare Trust found that a full-time nursery place for a child under two typically costs more than £7000 a year. It found that 90 per cent of lone parents say they would like to find paid employment but face barriers. They identify the main one as the cost and availability of childcare.

When lone parents do find work it is often low paid, so they merely replace workless poverty with working poverty. Therefore, lone parents have a high risk of living in poverty whether they are in work or not. According to research, nearly 86 per cent of working households who are in poverty are lone-parent households.

Women as carers

Whatever the structure of the family, women tend to bear a greater burden of the cost of bringing up children than men. Women experience poverty in different ways from men because the responsibility for managing household poverty usually falls on women. Most women see the well-being of their children as their major family priority. It often means that debt management becomes a daily as well as a long-term problem. Debt is often necessary to even out spending over a period of time, but it is often kept hidden from their partners.

Women are also more likely than men to be carers for elderly or disabled relatives and friends. Almost 6 million people – 11 per cent of the population – provide unpaid care. Of this, an estimated 4.8 million are women. Women with these caring responsibilities are much more likely than men to work part time or not at all. This means that they are more likely to have to survive on reduced incomes throughout their lives. At times when they could be earning and contributing to pension rights, some women are unable to do so because of the caring role they adopt or are expected to carry out. Ultimately this means they will continue to live in poverty past retirement age.

Dependence on welfare as they get older

As working-age women on average have lower incomes, they make fewer National Insurance contributions and so have fewer pension rights.

More than 80 per cent of women who retire are not entitled to a full basic state pension based on their own contributions. There are 26 per cent more women than men over the age of 60.

Women are less likely to have a pension than men, and part-time female workers are the least likely group to gain access to a pension. Lower-paid jobs are less likely to have occupational pension schemes. As women are over-represented in these jobs, they are less likely to retire with a decent pension and so have to rely on means-tested benefits. As a result, 44 per cent of single female pensioners depend solely on the state pension and have to seek pension credits, compared to only 28 per cent of single male pensioners. More male pensioners have occupational and personal pensions.

Access to the state pension will be increasingly later for both men and women, but this change will particularly affect women. Currently the pensionable age is rising for women so that by 2020 both men and women will access their pension only when they reach the age of 67. Then the plan is to increase both pensionable ages to 68 by 2046. These age increases also affect other benefits linked to age such as winter fuel payment and pension credit. A new higher flat-rate state pension of £144 per week at today's prices will be introduced from April 2016 for those who have contributed for 35 years or more. Women born between April 1951 and April 1953 who have 35 years' contributions will not receive the new pension and so may lose out financially.

Ultimately, far more women than men face poverty throughout their working lives because of lower wages and a lack of opportunities, and then they experience poverty in their retirement years as they rely mostly on basic welfare. This pensioner poverty lasts longer for women than for men because women tend to live longer.

Women serve different sectors in industry

During the early twenty-first century, women have experienced greater employment opportunities because of structural changes in the economy. The service sector or tertiary sector is growing, while primary sectors dealing with manufacturing have been in decline since the 1970s. Also, women's numbers are growing in occupations previously dominated by men. They now account for 75 per cent of pharmacists, 33 per cent of medical practitioners, nearly half of all lawyers and almost 40 per cent of accountants. The proportion of female managers and senior officials increased from less than 10 per cent in the early 1990s to more than one-third in recent times. Therefore, increasing numbers of women are entering occupations that offer higher earnings. Table 5.2 shows the recent trend in female representation in professional occupations.

According to the 2013 *Women in the Workplace Report* by the Business, Innovation and Skills Committee, 'some aspects of women's position in the workplace have changed for the better over recent years'. For example, Professor Jane Dacre, representing the Royal College of Physicians, states that '60 per cent of medical students are now female. Clever girls used to be nurses, now clever girls become doctors.' However, even in new industries there are several areas where women are poorly represented. Women account for only 14 per cent of professionals in science and technology industries.

Table 5.2 **Women in top posts in the UK, 2007 and 2012**

	2007 (%)	2012 (%)	Up/down 2007/2012
MPs	19.3	22.3	+3.0
MSPs	34.1	35.7	+1.6
MEPs	25.6	33.3	+7.7
Local authority council leaders	14.3	12.3	−2.0
Directors of FTSE 100 companies	11.0	16.7	+5.7
Editors of national newspapers	13.6	5.0	−8.6
Chairs of national arts companies	33.3	9.3	−24.0
Senior ranks in the armed forces	0.4	1.8	+1.4
Senior police officers	11.9	17.6	+5.7
Senior judges	9.6	13.6	+4.0
Civil service top management	26.6	31.0	+4.4
Head teachers of secondary schools	36.3	38.4	+2.1

Source: *Sex and Power 2013: Who Runs Britain?*, Centre for Women and Democracy

'Opportunities available to women depend on the level of wages, the choice of work, the flexibility of work on offer, maternity rights, the cost of local childcare, and the use of fair and open competition in job promotion. These factors are linked by perceptions of how women should be, what careers they should follow, and the roles that men take on. All these aspects of work are woven together, and they can either help or hinder women's prospects in their working and home life.' (*Women in the Workplace, 2013*)

Show your understanding

1 Explain how the following factors create wealth inequalities for lone parents:
    a) time constraints
    b) childcare
    c) family costs
    d) carer responsibilities.
2 What are the main reasons why women are more likely to be in poverty when they reach retirement? Explain why these factors affect women more than men.
3 Describe in detail the main changes taking place in the types of jobs women take on.

ICT task

Go to **www.sciencegrrl.co.uk** and discover some of the ways in which the group is trying to encourage girls to enter careers in STEM industries.

Inequalities in education

Since the 1990s girls have left secondary school with better exam grades than boys. In 2013, 26.7 per cent of S6 girls left school with five or more Highers, whereas only 19.2 per cent of boys were as successful. More girls are now going on to university and higher education than boys. As a result, females now outperform males at both undergraduate and postgraduate levels.

Table 5.3 shows that there are some subjects that are favoured by girls such as English, modern studies, administration and biology, whereas some subjects are dominated by boys such as physics, mathematics, chemistry and technological studies. Generally, more women than men study social science subjects such as

ScienceGrrl

ScienceGrrl (**www.sciencegrrl.co.uk**) is a broad-based, grassroots organisation celebrating and supporting women in science, a network of people who are passionate about passing on their love of science to the next generation. Members share the belief that science is for everyone; most of its members are women who are working as scientists but it also has plenty of non-scientists and men on board. The organisation is looking to address the under-representation of girls and women in science, technology, engineering and maths (STEM).

Dr Heather Williams is a senior medical physicist for nuclear medicine at Central Manchester University Hospitals and is a founding member of ScienceGrrl. She states: 'It is possible to have a career in STEM and related fields and other things you want in your life too; being "work-centered and careerist" is not the only route to professional success or personal happiness.' She believes that, in order to improve the number of girls entering STEM-related careers, action needs to be taken in the school curriculum. In addition, she states that we need 'more visible, accessible and inspirational female role models from a wide variety of careers, and to enable access to those role models for young women at all stages of their education.'

history, and arts subjects such as languages. On the other hand, women who do study STEM-related subjects gain entry into further education: nearly 60 per cent of students of medicine and dentistry are women.

Table 5.3 **2013 SQA examinations – Higher entries by gender**

	Girls (%)	Boys (%)
English	59	41
Mathematics	48	52
Biology	55	45
Modern studies	61	39
History	54	46
Chemistry	48	52
Administration	76	24
Physics	27	73
Technological studies	6	94

Source: Scottish Government

There has been a significant increase in the number of female graduates and so women are now earning more than men until the age of 30. However, these fortunes are reversed and a significant gap opens especially as men and women are promoted, where men take over from women.

Lack of women in senior positions

One of the issues for gender equality is the lack of women in senior positions in the public sector and in business. Some 20 per cent of the boardrooms of the FTSE 350 are made up of women and, as the Sex and Power 2013 survey (Table 5.2) shows, women are increasing their representation in the boardrooms of many businesses. However, when it comes to the positions of power within boards, the picture

becomes more bleak. Only 11 of the CEOs, the top executives, in the FTSE 350 are women. This means that 97 per cent of CEOs in the most successful companies are men. The UK Government has recommended to companies that they set voluntary targets to double the number of women on FTSE boards. However, although progress is being made, the positions are mostly non-executive which means that their actual power is very limited.

Show your understanding

1 Use Table 5.2 to create a bar graph showing the three greatest changes in women's senior positions.
2 Summarise the key gender patterns in education relating to pass rates and subjects studied.
3 'Women are making excellent progress in the boardroom.' How selective is this statement? Give reasons for your answer.

Ethnic minorities

Twenty-first century Scotland, and Britain as a whole, is a culturally rich and diverse country. Although the dominant group in the population in terms of numbers is still people deemed as ethnically white, multiculturalism is evident in every aspect of our lives. For example, the most popular dish consumed by people in Britain is curry and there are huge celebrations for cultural events such as St Patrick's Day and Chinese New Year.

However, although the UK could be described as culturally and ethnically diverse, those from black and minority ethnic (BME) backgrounds often suffer inequalities with regards to income, employment, education and even health as a result of poverty, discrimination and racism. According to the 2011 Census, the BME population is about 12 per cent of the total UK population. It has risen from 3 million in 1991 to almost 7 million in 2011. In Scotland the minority population is 4 per cent of the total population. The BME community consists of a variety of groups, each of which has different experiences of wealth and poverty. In Scotland the largest groups are Pakistani (30 per cent), Chinese (18 per cent), Indian (16 per cent) and mixed background (15 per cent). Glasgow's BME population – which includes Indian, Pakistani, Bangladeshi, Chinese, African, Caribbean and other Asian groups – has more than doubled between 2001 and 2011, from 31,510 to 68,684. A higher proportion of Bangladeshis, Pakistanis and black non-Caribbean groups are living in poverty than any other groups. Historically, reasons for poverty among the BME communities include:

- lower income
- culture
- employment
- education
- discrimination.

Lower income

With the exception of Indians, most minority groups earn less than the white British group. It is estimated that around two-fifths of people from BME backgrounds live in low income households, twice the rate of white British people. In the past, many migrants had lower qualifications or qualifications not recognised in the UK, so they were employed in low pay industries such as hotels and catering. Income inequalities vary by group and gender. Although black males earn considerably less than white males, black females earn considerably more than white females. Many white females work part time whereas more black females work full time. Indian males and females both earn more

than their white counterparts because they have higher levels of qualifications. Among those who are working, around 65 per cent of Bangladeshis, 50 per cent of Pakistanis and 30 per cent of black Africans are in low income jobs. This is much higher than the rates for white British, Indians and black Caribbeans, which range from 10 to 20 per cent.

In 2009 the Wealth and Assets Survey revealed that the 'average white household' had roughly £221,000 in assets, which is much higher than BME groups: black Caribbean £76,000, Bangladeshi £21,000 and black African £15,000. BME groups are also more likely to suffer homelessness. According to the Institute of Race Relations in 2011 in Wolverhampton 26 per cent of the population were from BME backgrounds, but they made up over 40 per cent of the homeless cases seen by the local authority.

In Scotland, the ethnic groups living in poverty vary slightly from the UK pattern. There are significantly fewer Indians and Chinese in the bottom 40 per cent of deprivation. Only 29 per cent of Indians and 30 per cent of Chinese compared to 42 per cent of white Scots live in deprivation, whereas 48 per cent of Pakistanis and 49 per cent of Bangladeshis are in this category.

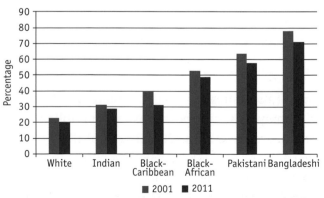

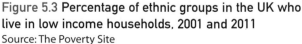

Figure 5.3 **Percentage of ethnic groups in the UK who live in low income households, 2001 and 2011**
Source: The Poverty Site

Culture

Reasons for inequalities are also cultural. The poorest groups, Pakistanis and Bangladeshis, are more likely to be married. Pakistani and Bangladeshi women are mainly Muslim and the cultural expectation is for them to stay at home and look after larger families. Three-quarters of Bangladeshi women and more than two-thirds of Pakistani women are economically inactive. Roughly 74 per cent of Bangladeshi households and 66 per cent of Pakistani households have dependent children, figures that are much greater than Indian (50 per cent), black African (48 per cent) and white British (28 per cent) households. Another possible reason why some Pakistani and Bangladeshi women stay at home is that they do not have the skills needed to work and, in the case of new immigrants, their English is poor, which is a major barrier to finding employment.

Employment

Traditionally, BME groups have always faced higher rates of unemployment than white British. All groups except Indians suffer almost three times the level of unemployment than the majority population does. First-generation migrants to the UK face several disadvantages that lead to higher unemployment, such as language difficulties, a lack of recognised qualifications and racial prejudice. Variations in the unemployment rate may also be a reflection of different skills and qualifications that each ethnic group possesses. Indian men have low unemployment rates: around 30 per cent of them have degree-level qualifications, and relatively few (15 per cent) have no qualifications. Pakistani and Bangladeshi men have high rates of unemployment. Only 11 per cent and 15 per cent respectively have degree-level qualifications, and 29 per cent and 40 per cent respectively have no qualifications.

According to the *Guardian*, unemployment figures from March 2012 reveal that the unemployment rate for black people aged 16–24 has increased at almost twice the rate for white 16- to 24-year-olds since the start of the recession in 2008. Young black men are the worst affected of all. Unemployment among young black men doubled in three years, rising from 28.8 per cent in 2008 to 55.9 per cent in the last three months of 2011. Generally, there is an acceptance that the recession has hit young black people disproportionately hard.

Education

In the last decade, all ethnic groups have improved their educational attainment. GCSE results in England show Indian and Chinese boys and girls gaining more passes than candidates from the white British ethnic group. These improvements are mirrored at degree level. The proportion of Chinese and Indians achieving a degree is now significantly higher than for the white British ethnic group. However, there are regional concerns.

In recent years there has been a huge increase in English university applications from BME students according to UCAS. There has been a big increase in applications from ethnic minority youngsters, particularly black teenagers, rising from 20 per cent to 34 per cent between 2006 and 2013. Chinese teenagers are the most likely to apply, followed by other Asian youngsters, with white teenagers the least likely to apply, with 29 per cent seeking places. These figures show the percentage of young people from BME backgrounds who are applying, rather than the absolute numbers. Most applicants will still be white students because this is a much larger group. For example, the Chinese figure is based on about 2000 youngsters, compared with about 500,000 white teens.

Discrimination

Younger members of BME populations face fewer barriers than their parents. This is because they are fluent in the local language, have a better grasp of UK social customs, have a wider social network and many have made good use of the education system.

The Race Relations Act was introduced in 1968, but it is accepted that despite this change in the law nearly 50 years ago discrimination persists. According to an investigation by the *Guardian* in 2012, a significant proportion of BME groups believed they had been refused a job because of their race. Asians also felt their religion led to discrimination. The report included comments from a number of young black men about their experience in the jobs market.

'Sometimes I have in the back of my mind that employers see my surname, see it's African and write my CV off straight away. I think about changing it because I wonder if they immediately think I might be trouble or I might be lying. I can count on one hand the amount of interviews I've had. I've been to university, I know how to write a CV, do application forms, but my [white] friends from university are getting jobs and I'm not. I've looked at their CVs and it's exactly the same as mine yet they're getting the job.' (*Nathan Atiko, aged 24*)

Black people and Asians reported that race and colour were reasons for being refused a job on a high proportion of occasions. Black people felt that their colour was twice as likely as Asians to be the reason for not getting a job, while it was 25 times more likely than white people. Asians felt it was ten times more likely their race had cost them work than a white person, while a black person felt it was 14 times more likely. Minorities also felt that they were denied promotion because of their race. Again, the unemployment rate for black Africans is greater than that for white people.

Research by the Equality and Human Rights Commission (EHRC) compares the success rate of job applicants with the same qualifications. All applicants had different levels of difficulty in getting a job interview but, as Figure 5.4 shows, white candidates were far more likely to be successful in gaining an interview compared to all other ethnic groups. Black people had by far the worst experience despite having equal or better qualifications and experience. This study demonstrates clearly the impact of discrimination in the job market as it exists today in the UK.

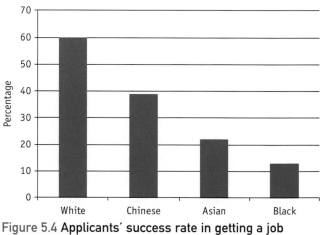

Figure 5.4 **Applicants' success rate in getting a job interview**
Source: Commission for Racial Equality

In Scotland, officers from BME backgrounds are under-represented in the police. According to the Supporting Ethnic Minority Police staff for Equality in Race (SEMPER) Scotland, the number of BME officers is still too low as a proportion of population. However, there have been year-on-year improvements.

Since police began recording racist crimes in 2000 in Scotland, the number of incidents has risen by 75 per cent. Part of this increase may be explained by a greater willingness on the part of victims to report these crimes. However, many organisations that represent BME groups say that most incidents still go unreported because the minorities have no confidence in the police. The clear-up rates are poor and with so few minorities on the force the communities do not feel it adequately represents them. A report by the Commission for Racial Equality Scotland stated: 'Verbal abuse … was so much a part of everyday life that most people did not think of reporting it.'

A lot of these attacks are concentrated in poorer areas of cities where many disadvantaged minorities live. So, many who are forced by low income to live in such areas become the target of racist abuse and violence. The perpetrators are mostly youths. However, racism and racist violence spill over into all areas of our cities and affect people from BME backgrounds at all economic levels.

Research has found that the volume of racism is so great that it is sometimes difficult for individuals to isolate specific incidents. The worst offenders were found to be children and youths, and the main victims were children and youths in BME communities. Most parents of the perpetrators were racists themselves and supported their offspring.

The impact of income inequalities leads many ethnic minorities to live and work in areas where they face emotional and physical abuse, which has a detrimental effect on their well-being. Race harassment and discrimination have an impact on health, both physical and mental. However, problems with mental health in particular often go unreported. Research has shown that there are high levels of unreported psychological distress in Asian communities, and particularly among Asian women.

Types of discrimination

Race discrimination in the UK takes three forms:

- Direct discrimination is when someone is denied an opportunity based purely on their race, ethnic origin, religion or belief. Denying someone employment or promotion because they are Asian, black or white, Hindu or Christian would be direct discrimination.
- Indirect discrimination occurs when everyone has to conform to the same practice that would deny a certain group the opportunity to practise its religion and celebrate its culture. For example, if the police were required to wear only standard-issue helmets this would indirectly discriminate against Sikhs whose culture requires them to wear a turban. The police issue special turbans when this situation arises.
- Institutional discrimination occurs when an organisation's procedures and policies disadvantage people from BME backgrounds. It came to the fore in the 1999 *Macpherson Report* into the Metropolitan Police following the Stephen Lawrence Inquiry where police attitudes to those from BME groups were described as 'institutionally racist' because of 'unwitting prejudice, ignorance, thoughtlessness and racist stereotyping which disadvantage minority ethnic people'.

Report reveals huge level of racial inequality in Scottish public sector workplace

A damning new report on workplace discrimination reveals huge levels of inequality when it comes to people from black and ethnic minorities getting a job within the Scottish public sector. Equality campaigners say not enough is being done to integrate people from black and minority ethnic (BME) backgrounds into the public sector workplace.

A report produced by the Coalition for Racial Equality and Rights (CRER) has revealed that just 0.8 per cent of staff in all of Scotland's local authorities are from BME backgrounds – despite making up 4 per cent of the general population of Scotland. Of all applicants for posts in the wider public sector just 4.4 per cent of people from a BME background are subsequently appointed, compared to 7.1 per cent for white candidates.

CRER say the situation in local authorities was 'more alarming' with white British candidates three times more likely to be appointed than BME applicants. Just 2.1 per cent of BME applicants end up being appointed compared to 6.1 per cent of white British applicants. The CRER study on staffing in 20 Scottish local authorities using freedom of information legislation, showed that of 146,774 total staff in post, just 1188 were declared as being from BME backgrounds.

It showed that the proportion of the Glasgow City Council workforce with a BME background is less than 2 per cent, although according to the latest census data, the BME population makes up 12 per cent of the city population. A council spokesman said it did not recognise the 12 per cent figure and believed 5 per cent was more accurate. Research shows that Glasgow's BME population, which includes Indian, Pakistani, Bangladeshi, Chinese, African, Caribbean and other Asian groups has more than doubled in ten years, from 31,510 in 2001 to 68,684.

Jatin Haria, executive director of CRER, said: 'I guess the picture I am painting of Scotland in 2014 is one of well-meaning people and policies, but a definitive lack of action. We seem to have moved on to a post-race society without acknowledging that "race" was ever an issue. Not only are white UK candidates three times more likely to be appointed than their equally qualified and experienced black counterparts, but if this situation is allowed to continue then the ethnic penalty faced by BME people in Scotland will continue to grow.'

Source: By Martin Williams, adapted from the Herald, *19 March 2014*

Mind, the mental health charity, states: 'It has been established and proven that black people face discrimination in the fields of employment, housing and education. This means that like other minority ethnic groups, Black people are often denied access to, or given second-rate, opportunities. These conditions must have an impact on mental well-being.'

Show your understanding

1 Explain in your own words the three different types of discrimination.
2 Describe, in detail, some of the negative experiences of discrimination felt by some BME groups when attempting to gain employment. Support your answer from evidence.
3 What are the main consequences of discrimination?

Attempts to tackle inequalities

National minimum wage, tax credits and pension credit

The national minimum wage, working tax credit and child tax credit have been used to increase the income of the lowest wage earners. These policies have particularly helped women and those from BME backgrounds as many ethnic minority workers and women workers suffer from low income employment. In addition, policies regarding childcare provision also help reduce the income gap. Child tax credit provides a working parent with up to 80 per cent of the cost of childcare up to a maximum of £140 a week for one child and £240 for two or more children. In 2014 the Scottish Parliament passed the Children and Young People (Scotland) Act, which increased free childcare for three- and four-year-olds, and vulnerable two-year-olds, from 475 to 600 hours: around 16 hours a week. This will help relieve some of the strain on mothers.

As women make up a larger proportion of the pensioner population, many government schemes have helped improve their incomes. Government policies aim to reduce the number of elderly living in poverty. Pension credit has helped improve the income of women who retire with reduced pension entitlement. In addition, the winter fuel payment is also paid to most elderly women who have reached qualifying age.

Equality Act 2010

The Equality Act 2010 consolidated the previous nine pieces of equality legislation based on protected characteristics to create, for the first time in Britain, unified equality legislation. The nine protected characteristics are:

- age
- disability
- gender reassignment
- marriage and civil partnership
- pregnancy and maternity
- race
- religion or belief
- sex (gender)
- sexual orientation.

The Equality Act 2010 gives women (and men) a right to equal pay for equal work. Previously the law ensured that men and women were paid the same rates for carrying out the same work. However, the Act means that women now have the right to the same pay as men, even if they both carry out *different* roles. For example, if a woman works as an administrative assistant in a council, she may be entitled to the same pay as a gardener for a local authority as both may require similar effort and a similar level of skill. This is intended to break down restrictions in pay based on certain roles being dominated by genders. The Act also states that companies with 250 or more workers have to publish information about the differences in men's and women's pay. The Government plans to do the same for public bodies with 150 or more workers.

The Act allows for positive discrimination. Job adverts can be aimed at different ethnic groups or women if the organisation does not have enough of that particular group. It can also train these groups to improve their chance of getting a better job within the organisation. The Act allows public organisations such as local councils to use their buying power to influence companies to include equality in the way they work. Public bodies spend £220 billion each year. They can use that power to influence companies that want their business to treat all their employees fairly. The following case study was created by the trade union Acas to help employers understand how to comply with the Equality Act.

Case study: Positive discrimination in recruitment

Loughton-on-Sea has a population of some 75,000, of which around 15 per cent at the last Census were from minority ethnic groups. The school is recruiting a new head of department. None of the existing ten departmental heads are from minority communities. The school runs an interview selection process where all candidates are scored against a range of job-based questions. The selection panel also objectively assesses the experience and qualifications of each candidate.

At the end of the selection process, two candidates have equal scores. Both are women, one of whom is black. The head thinks it is important that the school's senior leadership reflects the population of Loughton and the school, and so decides to use the provision in the Equality Act to appoint the black candidate. The head gives feedback to the unsuccessful candidate and explains the position the school has taken and why.

The Equality Act 2010 requires health organisations to eliminate discrimination in the provision of health care and thereby reduce health inequalities for BME groups. For example, health care providers should be aware of the language needs of people living in their areas and provide health promotion in languages other than English. One authority provided smoking cessation programmes in Hindi, Urdu, Punjabi and Polish as well as English. Another example is the employment of multilingual speech therapists for BME toddlers with speech difficulties.

In order to comply with the new law, NHS Scotland now publishes all materials in multiple language formats as well as offering the assistance of a translator in all medically-related appointments with health professionals.

Minister for Women and Minister for Equality

Following a Cabinet reshuffle in July 2014, Nicky Morgan was appointed Education Secretary and Minister for Women and Equality. Before 2010, there was no dedicated representation for both groups in the Cabinet. This puts equality at the heart of government and means that the Cabinet can dedicate more time to tackling inequalities.

Work and Families Act 2006

The Work and Families Act 2006 entitles women to statutory maternity pay (SMP) for 39 weeks. This is made up of 90 per cent of their salary for six weeks, and then £138.18 a week for the next 33 weeks (2014). Some women can take a further 26 weeks of maternity leave, which is usually unpaid. Fathers can currently claim two weeks of ordinary statutory paternity pay (OSPP) at £138.18 a week or 90 per cent of their average weekly earnings, whichever is lower.

The Work and Families Act 2006 gives people the right to request flexible working hours in order to care for children under six, disabled children under 18 and carers of disabled adults. It allows people to work while organising it around their caring role using such arrangements as flexi-time, compressed hours where you work your hours over fewer days, job sharing and home-working. As women have a far greater role as carers, this helps them more.

Equality and Human Rights Commission (EHRC)

According to its website, the EHRC has a 'statutory remit to promote and monitor human rights; and to protect, enforce and promote equality across the nine "protected" grounds – age, disability, gender, race, religion and belief, pregnancy and maternity, marriage and civil partnership, sexual orientation and gender reassignment.'

One important role of the EHRC is to monitor and report on pay divisions between the races and genders in unrepresentative public bodies. A major EHRC report of 2010, *How Fair is Britain?*, highlights the difficulties of disabled adults and BME women in finding work. Scotland's Commissioner Kaliani Lyle stated: 'What we have is a huge gap between our aspirations and our achievements. The Commission helpline takes calls every day from people experiencing real discrimination; women who are sacked because they are pregnant, people who face daily harassment because of their race and disability.' The report has been sent to every public body and government department and this provides a wealth of evidence that organisations can use to develop strategies to avoid discriminatory practices.

Success of government policies

Overall, it is clear that there have been some successes in addressing inequalities between genders and races. With several government policies aimed at the poorest in our society such as the national minimum wage, child tax credits, working tax credits and the pension credit, income has improved for low income households. However, women are still more likely to live in poverty than men and remain in poverty throughout their lives. As long as income inequalities remain, women will continue to be affected by health inequalities. In addition, despite government legislation and initiatives such as One Scotland: No Place for Racism, members of the BME community continue to face discrimination in employment. Some groups are using the education system to get access to higher income employment, but even here there is evidence of inequality.

The Equality Act 2010 in the long term may deliver greater equality of opportunity for women and BME groups in employment, income and health. A recent report by the EHRC looked at how local authorities have implemented the Equality Act. The Commission's first report, *Measuring Up? Monitoring Public Authorities' Performance Against the Scottish Specific Equality Duties* (June 2013), found that 92 per cent of listed authorities had published some information about the protected characteristics of their staff. The report found that 93 per cent of authorities reviewed had published information about the composition of their staff, broken down by protected characteristic. Authorities were assessed as reporting on the composition of their workforce if they reported on any of the relevant protected characteristics. Listed authorities were more likely to publish information relating to age, sex, race and disability than to sexual orientation, religion or belief. With this information now publically available, it is hoped that progress will continue in reducing inequalities experienced by women and BME groups.

However, in April 2012 Westminster's Equality Office published a report called *Evaluation of the Implementation of the Equality Act*. This found that two-thirds of organisations were unaware of the Equality Act, and smaller businesses said they found it difficult to get good quality information on equality issues. It revealed that among medium-sized employers (with between 50 and 249 employees), only two-fifths are well informed about the Act, while only one-third have detailed knowledge of disability limits in recruitment.

Figure 5.5 **Nicky Morgan, Education Secretary and Minister for Women and Equality**

Show your understanding

1 Summarise the main features of the Equality Act 2010.
2 In what ways does the Work and Families Act 2006 reduce the gender gap?
3 Create a table with two columns, one describing the arguments that improvements are being made in reducing gender/ethnic inequalities, and the other with arguments against.

12-mark question

Analyse government policies to tackle inequalities that affect a group in society.

6 The Scottish criminal justice system

Legal rights and responsibilities

As a member of British society you have legal rights and responsibilities. Essentially all citizens are permitted to live and work as they wish so long as they do not harm or interfere with the rights of others. All UK citizens have the right to be treated fairly and equally regardless of their gender, race, age, religion, sexual preferences, political persuasion or any disability that they may have. Citizens have the right to innocence until proven guilty and are protected by the police and judicial system. As well as enjoying rights, all UK citizens have a responsibility to respect the rights of others. UK citizens must also obey UK laws and regulations. UK citizens who are parents must protect and care for their children until they are at least 16 and must ensure that all children between the ages of 5 and 16 attend full-time education.

Overview of the judicial system

After the Act of Union in 1707, Scotland retained an independent legal system. This is often referred to as Scots law, which is distinct from the legal systems of other countries within the UK. Like most judicial systems, Scotland has two types of court: the civil court and the criminal court. In simple terms, civil courts exist to resolve the differences between two parties with a dispute, in a fair and unbiased manner. In contrast, the function of a criminal court is to provide a means of prosecuting those who are deemed to have broken the laws of society. In both courts, those accused are allowed to plead their innocence and present legal arguments and evidence central to the case. To ensure a case comes to a fair and just conclusion, it is up to a judge or jury to decide a verdict.

Before someone is summoned to appear in court, a process is followed after a person is presumed to have committed a crime. When the police identify a person or persons they think are responsible for a crime or offence, they can decide to take no further action, or issue a warning, or issue a fine, or send a prosecution report to the Crown Office and Procurator Fiscal Service (COPFS) for a procurator fiscal to review. Upon receiving a prosecution report from the police, the procurator fiscal can decide to take no further action (if there is insufficient evidence or prosecuting is not in the public interest), or issue a fine (or other direct measure), or begin court proceedings. If it is the latter, the procurator fiscal decides where the trial should take place based on the sentences the court can impose and the nature of the crime.

Crown Office and Procurator Fiscal Service

The COPFS is the civil service department responsible for prosecuting crime in Scotland, investigating suspicious deaths and investigating complaints about the police. The Crown Office employs around 1650 staff, including around 400 lawyers. Every year COPFS deals with more than 290,000 reports on offences committed, supplied by the police and other reporting agencies.

COPFS is headed by the Lord Advocate who, along with the Solicitor General, is the principal legal adviser to the Scottish Government. Both the Lord Advocate and the Solicitor General are government ministers appointed by the Queen on the recommendation of the First Minister. As they are both government appointments, these positions usually change with the government of the day. The current Lord Advocate is Frank Mulholland (Figure 6.1) and the Solicitor General is Lesley Thomson.

Figure 6.1 **Lord Advocate Frank Mulholland**

Working beneath the Lord Advocate and the Solicitor General are solicitors known as procurators fiscal. For most crimes in Scotland, procurators fiscal present cases for the prosecution. The most serious High Court prosecutions are conducted by the Lord Advocate himself. For other cases at the High Court, experienced solicitors called advocates depute carry out prosecutions.

> ### ICT task
>
> Visit COPFS's website and investigate its work at **www.crownoffice.gov.uk**.

Figure 6.2 (opposite) provides an overview of an offender's journey through the criminal justice system. This demonstrates the many processes involved and summarises the possible outcomes at different stages. What happens at each stage depends on decisions made by the accused (often on the advice of their solicitor), the various criminal justice bodies and individuals such as sheriffs. In reality, there are many variations in the route through the system and in what can happen at each stage.

> ### Show your understanding
>
> 1 Outline the judicial system and its purpose in Scotland.
> 2 Describe the work of COPFS.

The court system in Scotland

Within the court system there are two types of criminal procedure for hearing cases:

- Solemn cases are concerned with the most serious offences such as murder, rape or serious assault. Trials under solemn procedure are conducted in the High Court or Sheriff Court with a judge and a jury. A jury of 15 decides on the verdict of cases and a simple majority is needed to determine the outcome of the verdict. Citizens of Scotland over the age of 18 can be called at any time for jury duty.

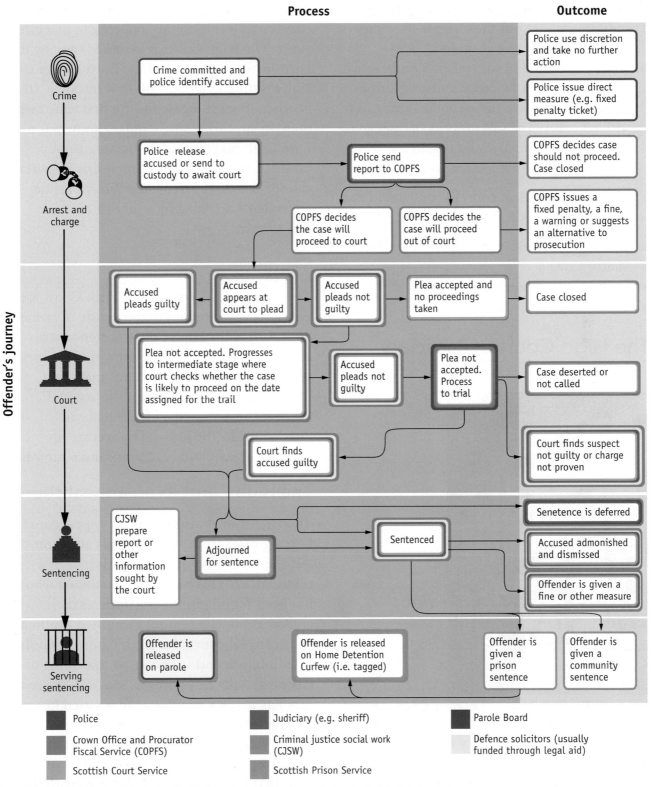

Note: Coloured borders round the boxes signify the different bodies generally involved at that stage of the process.
Source: Audit Scotland

Figure 6.2 **Overview of an offender's journey through the criminal justice system**
Source: Audit Scotland

In solemn cases, a document known as an indictment sets out the charges of crimes or offences against the accused.

- Summary cases deal with other criminal activity, such as breach of the peace, and are heard in a Sheriff Court or in a Justice of the Peace Court without a jury. The vast majority of cases going through the criminal justice system are summary cases – over 90 per cent in 2013.

There are four types of court in Scotland to deal with different levels and types of offence:

- the High Court of Justiciary
- Sheriff Courts
- Justice of the Peace Courts
- the Court of Session.

The High Court of Justiciary

Figure 6.3 **The High Court of Justiciary, Edinburgh**

The High Court of Justiciary is the supreme criminal court in Scotland. It deals with the most serious of crimes such as murder, rape, armed robbery and serious sexual offences, particularly those involving children. It sits in cities and larger towns around Scotland and has a permanent base in Edinburgh, Glasgow and

Aberdeen. There are periodic sittings in other courts and it is therefore referred to as a circuit court. The High Court is presided over by the Lord Justice General and the Lord Justice Clerk. When sitting as a court of 'first instance' (that is, when hearing a case for the first time rather than on appeal), a single judge, known as a Lord Commissioner of Justiciary, usually presides. In particularly complex or important cases, a bench of three judges may preside. Defendants are tried by a jury of 15 men and women.

Sentencing

The sentencing powers of the High Court are unlimited. On account of the nature of crimes dealt with at the High Court, sentences are always custodial. For the most serious crimes such as murder, statute dictates that life imprisonment is imposed on the accused. However, in Scotland a life sentence is determined by the judge. The average life sentence in Scotland is 13 years and 6 months.

The High Court as an appeal court

The High Court also sits as an appeal court, hearing cases from its own trials and from the Sheriff Courts of those convicted of a criminal act. This happens if someone who has been found guilty then appeals their conviction or the sentence imposed on them. As an appeal court, the High Court sits only in Edinburgh and is known as the Court of Criminal Appeal. However, in cases where a jury has made a decision, the accused has no right of appeal unless he or she brings forth fresh evidence which may then result in a retrial. Similarly, if the prosecution is of the view that a sentence handed down by the trial court is too lenient, they may appeal the sentence. Generally, for all appeals at least two judges preside, but this may increase to five in complex cases.

Crown loses appeal against 'lenient' sentence given to motorist who killed two cyclists

The Crown has lost an appeal against the 'unduly lenient' sentence on a motorist convicted of killing two cyclists in separate incidents. Gary McCourt was found guilty in April of causing the death of Audrey Fyfe by driving carelessly. The 75-year-old died two days after McCourt clipped the back wheel of her bike in Edinburgh in August 2011.

McCourt, 49, was banned from driving for five years and ordered to carry out 300 hours of community service by Sheriff James Scott. At the end of his trial at Edinburgh Sheriff Court, it emerged he was jailed for two years after being convicted in 1986 of causing another cyclist's death by reckless driving. George Dalgity, 22, was killed as he cycled along Edinburgh's Regent Road on 18 October 1985.

Mrs Fyfe's family and cycling charity CTC criticised Sheriff Scott's sentence and prosecutors lodged an appeal on the grounds that it was not tough enough. But at the Court of Criminal Appeal in Edinburgh today, Lord Menzies, sitting with Lady Smith and Lord Bracadale, refused the appeal. At an appeal hearing last month, Solicitor General Lesley Thomson argued McCourt should be sentenced to at least eight months' imprisonment and banned from driving for life. The trial sheriff had erred in applying the sentencing guidelines, resulting in an unduly lenient sentence, she said. He had been wrong to reach the conclusion that the accident had been the result of 'momentary inattention' on the part of McCourt, the court was told. The sheriff was wrong to take into account the fact that Mrs Fyfe was not wearing a cycle helmet, Ms Thomson said. No evidence had been led about the effectiveness of wearing a helmet and the sheriff had 'entirely formed his own view' on the matter. Insufficient weight had also been placed on McCourt's previous conviction for killing another cyclist, she argued.

But defence advocate Herbert Kerrigan QC said the sheriff had used his common sense and the sentence could not be criticised. McCourt had been travelling at a slow speed and had clipped the back of Mrs Fyfe's wheel, after which she toppled over, Mr Kerrigan said. 'The fact of the matter is she chose not to wear a safety helmet, which she was perfectly entitled to do,' he said. 'The sheriff has quite clearly weighed matters up with great care and concern.'

Mrs Fyfe's daughter Aileen Brown said the failure of the appeal left her 'lost for words'.

Source: Adapted from the Herald, *25 September 2013*

Sheriff Courts

There are six Sheriffdoms in Scotland with a total of 49 Sheriff Courts spread around the country. A sheriff presides over trials at a Sheriff Court. A sheriff is a solicitor or advocate who has over ten years' experience and considerable courtroom knowledge. Most criminal and civil cases in Scotland are dealt with in the Sheriff Courts. In criminal cases, depending on the gravity of the offence that the accused is charged with, one of two procedures will be adopted: solemn procedure or summary procedure. If the alleged offence is a serious physical assault, usually a solemn procedure is required, which means trial by jury. In civil cases, sheriffs deal with a variety of cases including cases involving debt, claims for compensation, bankruptcy, company liquidation and eviction. They hear almost all family actions – including divorce, child welfare and adoptions – and have important functions in relation to Children's Hearings (see page 95).

Sentencing

In solemn cases, the maximum sentence available to a sheriff is five years' imprisonment and/or an unlimited fine. In summary cases,

12 months' imprisonment and/or a fine up to £5000 are available. Note that the case can be remitted to the High Court of Justiciary for sentencing if the sheriff decides that his or her sentencing powers are insufficient.

Justice of the Peace Courts

Justice of the Peace Courts were formerly known as District Courts. Justices of the Peace (JPs) are lay magistrates (that is, not legally qualified) who sit with a legally qualified clerk who advises them in dealings with summary criminal cases. There are around 450 JPs, drawn from all walks of life. Justices usually sit alone and deal with less serious cases of assault, breach of the peace, theft and other less serious crimes. Further to this they deal with many driving offences such as speeding, careless driving and driving without insurance.

In Glasgow a slightly different system operates where Justice of the Peace Courts are manned by legally qualified stipendiary magistrates. They deal with more serious summary business, similar to sheriffs, such as drink driving and assault. This system only exists in Glasgow, mainly due to the high volume of crime in the city.

Sentencing

Sentencing powers are limited to 60 days' imprisonment and/or a fine of up to £2500, and the ability to disqualify drivers on a discretionary basis. In stipendiary courts magistrates enjoy greater sentencing powers akin to a sheriff in summary procedures.

In 2013 the Scottish Government announced that ten Sheriff Courts and seven Justice of the Peace Courts would be closed in cost-saving measures. Scottish Court Service (SCS) chief executive Eric McQueen said: 'Investing in fewer courts will enable us to improve facilities and technology, which will provide better services for all court users, and in particular victims and witnesses.'

The Court of Session

The Court of Session is the supreme civil court of Scotland. It sits in Parliament House in Edinburgh and is both a trial court and a court of appeal. The vast majority of civil cases such as small claims cases are heard at the Sheriff Courts, but high profile cases involving large companies or sizable sums of money are heard at the Court of Session. For example, much of the legal wrangling centring on Rangers Football Club has been heard at the Court of Session.

Show your understanding

1 Explain the difference between solemn and summary procedures.
2 Describe the following criminal courts and the sentencing powers in each:
   a) High Court of Justiciary
   b) Sheriff Court
   c) Justice of the Peace Court.
3 Outline the work of the High Court as an appeal court.
4 Outline the work of the Court of Session.

UK Supreme Court

The role of the UK Supreme Court in Scottish judicial affairs is somewhat controversial. The Scottish Government has recently accused the UK Supreme Court of undermining the independence and distinctiveness of the Scottish legal system by becoming involved in Scottish criminal appeals. The Supreme Court, as the UK's highest court of the land, argues that it can judge Scottish appeals if the accused is appealing under European Court of Human Rights (ECHR) legislation. For example, in 2011 Nat Fraser, who was found guilty of murdering his wife in Elgin in 2003, argued there had been a miscarriage of justice, centred on claims that evidence in his case was tampered with and prosecutors had not been given all of the facts.

He appealed to the UK Supreme Court, which recommended that his conviction be quashed, and he was retried in May 2012 in the High Court in Edinburgh. Fraser was found guilty for a second time and will spend 25 years behind bars.

Verdicts in Scottish courts

There are three verdicts that a jury can arrive at in the Scottish criminal courts: guilty, not guilty and not proven. Both 'not guilty' and 'not proven' lead to the acquittal of the accused. The 'not proven' verdict is unique to Scotland and has caused controversy since it was established in 1728. In 2012 MSP Michael McMahon launched a consultation into the 'not proven' verdict, as he believes it is 'illogical, inconsistent and confusing'. Some of the main criticisms of the 'not proven' verdict include:

- The effect of a 'not proven' verdict is the same as that of 'not guilty'. The accused is acquitted, but the implication is that they have escaped conviction *only* because of some doubt or lack of evidence. Therefore, not proven is incompatible with the presumption of innocence.
- The 'not proven' verdict can be confusing for jurors, especially as they are not allowed to receive guidance on the difference between the two acquittal verdicts.
- It can be argued that 'not proven' is not conclusive and does not give closure to the families of victims or the accused.
- Some see the verdict as a 'cop-out' – a means for jurors who are fearful of wrongly sending someone to jail for life to acquit in the face of considerable evidence.

However, there are arguments to keep the 'not proven' verdict:

- The current system works, there is no need to change it – Scotland has had it for nearly 300 years.

- It leads the jury to fully focus on the evidence presented and to analyse whether this evidence is sufficient to lead to a criminal conviction.
- It gives the jury another option and therefore allows jurors some degree of flexibility.
- If the 'not proven' verdict is abolished, there is a possibility of an increase in miscarriages of justice.

Show your understanding

Create a mind map outlining the arguments for and against the 'not proven' verdict.

Added Value idea

The controversies and debate surrounding the 'not proven' verdict would make an ideal topic for your Assignment.

Other issues in the Scottish judicial system

Double jeopardy

Double jeopardy is a legal principle that prevents people being tried for the same crime twice. The idea behind the centuries-old principle is that it protects citizens from being repeatedly pursued by the state for a crime they may or may not have committed. However, in 2011 the Scottish Government made reforms to the double jeopardy law to bring it into line with twenty-first century society. The key elements of the Double Jeopardy (Scotland) Act include allowing a second trial in very serious cases where, after an acquittal, compelling new evidence emerges to substantially strengthen the case against the accused. This is particularly important in recent decades with the technological advancement of sophisticated DNA evidence.

World's End pub murders: Angus Sinclair could face retrial over 1977 deaths of teenagers Christine Eadie and Helen Scott

The Crown have been granted authority to bring a new prosecution against the 68-year-old following the introduction of the Double Jeopardy law in 2011 which allows suspects who are found not guilty in court to face a retrial.

A man cleared of the 1977 World's End murders faces standing trial again following a ruling by judges. The Lord Justice Clerk, Lord Carloway, sitting with Lady Dorrian and Lord Bracadale, have granted the Crown authority to bring a new prosecution against Angus Sinclair. They granted an application under the Double Jeopardy (Scotland) Act 2011 and set aside his earlier acquittal, paving the way for a new trial.

The bodies of 17-year-olds Christine Eadie and Helen Scott were found in East Lothian in October 1977 after they had earlier been seen at the World's End pub in Edinburgh's Royal Mile.

Sinclair, 68, stood trial at the High Court in Edinburgh charged with their murders in 2007. The judge, Lord Clarke, brought proceedings to an end by ruling there was no case to answer. After the 2011 law was passed, the Crown went to the appeal court to ask for the acquittal to be set aside, and to seek authority for a fresh prosecution. The law change, passed unanimously by MSPs three years ago, allows suspects found not guilty in court to face a retrial.

Justice Secretary Kenny MacAskill said at the time the law was passed that the principle of double jeopardy had stood for 800 years but the law had to be modernised to ensure it was fit for the twenty-first century.

Source: Adapted from the Daily Record, *16 April 2014*

Corroboration

Scottish Government Justice Secretary Kenny MacAskill is attempting to pass legislation through the Scottish Parliament abolishing the historic rule of corroboration, which requires at least two pieces of evidence for a criminal conviction to succeed. Corroboration has been blamed for low conviction rates in rape and domestic violence cases, where it is more likely to be one person's word against another's. The recommendation to scrap corroboration is supported by the Scottish Government, the Crown Office, Police Scotland and campaigners for victims of domestic violence and rape. However, the Faculty of Advocates warned against the move and advised appropriate safeguards be put in place, such as increasing the jury margin required to find the accused guilty from a simple majority of 8/15 to 12/15. A decision on corroboration will be made in 2015/16.

Clare's Law

The Scottish Government is considering implementing the Domestic Violence Disclosure Scheme (DVDS), more commonly known as Clare's Law, which was introduced in England and Wales in 2014. This law gives people the right to know if their partner has a history of domestic violence. In 2009 Clare Wood was murdered by her ex-boyfriend George Appleton in Greater Manchester. Unknown to Clare, Appleton had a disturbing history of savage violence towards women. Her family campaigned for greater disclosure and pilot schemes were introduced in 2012, which led to the Government passing this new law. Requests for information are considered by a panel of experts to ensure that what is passed on is lawful and necessary (see page 120).

The Children's Hearings System

The Children's Hearings System (CHS) is unique to Scotland, combining justice and welfare for vulnerable and troubled children and young people. It is important that children who commit offences, and those who need care and protection, are dealt with in the same system as these are often the same children. In 1971, the CHS took over responsibility from the courts for the welfare of children and young people under 16, and in some cases under 18 who need care and protection or who have committed an offence. In June 2013, a new Act came into operation that strengthens and modernises the Children's Hearing System.

A children's hearing (sometimes called a children's panel) is a legal meeting arranged to consider and make decisions about children and young people who are having problems in their lives. The hearing consists of three members of the local community who act as lay tribunal members, called panel members. The panel must have at least one male and one female member. The child and their parent(s) are also present, as well as a lawyer in some cases. The hearing, which is set up to create a comfortable setting for the child, listens to the child's circumstances and then decides what course of action is required regarding the needs of the child.

Children and young people are most commonly referred to the Reporter by social work and the police, but other agencies in health and education sectors can make a referral. The outcome of a panel meeting varies from case to case depending on the child's circumstances and/or the offence. The most common grounds for referral in 2012–13 were children at risk, with the number of children referred on grounds of offence declining for the sixth consecutive year. The most common types of alleged offence are assault, vandalism and threatening or abusive behaviour.

What decisions can be made?

The hearing can:
- decide that no further action is required
- request further background information and defer making a decision until a subsequent children's hearing
- decide that a compulsory supervision order (CPO) is required which may require the child to avoid certain locations or individuals or attend and co-operate with specialist programmes to address his or her offending behaviour
- decide to place the child in care, perhaps with foster parents, in a residential establishment or in secure accommodation if that is necessary.

Only in cases where the young person has committed a serious criminal offence such as murder or serious assault will he or she be dealt with through the court system. The Scottish Government raised the minimum age of prosecution from 8 to 12 in the Criminal Justice and Licensing (Scotland) Act 2010. However, the age of criminal responsibility is still 8 years old.

Section 67 of the Children's Hearing (Scotland) Act 2011

A child or young person may be called to a children's hearing if:

- the health or development of the child/young person is likely to be seriously impaired due to lack of parental care
- a Schedule 1 offence has been committed in respect of the child/young person
- the child/young person has committed an offence
- the child/young person has failed without reasonable excuse to attend regularly at school
- the child/young person is beyond the control of a relevant person
- the child/young person has misused alcohol or drugs.

Show your understanding

1 Define the term 'double jeopardy' and outline the 2011 reforms to the law.
2 Define the term 'corroboration' and outline the Scottish Government's proposals regarding this rule.
3 Why is the Scottish Government considering implementing Clare's Law?
4 Describe the work of Children's Hearings System in Scotland.

12-mark question

Analyse how the Scottish court system deals with a variety of offenders.

7 Theories and causes of crime

Criminology is the study of why people commit crime and it is the fastest growing degree in UK universities. Those who practise in this field are known as criminologists. Ultimately, the reason why we have crime is because of the actions of individuals who break the rules of society. While excuses can sometimes be made for criminal acts, justice dictates that the individual is responsible for their own actions. However, there are trends and patterns that suggest that the conditions in our society have a huge influence over the motivations behind crime and therefore society has a responsibility to provide conditions to minimise crime. These theories are known as sociological explanations for crime and relate largely to the impact of experiences in life and how people are affected by the environment around them, sometimes referred to as nurture. Contrastingly, there are occasions when there are no sociological explanations for some crimes. In some cases crime is because of psychological or physiological reasons. These theories offer a biological explanation for crime and consider the nature of individuals and their innate desire to commit an offence.

Sociological explanations

When considering the impact of society in developing criminality in individuals, it is important to understand that the aspects involved are rarely in isolation of each other. It is a complex combination of factors that lead people to commit crime. For example, the vast majority of people who suffer poverty will never commit a crime. However, for a young person,

the influence of sustained poverty combined with poor upbringing and peer pressure may lead them down a path of offending. Criminologists look at this combination of factors when trying to form theories behind offending and criminal behaviour. Figure 7.1 gives some of the sociological causes of crime.

Economic factors and poverty

Poverty creates conditions that make it more likely for someone to commit certain crimes. The wider impact of poverty on someone's life experiences can be vast. When we describe a group of people from poorer backgrounds we often use the term 'disadvantaged' and this relates to education, housing, social exclusion and even self-esteem. Although there is no direct link between poverty and crime, there are trends which would suggest some sort of relationship.

When looking at the Scottish Index of Multiple Deprivation (SIMD), which looks at a variety of factors that define how much poverty is experienced in different areas in Scotland, we can see that Scotland's most deprived areas experience more crime than other areas. Glasgow, West Dunbartonshire and Renfrewshire contain some of the largest areas of social deprivation and as a result suffer the highest violent crime rates. According to the 2013 Scottish Crime and Justice Survey (SCJS), 'More property and violent crime have consistently been found in areas with higher levels of deprivation. Urban areas, where areas of higher deprivation tend to be, have higher crime

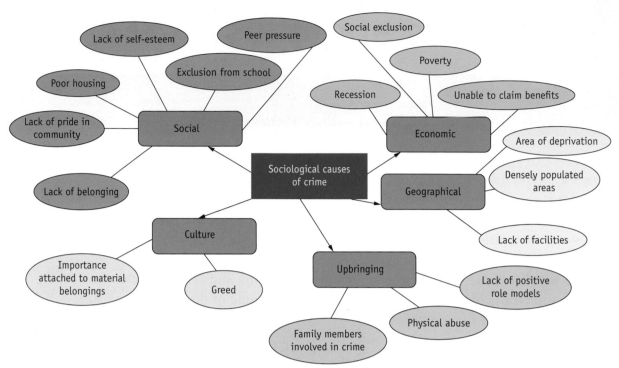

Figure 7.1 **Sociological causes of crime**

rates.' However, the report also highlights that 'In high crime areas, the risk to an individual household is relatively low, but those that are victims more often suffer repeated victimisation.' As we can see from Figure 7.2, crime is more prevalent in poorer areas and so people from a young age are more likely to live in an environment of crime. This also alludes to

victims of crime, which is discussed in Chapter 8. According to a report by the Institute for Economics and Peace called the *UK Peace Index*, Glasgow was ranked as the UK's most violent area. The report highlighted that gangs and knife crime contribute to Glasgow's position and drew attention to the link between crime and poverty by describing Glasgow as one of the poorest areas of the UK.

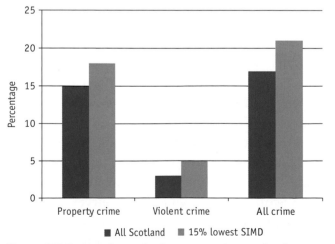

Figure 7.2 **Comparison of crime percentage rates by area of deprivation**
Source: Scottish Crime and Justice Survey, 2013

Strain theory

Poverty does not directly cause criminality, but it is poverty's consequences that can lead a person down a criminal path. This hypothesis was developed by American sociologist Robert K. Merton (1910–2003) in his strain theory. People engage in criminal activity as a means to escape the strain of a bad experience. For example, someone who is having financial difficulty may engage in stealing to reduce his or her financial problems. Failure to achieve certain goals such as respect, money and self-sufficiency can all lead to criminal activity.

Social factors

Youth crime

Youth crime is a controversial subject and is heavily present in the media. In the last half of the twentieth century, we saw an increase in youth crime through gang violence and this contributed to a general demonisation of young people in the press. Terms like 'ned', 'yob', 'ASBO' and 'hoodies' were used to grab headlines. However, when looking at the reasons behind this movement towards increased coverage of youth crime, it is important to understand some of the reasons for offending. Many people blame external factors such as poverty, poor parenting and peer pressure as reasons for young people committing crime. Young people generally are finding their way in the world and in Scotland they are not considered to be fully responsible for their actions until they are 16. Therefore, more responsibility is given to external factors that may lead them on a path of criminality. There is no easy answer to the reasons for young criminals, but there are a number of key risk factors that may result in youth offending:

- being male – 87 per cent of youth crime is committed by males
- having parents or other family members who are offenders or imprisoned
- suffering bereavement or family breakdown
- drug and alcohol abuse
- neglect and physical, sexual or emotional abuse
- associating with other young criminals
- witnessing domestic violence.

In 2010 a record 54,000 youths were referred to a Children's Hearing (see page 95). For the first time, more children were referred because of a lack of parental care than purely for committing offences. Alcohol and drug abuse among parents was identified as one of the main reasons for these 'troubled youngsters'. Of those committing offences, the types of crime committed most regularly were breach of the peace, followed by vandalism and assault. According to the Scottish Government, in 2013 43 per cent of all crimes and offences in Scotland were attributable to young people under the age of 21. Young people are responsible for higher proportions of offences such as fire-raising (86 per cent), vandalism (75 per cent), theft of motor vehicles (75 per cent), handling offensive weapons (59 per cent) and housebreaking (55 per cent). Young people seem less likely to commit crimes of indecency (41 per cent), other crimes of dishonesty such as fraud (30 per cent) and motor vehicle offences (26 per cent). It is estimated that the bulk of youth crime is attributable to those aged 18–21 (49 per cent). The under-15s commit over one-third of youth crime, with the remainder attributable to those aged 16–17.

Gangs

When considering young criminals, we often associate their actions with gangs. Recent studies have found that up to 3500 young people between the ages of 11 and 23 have joined one

Glasgow gang violence: David's story

David was born in the 1980s; his mother was an alcoholic and lived on income support in one of the 20 most deprived electoral wards in Scotland. When he was three, he moved with his mum to a more deprived ward because of domestic abuse. Over the next five years, they moved twice more following harassment from his mother's ex-partner.

Aged eight, David moved in with his maternal grandmother through the week; his mum couldn't cope. In the same house lived three adult uncles with some 120 previous convictions between them, mostly for drugs and violence.

Between the ages of nine and 12, he moved home a further three times owing to local authority regeneration. At secondary school he started to get involved with gangs, was a frequent truant and considered 'outwith parental control'.

At 13, he committed two breaches of the peace. At 14, after moving house yet again, he was described as classroom disruptive and abusing solvents.

He was excluded from school intermittently and also charged with housebreaking.

At 15, David was drinking; he was on a home supervision order, and in trouble three times for assault, shoplifting, theft and breach of the peace. The following year he was charged with assault, assault and robbery and finally attempted murder and murder.

He was found guilty of culpable homicide, and sentenced to seven years.

David went to prison. When he was 19, his mum died of a heroin overdose. Aged 21, David was released on licence to his grandmother's house, where his uncles still lived. In the same street live a heroin dealer, an ecstasy dealer, an amphetamines dealer, a Valium dealer, a man who makes counterfeit DVDs, a woman who is a known knife carrier, and a man who attacked another man with a baseball bat and axe. David is now a father, with a baby son, living on the same street he left when he went to prison.

Source: By Jon Henley, adapted from the Guardian, *19 December 2011*

of the 170 street gangs within Glasgow's borders. Furthermore, the homicide rate for Glasgow males aged between 10 and 29 is comparable to rates in Argentina, Costa Rica and Lithuania.

The issue of gangs and violence was brought to the fore in 2007 when Garry Newlove, a father of three, was beaten to death as he stood up to a street gang in Warrington. He confronted the gang because of the damage he suspected they had caused to vehicles in the neighbourhood. He suffered severe head injuries and died in hospital two days after the attack. Three young men were convicted for his murder.

The reasons why young people join gangs are varied, but invariably they are caused by problems in their lives and local area. According to the Gangs Alternative Programme (GAP) based in Los Angeles, USA, a city notorious for its gangs, some common reasons for joining gangs include:

- A sense of 'family' – young people might feel that they do not receive enough support or attention at home. They may be trying to escape a negative home life, or may be looking for a father figure. Gangs often make promises to give unconditional support and to become the 'family' they never had.
- Need for food or money – gangs may present themselves as a means of survival to youths who lack basic essentials such as food, clothing and shelter. Gang members use

their affiliation to make a profit through illegal activities, such as selling drugs and theft.

- Desire for protection – communities with high gang activity often see young people join a gang just to survive. It is usually easier to join the gang than to remain vulnerable and unprotected in their neighbourhoods, especially when considering the welfare of their own families.
- Peer pressure – kids and teens face constant pressure to fit in. Peer pressure can come in the form of intimidation, coercion, a dare, harassment, friendly persuasion or repetitious begging.
- Family history or tradition – families can have gang involvement spanning multiple generations. This is one of the toughest forms of pressure to escape, as the gang lifestyle is deeply rooted in family traditions and values.
- Excitement – some young people get a rush out of defying authority or committing crimes. They may be attracted to the gang lifestyle, as it lives outside the law and participates in many illicit behaviours. Many teenagers from areas of deprivation

cannot afford to take part in activities that stimulate them or they may not be available in their areas. This social exclusion can lead youngsters to seek thrills elsewhere.

- To appear cool – gangs have mastered the art of manipulation to attract potential recruits. Being part of a gang offers instant respect and a way to access loyal friends.

Figure 7.3 **Gang violence is a serious issue for Scotland**

Subculture: status frustration and the Chicago School

Theorists and criminologists have attempted to explain youth crime and gang culture, but they recognise that there cannot be a one-size-fits-all explanation. Albert Cohen (1895–1981) developed the idea that young people create their own subcultures separate from the dominant culture. These subcultures have their own norms, values and beliefs. Gangs are subcultures as their members feel that they

cannot succeed in 'normal' society. This 'status frustration' leads them to reject mainstream goals and adopt delinquency as this is achievable and valued highly by the subculture created by gangs. This theory was also developed by the Chicago School of thought on the organised crime of Chicago gangs that existed in the 1920s and 1930s. For Scotland, this takes shape in 'young teams' where opportunities exist for young people to become successful by taking part in dangerous and criminal behaviour. Any valued success is out of their reach in mainstream society because they are in poverty and experiencing social exclusion.

Show your understanding

1 The media often use labels such as 'neds' and 'hoodies' when explaining delinquents. In pairs, discuss and write down ways in which you feel labelled by society. Do you have any particular examples? Be prepared to share your answers.
2 Look at the list of key risk factors. For each one, expand on how this factor may lead a young person into crime.
3 Read the article from the *Guardian* on David's story. Create a timeline of events that shows the influences on his life and his record of offending. Can you think of how, with the benefit of hindsight, the authorities could have prevented his life path?
4 Create a mind map explaining some of the key reasons why some young people join a gang. Your diagram should be detailed and can be supported by illustrations.

Education

Those from areas of deprivation will generally perform less well in school. Pupils from the most deprived areas are more likely to have additional support needs, to leave school as a NEET (not in education, employment or training), and to have lower levels of attainment than those from better-off areas. Exclusion rates are higher in local authorities with multiple levels of deprivation. These points are backed up by Table 7.1, which summarises the figures for school exclusions in Scotland in 2013.

'The exclusion rate per 1000 pupils, for pupils who have an additional support need, is more than four times higher than those who have no additional support needs. Deprivation also plays an important factor in the likelihood of exclusion. Rates of exclusions per 1000 pupils are more than six times greater for pupils living in the 20 per cent of areas associated with most deprivation, compared with pupils living in the 20 per cent associated with least deprivation, as defined by the SIMD.' (*Scottish Government*)

Table 7.1 Summary of school exclusions in Scotland, 2013

	Number of exclusions	Rate per 1000 pupils
Male	17,104	50.1
Female	4,851	14.8
Pupils with additional support needs	10,539	90.0
Pupils with no additional support needs	11,266	20.0
Lowest 20% of SIMD (most deprived)	9,298	65.0
Highest 20% of SIMD (least deprived)	1,271	10.0

Source: Scottish Government

Pupils get excluded from school for a variety of reasons. Many young people in this situation may feel abandoned by their teachers and their parents, and may find more comfort in belonging to a gang (see pages 98–100). This pattern is also reflected in attainment. Attainment is measured through an average tariff score which is calculated by SQA course examination results. For pupils from the most deprived backgrounds, the average score is much lower than those from areas that suffer least deprivation. According to the Scottish Government, 'there remains a gap in the attainment between leavers from the most deprived areas and those from the least deprived areas. In 2011/12 the average tariff score for the most deprived 20 per cent was 268 compared with 552 for the least deprived 20 per cent.' Figure 7.4 shows that there is a large gap between the attainment of those from poorer backgrounds compared to those from well-off backgrounds. It also shows that improvements are slowly being made in attainment for all pupils, but the gap in attainment between the richest and poorest remains wide.

The reasons for these statistics are wide-ranging and extremely complex. Pupils from low SIMD

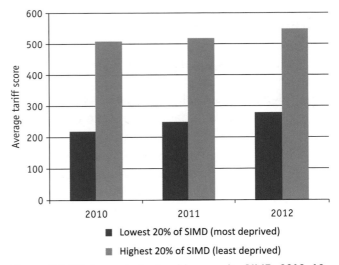

Figure 7.4 Attainment of school leavers by SIMD, 2010–12
Source: Scottish Government

areas such as Drumchapel in Glasgow and Bowbridge in Dundee may find that education is not a priority in life. Gang culture, criminality in parents, family violence and abuse, and poor upbringing could all contribute to a lack of focus on attainment. For some of these young people who perform poorly in school, a life of crime is seen as a preferred route to wealth and material objects than struggling on low income and perhaps a greater risk of unemployment.

Case study: The riots in England, August 2011

The one consolation to be taken from the August 2011 riots that engulfed London and cities such as Manchester over three or four nights is that they were not a conflict between black people and the police (as happened in 2001 in Bradford). Although it was the death of a black person in police custody that sparked off protest, what followed became an opportunity for people of all races to rampage the streets and empty the shops. Over 2000 people were later charged for their part in the riots, including murder charges against those who had run over and killed three Asian men in Birmingham. High youth unemployment, grim council estates, generations of toxic families living on welfare and gang activity were all blamed. Yet Glasgow and Scotland – with some of the highest levels of deprivation – were spared the riots.

The Economist, in a September 2011 article, argued that race did play some part in the riots. Although black people make up only 3 per cent of the UK population, CCTV placed on the internet by the police displayed a significant number of black rioters. In contrast there was no disorder in districts with large Asian populations.

⇨

Case study continued...

Timeline of the riots

- 4–6 August: Mark Duggan was killed in Tottenham, London, after police stopped the car in which he was a passenger. Saturday's protest march sparked unrest and by the end of the night Tottenham was ablaze, with cars and shops set on fire and looters running free.
- 7–8 August: more disturbances took place on Sunday night, but it was on Monday afternoon that they began to escalate. The violence spread first to Hackney, then to other parts of London, and then to major cities outside London.
- 9 August: an extra 10,000 police meant the streets of London were quieter, but rioting and disorder took hold in Manchester, Birmingham, Nottingham, Wolverhampton and Liverpool.
- 10 August: looting and clashes with police continued into the early hours in many areas outside the capital. London remained calm. Three Asian men died when they were hit by a car in Birmingham – they were trying to protect their community. Meanwhile, hundreds were arrested in the capital and elsewhere as the clean-up continued.

By the end of August over 2000 arrests had been made and 1400 jailed:

- 25 per cent of those charged over the riots had committed more than ten past offences
- 75 per cent had a previous caution or conviction
- 46 per cent were black mixed race and 42 per cent were white
- 60 per cent were claiming benefits
- 90 per cent were male.

'These riots were not about poverty. That insults the millions of people who, whatever the hardship, would never dream of making others suffer like this ... [it comes down to] a lack of proper parenting, a lack of proper upbringing, a lack of proper ethics, a lack of proper morals.' (*David Cameron, UK Prime Minister*)

Figure 7.5 An iconic London bus set ablaze during the riots

Show your understanding

1. What statistical evidence is there to suggest that exclusion rates are higher for those from areas of deprivation?
2. Describe the trends in attainment for pupils in Scotland.
3. Explain, in your own words, why those from the most deprived backgrounds have a poorer record than those from less deprived backgrounds. Give as much detail as possible for your reasons.

12-mark question

Analyse the main causes of youth crime.

Added Value idea

The debate over the riots of August 2011 is still topical and worthy of further research. This could be a good opportunity for your Added Value unit assignment. You will need to research and develop your own sources and present your findings of the causes of the riots in the form of a report. Discuss this with your teacher.

Family structures

Another explanation put forward by some criminologists for an increase in youth crime is the changing nature of families in modern-day Britain. The stereotypical family image – mother, father and two children in a detached or semi-detached house – is fast becoming less likely in British homes. The 2011 Census revealed that a greater proportion of the UK's households now comprise single parents, adult children living with their parents, or pensioners than in 2001. There was a 6.4 per cent rise in the number of families over the past decade, up from just over 16 million in 2001 to 17 million in 2011. However, there was a 9.5 per cent increase in lone-parent families, up from 2.6 million to almost 2.9 million. Single-parent families comprise almost 17 per cent of all families in the Census, up from 16.3 per cent in 2001.

There is great debate over the impact of these changes on society and specifically on the prevalence of youth crime in urban areas within the UK. David Cameron made waves during the 2010 General Election campaign by claiming that a Conservative Government would fix 'broken Britain'. Following this, Work and Pensions Secretary Iain Duncan Smith visited Easterhouse on the outskirts of Glasgow. During the trip he alluded to changing family structures as being a main contributor to 'broken Britain'.

Figure 7.6 Iain Duncan Smith visiting Easterhouse in Glasgow

'We have the fourth largest economy in the world, but within that economy, reasonably close to areas of affluence, you have areas with concentrated levels of deprivation. These include a growing number of dysfunctional families who are progressively cut off from what you and I might consider to be the norms of society – the normal processes of education, aspiration, work, and of balanced families that are themselves generally productive and positive.' The rest, the more dysfunctional family units, are growing in number 'by nature of the fact they have high numbers of children, and their children go on to have high numbers of children, and early. So you get a natural growth compared to the rest of society, which has on average fewer children.' (*Iain Duncan Smith, Work and Pensions Secretary*)

Iain Duncan Smith has also alluded to deeper biological reasons why some children from poorer areas may be more likely to turn to deviant behaviour. 'There is a physical effect taking place in children growing up in abusive households, in places where they witness a lot of abuse, perhaps their mum having different, multiple partners. These children's brains will develop physically at a rate which is quite different from those who are growing up in a normal, balanced environment in which there is attunement and empathy, reading and conversation; in which somebody has aspirations for that child and has a set of values that they pass down to that child,' he says. 'In those very abused families, you will find that the child's brain simply doesn't develop.'

Alcohol and drugs

Alcohol abuse is linked to many crimes, especially violent offences. Nearly half of all of Scotland's prisoners say that they were under the influence of alcohol at the time of their offence. Although this is a problem across the UK, it has been identified as a particular issue for Scotland. According to the Justice Secretary Kenny MacAskill, 'We in Scotland have a cultural problem with alcohol. Too many Scots think it is acceptable to get drunk. Abused partners, random assaults, stabbings and vandalism – the impact is there for all to see – on the streets, in the police stations, in hospital emergency departments, and in the courts.' Alcohol may create the sort of dysfunctional family from which children are more likely to turn to violence.

According to a report in the *Herald*, academics at Glasgow University have found that people living in an area with six alcohol outlets or more can expect crime rates twice as high as those in an area with only three.

The 2013 Scottish Crime and Justice Survey found that in 59 per cent of violent crimes the victim said the offender was under the influence of alcohol. According to the same report, the numbers under the influence of drugs accounted for 29 per cent of violent crimes. In a similar way to alcohol, drugs may have a much larger role in the causes of crime, especially for young people brought up into an environment of drug abuse. Drug abusers are also more likely to commit crimes such as burglary and theft in order to fund their habit. However, it is highly debatable whether drugs actually lead people to commit crimes or whether those who use drugs are predisposed to such activities anyway.

'Scotland has an incredibly complex relationship with alcohol. People drink for so many reasons but that includes alienation and hopelessness. Too many places are selling alcohol and alcohol is linked to crime.

'There is an overprovision of alcohol and I can't believe it is sold in petrol stations, but I don't think the problem is just about provision. Just because there is a McDonald's at the end of my road doesn't mean I eat there.' (*Karyn McCluskey, co-director of the national Violence Reduction Unit*)

Show your understanding

1 Describe the main changes to family structures in recent years.
2 What did David Cameron mean by 'broken Britain'?
3 Look at Iain Duncan Smith's comments during his visit to Easterhouse. Do you agree with his views? Use quotes from his comments to explain your thoughts.
4 What evidence is there to suggest that alcohol and drugs are a key cause of crime?

Added Value idea

A key proposal brought forward by the SNP Government in 2011 was the introduction of a minimum pricing unit (MUP) on alcohol. Research and investigate the wider effects of trying to restrict alcohol consumption. Consider not only the impact on crime in Scotland but also people's health (see also Chapter 4).

Biological explanations

Mental health issues

There are many theories and explanations of how society influences crime and how someone's life experiences can lead them down a path of criminality. There is, however, another school of thought that looks at the biological profile of offenders and attempts to make links that would suggest that some of us are more likely to commit criminal acts from birth – that is, sociological experiences bring out only something that already exists within us. For example, many people with mental health needs end up in the criminal system. Derek McGill, governor of HMP Barlinnie, said he could fill an entire hall at the prison with people who have mental health problems. A 2008 report from Scotland's then chief inspector of prisons, Andrew McLellan, warned that high numbers of people with mental health problems were ending up in prison and that it was not the appropriate place for them.

Evidence also suggests a link between imprisonment and those with conditions such as ADHD and depression. A young person struggling to control their ADHD may fail first at home, then at school, next at work and then finally with the law. This pattern of troubled lives for children with ADHD is a growing concern, and the proportion of people in jails who have ADHD is estimated to be high. However, this is an area of huge debate. A study conducted by Edinburgh University into all of Scotland's prisons found little evidence that major mental illness is common in the prison population. However, it highlighted the poor educational background of many Scottish prisoners, and in

particular the high levels of alcohol and substance abuse.

Gender

There are key patterns of criminal behaviour between men and women. Men commit far more crime than women. According to the latest statistics, men committed 88 per cent of all crimes in Scotland in 2013. Men almost dominate violent crimes such as homicide and serious assault. Of women convicted of crime, the largest proportion committed theft. Women are more likely to commit low level, non-violent offences and therefore pose a lesser risk to society. This may be explained through biological differences between men and women. As a result of hormonal differences, women tend to be less aggressive as they have lower testosterone levels.

However, although crime rates for men have gradually declined, we have seen crime rates for women increase, especially for more serious offences such as assault. This is sometimes referred to as the rise of the 'ladette' culture – young women acting in a way that is usually associated with deviance in young men, such as heavy drinking, drug abuse and assault. UK government statistics show that youth offending has increased for young women, with 22 per cent more crimes committed by girls aged 10 to 17. Although the number of offences dealt with involving girls under 18 has risen by 22 per cent, the number of offences for teenage boys has fallen by 9 per cent. There are many factors that have been blamed for the cause of increased violent crime in women. Many people point to a dilution of society's expectations for women as well as the influence of famous young women promoted in the media who partake in heavy drinking and general 'laddish' behaviour. Reality programmes such as *The Only Way is Essex* and *Big Brother* often feature young women becoming drunk and acting aggressively. However, there are arguments over whether they truly influence other young women or whether they are a reflection of a general change in society.

Nature versus nurture

On 12 February 1993, James Bulger, a toddler, was abducted from a Merseyside shopping mall by two 10-year-old boys. Two days later, his body was found on a railway line. The article below looks at how James's murder changed the way the UK thinks about its children and wonders if any lessons were learned.

Labelling theory

Howard S. Becker (1928–) noted that when it becomes known that someone has acted in a way not acceptable to society in general, they are cast as outsiders. This process of segregation creates 'outsiders' who associate with other individuals who have been cast out. Once more and more people label this person as deviant, they respond to them by continuing to engage in the behaviour society now expects of them. They become a 'self-fulfilling prophecy'. This relates to many groups in society and can be associated with 'lads' and 'ladettes'.

Life after James

Figure 7.7 *CCTV photo of James Bulger as he is led away by Thompson and Venables*

The BBC called it a 'landmark case', and so it was. It came to symbolise a moral panic about children – the threat of other people's, the defencelessness of our own. But for the first few hours after James Bulger went missing, it was assumed that the abductor was an adult. And had the child, following the usual pattern, been killed by someone he knew – a father, stepfather, uncle, neighbour or family friend – the story would have rated only a passing mention.

What put it on the front page was an image. A shopping-centre surveillance camera had caught two shadowy figures leading away a smaller figure, his hand placed trustingly in theirs. Two days later a body was found on a railway line. The two-year-old child had been attacked with bricks and an iron bar, then laid across the tracks to make it look like an accident. That was Sunday, 14 February, Valentine's Day. The surveillance images convinced the police that they were looking for two teenagers. Until Robert Thompson and Jon Venables were taken in for questioning on the Thursday morning, no one imagined that the killers would be as young as 10.

The image of abduction, the horrific death, the grieving parents, the raging crowd outside Sefton magistrates' court, the tender age of the accused – these guaranteed massive news coverage. In some countries, the media are prevented from reporting cases involving child offenders. Even in Britain, reporting restrictions prevented the naming of the two boys until the end of their trial. But this didn't stop the tabloids printing horror

⇒

stories about them and their families, including wild tales of tortured animals. Why not? This was a landmark case.

Most of us were haunted by that image from the shopping centre, with its allegory of innocence betrayed. Sales of toddler reins rose sharply, and in a survey of parents by the children's organisation, Kidscape, 97 per cent of respondents put abduction as their biggest worry, ahead of traffic accidents, glue-sniffing and Aids. The message of Bulger was that we were living in a violent new world, where you couldn't trust your children with anyone, not even other children.

Single mothers, absent fathers, school indiscipline, the decline of churchgoing, the 60s, the pill – all were blamed for the emergence of a new generation of child-hoodlums. News reports completed the picture. I still have cuttings collected from that time. Ten-year-old boy abducts 10-month-old baby. Boys aged 10 and 11 charged with rape. Boy of 13 accused of murdering 85-year-old woman. Boy, eight, attempts armed robbery. Boy, 13, denies rape in sandpit. Boys aged 10 and 11 drop five-year-old 14 storeys to death after he refuses them sweets. Boy burglar, six, batters baby to death.

But most of these cases dropped from view or never came to court. And UK statistics don't suggest that violent crimes by juveniles, especially schedule one offences such as rape or murder, were any worse in the 1990s than they had been previously. Recorded killings by children in Britain go back as far as 1748. The last notorious child-killer before Thompson and Venables was Mary Bell, in 1968. And though a dozen other cases of homicide by children were recorded over the next quarter-century, the pattern suggests that it is a crime that happens comparatively rarely – and not that we have bred a new generation of child-monsters.

The Bulger case was iconic. But in hindsight, its lesson is almost the opposite of what it was taken to be at the time – not that children had grown big and dangerous, but that adult society had lost sight of their smallness and vulnerability. The 38 witnesses who claimed to see two boys kicking and beating a smaller boy but who didn't intervene; the failure of teachers and others to halt Robert Thompson's extraordinary level of truanting or notice Jon Venables' sense of neglect; the barbarism of a legal system which demanded that 10-year-olds be tried as adults in a public courtroom: all these point to a failure to protect children, or act in their interests. Amid the hysteria in 1993, Thompson and Venables lost the right to be seen as children, or even as human. The kids who had killed the kid had to be killed, or at any rate locked up for life. The word used about them stopped all arguments. They were evil.

The tabloid verdict was that Thompson and Venables were aliens from the Planet Evil, or (no less Gothic) video-junkies mimicking Chucky Doll in *Child's Play 3*. The truth is more humdrum. Their family backgrounds exhibited classic 'risk factors' – dysfunction, poverty, alcoholism, marital breakdown, neglect and bullying. Both boys had been held down a year at school, a humiliation which made them team up. Both resented their siblings, and may have punished James for it. Most important, having bunked off school and walked the toddler the two miles back to their school and homes in Walton, they were terrified of getting into trouble with their mothers – and scrambled up on the railway line, where they killed him, to avoid it. The police saw evidence of sophistication and premeditation in the crime. But why, then, did they take the victim to their own neighbourhood, where people knew them? I see damaged children, not cunning adults. They were 10.

Source: By Blake Morrison, adapted from the Guardian, *6 February 2003*

Both Jon Venables and Robert Thompson were found guilty of the murder of James Bulger. Both were released on licence when they turned 18 and given new identities. Although it is thought that Thompson has been rehabilitated successfully, Venables has since been convicted of several charges and has been in and out of prison.

Other reasons

While academics and commentators continue to develop explanations for why people commit crimes and the underlying motivations for deviant behaviour, there are some crimes that cannot be explained easily through sociological and biological theories. Many of these offences are new to the scene such as identity theft or computer hacking using modern technologies. Some crimes are carried out in protest. Green Party MP Caroline Lucas was arrested at an anti-fracking protest for disturbing the peace, and members of the pressure group Fathers4Justice have been arrested on anti-terrorism charges. It would be ambitious to try to link their crimes to nature or nurture. They simply committed the crime for publicity or belief in their causes.

White-collar (corporate) crime

Some crimes are committed purely out of greed. Some of these perpetrators may be comfortably rich, but they continue to break the rules in an attempt to increase their wealth. White-collar crime is when fraud, embezzlement or other illegal schemes are used in the financial sector. Tax evasion is the most popular white-collar crime and there have been a number of high-profile cases in recent years.

According to accountancy firm KPMG, the typical white-collar fraudster is male, aged 36 to 45, holds a senior job in finance, has worked for his company for more than a decade and acts in collusion with a partner. The problem with white-collar crime is that it is non-violent, not obvious and rarely committed against one victim, so it is hard to detect and prove. A few recent examples are Jurgen Whitehouse, IT services boss at Ofcom, who was sentenced to two and a half years in prison for defrauding the telecoms regulator out of more than £500,000, whereas a Sainsbury's IT manager who stole millions of Nectar points after finding a loophole in the system was jailed for 20 months.

Show your understanding

1. What are some of the main reasons why women commit fewer crimes than men?
2. 'The rise in women offending is because of the emergence of a ladette culture.' Do you agree with this hypothesis? Explain your answer.
3. Explain what is meant by white-collar crime.

Added Value idea

Hold a class debate on the following motion: 'Nature not nurture creates the murderers of innocent people.'

Impact of crime on society

The impact of crime on society can be far-reaching. Of course there are human costs to consider. For most crimes there is a victim or group of victims and the financial and emotional impact of this can be impossible to measure accurately depending on the circumstances of the crime. Some groups of people are more likely to be victims of crimes than others. There are also financial costs to crime. The criminal justice system is not cheap and costs have to be considered for the police service, court service and the financial costs of any punishments that may be required. In addition, for some crimes there may be a wider cost to community confidence and this can have a knock-on effect to businesses in areas perceived to have high crime rates. There are also increased financial costs for individuals such as home, business and car insurance. Therefore, crime can have a huge impact on society.

Personal impact

Crime has a huge impact on the individuals involved. There are obviously consequences on the victims of crime. For some crimes there may be physical damage or harm. Victims also respond emotionally to crime, the degree of which depends greatly on the type of crime experienced. Many people feel a sense of annoyance at property crime. The idea that someone would damage or steal the things that someone else owns often brings out a sense of anger. Conversely, other crimes that are violent can bring out deep reactions in people such as anxiety and depression.

Table 8.1 shows the emotional impact of crime on the victims: the most common reactions are annoyance, anger and shock. Although there are different emotional responses depending on the type of crime, this varies hugely depending on different groups of victims.

Table 8.1 Emotional impact of crime on the victims (%)

	Property crime	Violent crime	All crimes
Annoyed	56	47	53
Anger	52	47	52
Shock	16	38	22
Fear	6	22	11
Lost confidence/felt vulnerable	5	19	9
Anxious/had panic attacks	5	13	7
Difficulty sleeping	4	11	6
Depressed	3	9	5

Source: Scottish Crime and Justice Survey, 2013

Victims of crime

Those in poverty

According to the 2013 Scottish Crime and Justice Survey (SCJS), adults who live in the 15 per cent most deprived areas of Scotland are more likely to be a victim of crime: 21 per cent compared to 16 per cent for those living in the rest of Scotland. The risk of poverty crime was higher for those living in the 15 per cent most deprived areas compared to the rest of Scotland, as was the risk of experiencing violent crime. Not only are those who live in poorer areas more likely to be victims, they are also most likely to be repeat victims.

In addition, most of the poverty in Scotland exists in urban areas such as the east end of Glasgow. According to the SCJS, more property and violent crime have consistently been found in urban areas. There is a higher than average risk of victimisation to adults living in urban areas compared with those living in rural locations.

According to a 2006 report called *Crimeshare: The Unequal Impact of Crime* by the Institute of Public Policy Research, the poor and the unemployed are twice as likely to be victims of crime. The report also found that fear of mugging and violent attacks makes people in more deprived areas 'very worried' about living in their area. Former director of the Institute, Nick Pearce, commented that 'People in poorer households have less choice over where to live, they cannot afford to pay for expensive alarm systems or the safety of a taxi ride home. They are less able to control the risks they face and often have no option but to expose themselves to greater danger.'

The young

According to the 2013 SCJS, 8.2 per cent of those aged 16–24 reported being victims of violent crime. This is nearly double the rate of those aged 25–44. Only 1.9 per cent of those aged 45–59 reported being victims of violent crime.

The most common form of victimisation for young people is assault without injury followed by personal theft. This may be because young people have many desirable and expensive goods in their possession. Mobile phone theft is the most common type of theft in the UK today. Young people are more likely to feel pressurised into joining gangs. In some areas, these who refuse face greater victimisation, and for those who do join there is a greater risk of committing crime as well as being a victim of crime.

It is generally thought that young people who are victims of crime at the hands of other youths are unlikely to report such crimes because of fear of repercussions such as further attacks, the safety of their friends and families and, in some cases, fear of not being believed. In addition, in the case of knife crime and gangs, many young people report that they carry a weapon because of their experience of being a victim of assault involving the use of or threat of a knife.

Young people are more likely to be victims of crime because of events at school. Bullying is a well publicised problem in some secondary schools. When a crime occurs at school, victims cannot escape the school grounds, their classroom or their changing room. For some young people this can generate feelings of isolation and alienation, and school work often suffers. Children are also more likely to be victims of mental, physical and sexual abuse. According to the children's charity the NSPCC, the police recorded over 23,000 sex offences against children aged under 18 years in England and Wales between April 2012 and March 2013. In 2013 ChildLine counsellors dealt with 1.4 million contacts from children about various problems including bullying, sexual abuse, violence and mental health issues.

The elderly

Although older people are statistically less likely to be victims of crime, the impact of crime against them can be devastating. The charity Age UK found that almost half of those aged over 75 are too afraid to leave their homes after dark because they believed they would be subject to verbal abuse or mugging. Two-thirds felt they would inevitably become victims of crime as they got older, whereas one-fifth stated that this fear has caused a sense of loneliness and isolation. According to the Crown Prosecution Service, 'Older people can be targeted because of their perceived or actual vulnerability or their unequal access to safety. For example, an older man walking along a street may be robbed of his wallet because the suspect chose him because, on that basis, he was an "easy" target.'

In recent years criminal gangs have targeted the elderly, attempting to trap them in a financial scam by using their vulnerability to extract life savings and other assets that they might possess. At times these gangs target individuals who appear to live alone. They also sell details of these individuals to other fraudulent groups, making some elderly people's lives a misery.

Show your understanding

1 What are the key statistics that show that people in poverty are more likely to be victims of crime?
2 a) In your own words, create three scenarios to explain why living in poorer areas makes it more likely for someone to be a victim of crime.
  b) Share your scenarios with a partner. Discuss any similarities between your examples.
  c) From this discussion, create a list of five key factors that result in a stronger likelihood that those in poverty are impacted by crime.
3 Explain some of the reasons why younger people are more likely to experience crime.
4 Why might crime among young people be under-reported?

Case study: Think Jessica

Think Jessica is a charity pressure group which aims to raise awareness of financial scams that target the elderly. It also aims to make Jessica Scam Syndrome a recognised condition. According to the charity, it believes that some elderly people become addicted to these scams and even develop a mental condition that can cause ill health and death. Think Jessica was started by Marilyn Baldwin in 2007 after her mother was caught up in a vicious cycle of scams that Marilyn believes contributed to her death.

Elderly hit by new telephone scam

Elderly people are being targeted with a new telephone scam that involves con men posing as bank staff or police, a fraud watchdog has warned. The fraud, which has cost victims £7m in a year, is difficult to detect when well-executed, Financial Fraud Action UK said. The criminals instruct the victim to disclose credit and debit card information before emptying the person's bank accounts. Those who have fallen into the trap have had their life savings wiped out within 24 hours.

Around one in four adults in the UK has received a cold call like this. Financial Fraud Action said 43 per cent of victims have been aged over 50. The new con is dubbed 'vishing'. It involves a fraudster posing on the phone as someone from a bank or building society fraud investigation team, the police or another legitimate organisation such as a telephone or internet provider.

An automated system calls the unsuspecting victim. Once they pick up the receiver the criminal, posing as a representative of a reputable organisation, claims an urgent need for their debit or credit card. In a cruelly ironic twist, this typically involves telling the bank customer their card has been cloned and fraud is about to be enacted on their account. The crook urges the victim to act straight away to avoid the disaster. If he or she can sense doubt, they urge their victim to put down the phone and ring back. However, the criminal simply stays on the line and either pretends to answer the phone or passes the receiver to another member of the gang. It may sound far-fetched, but the scam is so believable that four in ten people fail to see through tricks, Financial Fraud Action said.

Once the details have been handed over, the criminal simply empties the account. In some circumstances, victims are being persuaded to go into their bank, withdraw their life savings and then hand them over to a courier who arrives at their front door later in the day.

Source: By Kyle Caldwell and Jessica Winch, adapted from the Telegraph, *28 August 2013*

Women and families

Although women in the UK commit far fewer crimes than men, they are often victims when it comes to violent crime. According to the pressure group the Fawcett Society, at least one in four women will be a victim of domestic violence in their lifetime, and between one in eight and one in ten women experience it annually. This figure relates only to reported crimes as fewer than half of all incidents are reported to the police, yet they still receive one domestic violence call every minute in the UK. Violence against women is still persistently high despite a number of high profile government campaigns. The Fawcett Society claims that violence, including sexual violence against women and girls, is still not being treated with the same professionalism as other crimes. Even before the current austerity measures that have seen funding for violence-against-women's services cut, over one in four local authorities in Britain had no specialised violence-against-women support services at all.

Figure 8.1 In the UK, two women a week are killed by a current or former male partner

Domestic violence

Domestic violence is still largely a hidden crime. Those who have experienced abuse from a partner or ex-partner often try to keep it from families, friends or the authorities.

- They may be ashamed of what has happened.
- They may feel they were to some extent to blame.
- They may love their partner and do not want him to be criticised or punished for what he did.
- They may think it was a one-off event that will not happen again.
- They may be frightened that if they tell anyone about it, their partner will find out and they will be in danger of further and perhaps more severe violence from him.

For all these reasons, and others, victims of abuse are likely to experience repeated attacks before they report the abuse to anyone – and statistics can only be based on known data. On average, 35 assaults happen before the police are called.

Women also feel the impact of crime with regards to their traditional position in households. They are traditionally the head of a family and so have added pressures when it comes to the impact of criminality on their families and the impact of criminality within their families. In some cases, women are left to pick up the pieces after criminal behaviour from teenage sons or are raising families on their own because absent fathers are in prison.

Show your understanding

1   Consider the impact of crime against the elderly. In pairs, create a PowerPoint presentation for the campaign group Think Jessica. Include:
   a) the ways in which crimes can affect the elderly
   b) some of the reasons why they are targeted
   c) advice for elderly people on how to avoid being a victim of crime.
2   In your own words, explain the issues surrounding domestic violence.
3   Give some of the reasons why domestic violence is under-reported.
4   Explain the other, less obvious, impact of crime on women.

Impact on the offender

One area of impact that has received little attention is the impact of crime on the offender. Many people feel it is part of the punishment of committing a crime. Criminals spend time in prison, which should act as a deterrent for committing future crimes as well as a rehabilitative step towards becoming a law-abiding citizen. However, committing a crime can have huge personal consequences as well as impacting on the offenders' families.

Once their punishment has been served, many convicted criminals find life extremely difficult.

They suffer from a lack of employment opportunities; it is estimated that seven out of ten employers would not employ a convicted criminal. If you are a convicted criminal you must reveal your criminal past when applying for jobs. However, if only a short amount of time has been spent in prison, offenders do not have to reveal their criminal past if the employer does not ask them. But if, as part of an application form, an employer asks for previous criminal convictions, they have to be declared. This rule also applies to many university courses, so this has a particularly negative effect on young offenders who may be attempting to improve their life chances. Travel to and from other countries can also be affected. The USA and Australia have particularly robust visa application procedures and if an applicant has a criminal record it is likely that he or she will be denied access. Mortgage and insurance applications require people to detail any previous convictions and, again, this can result in rejection or increased costs. For offenders there can be a personal impact on their personal lives after conviction. Their ability to hold down long-term relationships can be impacted, as well as the ability to build up trust in friendships and within their community.

The families of offenders can also be affected by their crimes. Depending on the specifics of the offence, some families experience a great deal of shame and embarrassment. They are sometimes targeted in bullying or revenge attacks, or even forced out of communities altogether. For parents, having a child who is a convicted criminal can impact on their position within their community for the rest of their lives.

Impact on the community

Crime can have a hugely negative impact on local communities. Once an area experiences high crime levels, the impact may be long lasting and span generations. It can cause many law-abiding citizens, given the chance, to move out of these areas. Dalmarnock in the east end of Glasgow used to be a thriving community with over 10,000 inhabitants. It provided many of the workers for Glasgow's famous shipbuilding industry. However, with the decline of shipbuilding and high unemployment rates, the area has been branded a 'ghetto', with only 2500 people now living there. This depopulation leaves a concentration of deviant individuals who often wreak havoc on communities. High levels of crime may also damage community spirit and result in less neighbourliness. It leads to people wanting to 'keep themselves to themselves' for fear of harassment or becoming involved in arguments that may result in them becoming part of a criminal act.

High crime levels can also contribute to 'environmental poverty' – that is, areas with high crime levels often suffer from vandalism and graffiti. This makes the area less desirable and more dangerous. Fear of crime also deters people from using public facilities such as parks and public transport. Many people in the most deprived areas of Scotland with the highest crime rates suffer poor health as a result of a lack of decent facilities and through the lifestyles, stresses of fear and anxiety that exist in 'bad' communities. In May 2010 the *Herald* ran the headline 'Springburn Tops League as Nation's Most Feared Area for Violent Crime'. The article detailed how 42 per cent of residents in Springburn feared being attacked by neighbours, which is more than double the figure for areas such as Perthshire.

Once a region with a high level of crime is labelled as a 'bad' area, it may be almost permanently damaged with regard to public perception. This leads to a lack of 'new' families entering areas to try to dilute tensions that may exist in that community. One example of this is Easterhouse in Glasgow. In the 1980s and 1990s, this suburb developed a bad reputation for gangs and violent crime. The community was divided, with several gangs protecting their 'patches', and there was a high drug crime rate. However, through investment over the past two decades,

Easterhouse has seen a severe drop in crime and very little gang activity. There has also been investment in community facilities such as the building of the Glasgow Fort Shopping Centre and new house-building. However, the area still suffers from a reputation of being a 'bad' area. House prices are lower than average and unemployment rates continue to be high.

However, we have seen on occasion that some crimes can bring communities together. For example, in February 2011 thousands of people from communities around Blantyre marched in support of murdered teenager Reamonn Gormley's family. Reamonn was brutally attacked while walking home with a friend. Both men were stabbed; Reamonn died of his injuries. John Tierney, a local who helped to organise the march, said at the time that 'The good people of Blantyre have come out in tribute to one of their own. One of the most important things is the Gormley family know the community are behind them. Hopefully they can take a bit of strength from this.'

Another example of crimes that ultimately helped to bring communities together was the riots of 2011 in England. A government report into the impact and action to be taken as a result of the riots, called *Response to the Riots*, was published in 2013. It found that:

- Following the riots, local communities were quick to respond in doing all they could to get their local areas back to normal.
- If the rioters demonstrated some of what is worst in our communities, the actions of many citizens the morning after the riots showed the best.
- Neighbours gave their time and energy in a variety of ways – cleaning up the streets and making donations to local victims, and workers turned up early to get shops back in business.
- In Croydon, over 100 young people came together and revamped waste land in the worst affected areas.
- Residents in Lewisham called for a show of community support and contacted the Mayor and council with offers of help, including organising clothes collections for those made homeless and supporting local market traders and businesses.
- Hundreds of people in Liverpool got together to sweep up piles of broken glass and debris following the set-up of a Facebook group.

Figure 8.2 Around 1000 people marched through Blantyre to honour Reamonn Gormley and to demand action against knife crime

Economic impact

As well as the emotional and physical impact of crime, there is an obvious financial impact. According to the Scottish Government, over £2.5 billion was budgeted for criminal justice in 2013–14. This represents the third highest area of spending behind health and local government. The largest outlays were over £1 billion for the set-up of a single police force, over £346 million for the Scottish prison system and over £73 million for the Scottish court system. The prison service estimates it costs £119,000 to set up an initial prison place for a long-term prisoner and nearly £40,000 per prisoner per year after this. With reconviction rates for short-term offenders taken into consideration, it is estimated that the failure of prison to rehabilitate offenders costs around £11 billion in the UK.

Of course dealing with offenders incurs a cost to the taxpayer, but there are also financial costs to the victims. Theft obviously creates costs for victims with regard to robbery and burglary, as well as criminal damage. The true amount varies depending on circumstances, but there is also the emotional value attached to some belongings which cannot be replaced. For some individuals losses are covered by insurance, but in the long term this increases insurance costs for everyone. Another example is the 'crash for cash' scam used by criminal gangs to make fraudulent claims to insurers for accidents. Criminals stage accidents, typically at roundabouts, by slamming on their brakes and causing the car behind to crash into them. The fraudsters then claim for the cost of repair or replacement of their vehicle on the innocent driver's insurance. Criminal acts such as these have resulted in car insurance costs rising by more than 20 per cent since 2010.

For businesses, there is the cost of theft through crimes such as shoplifting, This is added to the cost of crime prevention measures such as CCTV and other security solutions. In January 2013 the *Guardian* reported that retail crime is estimated to cost the sector over £1.6 billion per year. It found that nearly 1 in 20 stores was robbed during 2013. Customer thefts remain the most common retail crime, accounting for 83 per cent of all incidents. There are on average 2 million incidents of shoplifting a year in the UK retail sector as a whole. However, it is not just the cost in lost goods or the cost involved in insurance that has an impact. The overall economy suffers as employers pass on these costs to consumers, raising prices for everyone. It also restricts businesses' ability to expand and take on new workers, thereby restricting employment rates for everyone. Violent crime costs the UK economy more than £124 billion a year, equivalent to £4700 for every household. This figure, which equates to 7.7 per cent of the UK's GDP, includes the cost of police investigations, courts and prison expenditure as well as damage to the overall economy with absences in work.

According to Joe Perman, Assistant Economist for the Scottish Government, every crime has a financial impact on the economy. Less obvious crimes that have an economic impact are murder (£148 million a year) and minor assault (£1.7 billion a year).

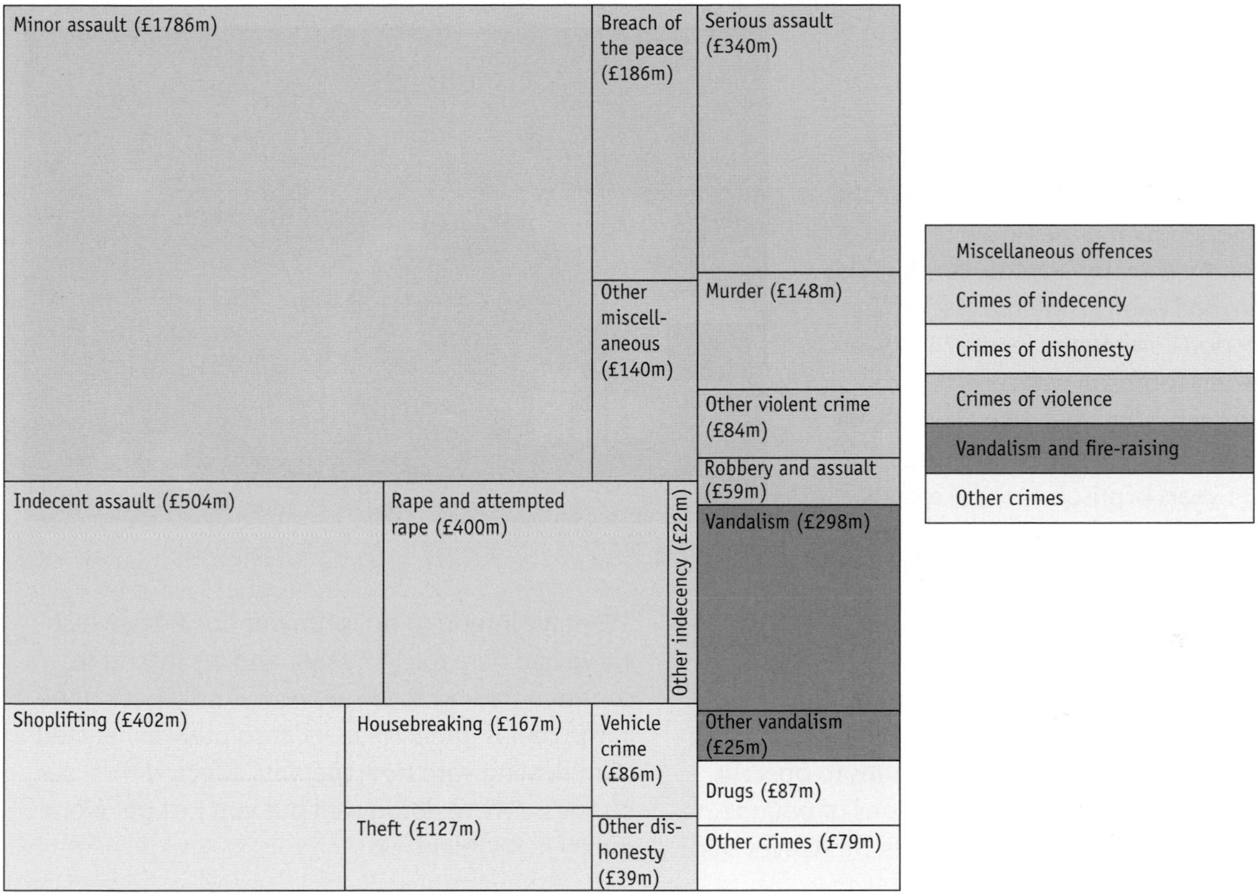

| Minor assault (£1786m) | | Breach of the peace (£186m) | Serious assault (£340m) |
| Other miscell-aneous (£140m) | | | Murder (£148m) |

Miscellaneous offences

Crimes of indecency

Crimes of dishonesty

Crimes of violence

Vandalism and fire-raising

Other crimes

Other violent crime (£84m)

Robbery and assualt (£59m)

Indecent assault (£504m)

Rape and attempted rape (£400m)

Other indecency (£22m)

Vandalism (£298m)

Shoplifting (£402m)

Housebreaking (£167m)

Vehicle crime (£86m)

Other vandalism (£25m)

Theft (£127m)

Other dis-honesty (£39m)

Drugs (£87m)

Other crimes (£79m)

Figure 8.3 Total cost of various crimes in Scotland
Source: Scottish Government

Identity theft costs the UK £2.7 billion

According to the financial services comparison website confused.com, identity theft is creating huge economic costs for individuals and businesses in the UK. It estimates that identity thieves are getting their hands on £1.9 billion of other people's money every year. The National Fraud Authority (NFA) estimates that identity fraud costs more than £2.7 billion and affects more than 1.8 million people. Of this, at least £1.9 billion is the amount gained by the fraudster, which means on average ID thieves gain over £1000 from every stolen identity.

As part of National Identity Fraud Prevention Week, the NFA is reminding individuals and businesses how important it is to take responsibility for protecting their own identity.

Action Fraud offers the following advice to help protect against ID theft:

- Don't throw out anything with your name, address or financial details without shredding it first.
- Check your bank and credit card statements carefully and report anything suspicious to the financial institution concerned.
- Make sure your computer has up-to-date anti-virus software installed.
- Make sure you use all the privacy settings available on social networking sites, but don't put too much personal information up there.
- If you move house, always get Royal Mail to redirect your post.

Source: Adapted from Confused.com

House of Reeves furniture store

One of the most iconic images of the riots in England in 2011 was that of the flames engulfing the House of Reeves furniture shop in Croydon, London. The store had been an integral part of the Croydon community for over 144 years. Gordon Thomson was convicted of starting the fire by setting alight a sofa in a display window. He was sentenced to 11 years in prison. He now regrets starting the fire, saying: 'If I had known what I know now then I would have gone round the corner and pulled that burning sofa out before the whole store came down.'

In 2013 the Reeve family announced that they were giving up attempts to rebuild the store. The furniture business, which continues to operate from another building, lost millions of pounds over the two years since the riots. Mr Reeves said:

Figure 8.4 House of Reeves during the riots, 8 August 2011

'What we intend to do is run our business, which we've had here for 147 years, and we intend to continue trading as we are now. And what's gone in the past is gone.' He feels 'absolutely exhausted' from dealing with how the riots affected the business. 'We're doing well but you just get worn out by it, it's relentless.'

Show your understanding

1 Describe what is meant by the term 'crash for cash'.
2 In your own words, explain the term 'identity theft'.
3 Explain, in detail, how crime impacts the economy. In your answer ensure you refer to profit, employment and prices.

Political impact

The problem of crime in society is an emotive issue and it plays a central part in the Government's work. Crime has a personal and at times brutal impact on people's lives, and the general public, as well as the media, demand that politicians deal with those who commit crime in appropriate ways.

One of Tony Blair's most iconic sound bites was 'tough on crime, tough on the causes of crime' and during his Labour administration a huge increase in the prison population took place. Since then we have seen a 'rehabilitation revolution' in which the Coalition Government has attempted to reduce the prison population in an effort to reduce costs while still ensuring a tough approach to criminals. Generally, the public demands that criminals are dealt with firmly and that they are appropriately punished. There are, however, certain cases where particular criminal acts or issues become central to public debate and as a result the Government must react in order to ensure that they retain the support of the electorate.

One such issue that has arisen is corroboration in Scots law (see page 94). Corroboration is a rule that two pieces of supporting evidence are needed in order for a case to go to court. For example, if someone was assaulted, evidence of the victim's injuries or another witness, as well as their own testimony, would be needed for that case to be tried in Scottish courts. This is not the case in England and Wales. This rule is particularly relevant in rape and sexual assault claims where attacks are usually carried out in private and, for some, the assault may not be reported until some time after the event. In these circumstances it can often be the word of one person against another. Many groups such as Rape Crisis Scotland have been campaigning for years to have corroboration removed from Scots law. In a statement made in July 2013, Sandy Brindley, National Coordinator for Rape Crisis Scotland, said: 'It can't be right to have a justice system where three-quarters of rapes reported to the police can't be prosecuted. However, we need to be realistic about prospects of this leading to increased convictions – this bill will remove a barrier to cases getting to court but it will still be for juries to make a decision beyond reasonable doubt.'

Removing corroboration is part of the Criminal Justice (Scotland) Bill introduced to parliament in June 2013. Since then there has been huge public and media interest in the bill. The change is backed by many members of the public, police and prosecutors, but there has been fierce opposition from other sections of the legal profession, who have raised concern of an increased risk of miscarriages of justice. Following a vote in the Scottish Parliament in April 2014, it was announced that the bill will be delayed until at least after April 2015. This shows that crimes can have an impact on politics as governments try to find the solutions that the public demand.

Clare's Law and Sarah's Law

Another example of a crime that has had a political impact is the Domestic Violence Disclosure Scheme (DVDS), more commonly known as Clare's Law. It was named after Clare Wood, who in 2009 was murdered by her ex-boyfriend George Appleton in Greater Manchester. Unknown to Clare, Appleton had a disturbing history of savage violence towards women. Her family campaigned for greater disclosure and, after a series of pilot schemes in four police areas, the DVDS became law in England and Wales in March 2014. This law allows the police to disclose information on request about a partner's previous history of domestic violence or violent acts. Domestic Violence Protection Orders have also been introduced to enable the police and magistrates courts to provide protection to victims in the immediate aftermath of a domestic violent incident.

In a response to a similar campaign in Scotland, the First Minister announced in May 2014 that a pilot scheme would be introduced in Scotland. In 2012–13, the police recorded 60,080 incidents of domestic abuse, a slight increase from the 59,847 incidents in 2011–12.

Clare's Law is another example of the media and public opinion leading to a change in the law. It echoes the success of Sarah's Law, so-named after Sarah Payne, an eight-year-old girl who was abducted and murdered in 2000 by Roy Whiting. Whiting had previously been convicted of abducting and indecently assaulting a young girl. The story was picked up by the *News of the World* newspaper and attempts to get the law put into place became a massive nationwide campaign. Following this, the Child Sex Offender Disclosure Scheme for England and Wales and the Keeping Children Safe Scheme for Scotland were both set up so that parents and carers can request criminal records held by police for people who have access to children.

Riots in England, August 2011

A crime incident that has perhaps exposed the political impact of crime most clearly is the riots of 2011 in England. Such was the public outcry at the televised destruction caused by rioters that many media outlets wanted the Government to take swift action against the assailants. Christine Piper of the Open University highlights the impact of public pressure on the Government to take action. She stated that Prime Minister David Cameron's first message to the rioters appeared to anticipate the outcomes in sentencing courts when he told them that 'You will feel the full force of the law and if you are old enough to commit these crimes you are old enough to face the punishment.' She commented that 'One of the judges imposing allegedly tough sentences (Andrew Gilbart QC) explicitly justified his approach, explaining that such criminal behaviour "must be met with sentences longer than they would be if the offences had been committed in isolation".'

Miss Piper questions whether the Government, as well as parts of the press, exerted untoward pressure on the courts and whether this has resulted in sentences that would not 'normally' be imposed. An analysis of 1000 riot-related cases heard by magistrates suggested that those sentenced received prison terms 25 per cent longer than normal and that the overall imprisonment rate of 70 per cent was much higher than the previous rate. Those convicted of theft received sentences of 7.1 months, compared with the normal tariff of 2.4 months, and for violent disorder, 10.4 months instead of the normal 5.3 months.

Show your understanding

1 'Corroboration must be removed from Scots law.' Do you agree with this statement? Explain your reasons in detail.
2 Explain what is meant by Clare's Law and Sarah's Law.
3 With regard to the riots in England in 2011, in what ways could it be said that these crimes had a 'political impact'?

Added Value idea

Corroboration is a key part of Scots law. Opinion is hugely divided on whether it should be removed so that more cases are able to go to court. However, there is also a feeling that it could create miscarriages of justice.

9 Efforts to tackle crime – the police

The impact of crime is deeply detrimental both to society and to the economy. Since the establishment of the UK's first professional police force in 1829, society has relied on the police to ensure the rule of law. The police have been described as 'citizens in uniform', but this image is becoming harder to maintain with Police Scotland's decision in 2013 to allow armed police to attend non-conflict situations (see page 132). Laws are created and approved by the various parliaments in the UK to the benefit of society.

The role of the police

The role of the police is vital in ensuring law and order are kept in society. All police forces throughout the UK want to record a trend of decreasing crime rates as it shows they are doing their job well and ensures positive press coverage. In maintaining law and order, the police's role covers preventing crime, protecting the public and detecting criminals. Scotland's police service, Police Scotland, is centred on one fundamental aim of 'Keeping People Safe'.

The structure of policing in the UK is complex, with Scotland having its own separate police service and justice being a devolved power. The Scottish Parliament is responsible for most of the powers and functions of the police in Scotland and the formulation of new laws. However, the UK Government retains responsibility for passing laws on terrorism, security, firearms and drugs.

Police Scotland is the second largest force in the UK after the Metropolitan Police. There are 14 local policing divisions (Figure 9.1), each headed by a local police commander who ensures that local policing in each area is responsive, accountable and tailored to meet local needs. Each division encompasses response officers, community officers, local crime investigation, road policing, public protection and local intelligence. Alongside local policing divisions there are a number of national specialist divisions. The Specialist Crime Division (SCD) provides specialist investigative and intelligence functions such as major crime investigation, public protection, organised crime and counter-terrorism. These functions may not be required often, but when a serious crime takes place or public safety is under threat from criminals, the most professional response is available, regardless of where you live. The Operational Support Divisions (OSDs) provide specialist support functions such as road policing, air support, dog branch, marine policing and the mounted branch.

Critics of having one police force are concerned that it takes away local accountability and makes the police a remote organisation out of touch with local concerns. Centralisation weakens local democracy; concern has already been expressed that the former Strathclyde police force is imposing its target-driven approach and former priorities throughout Scotland. Councillors and MSPs in Highland constituencies question the need for armed police patrolling the rural peace of the Highlands and argue that it is a central-belt solution being imposed on parts of Scotland with low crime figures (see page 132).

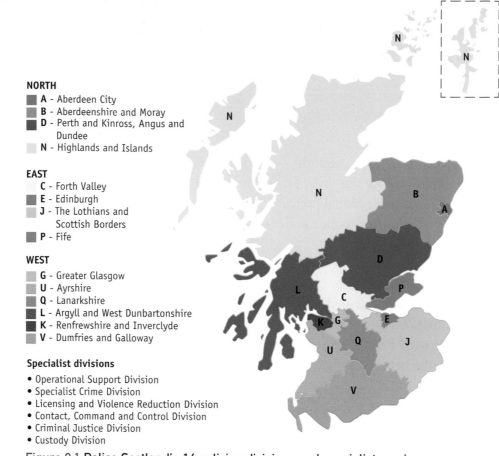

NORTH

- **A** - Aberdeen City
- **B** - Aberdeenshire and Moray
- **D** - Perth and Kinross, Angus and Dundee
- **N** - Highlands and Islands

EAST

- **C** - Forth Valley
- **E** - Edinburgh
- **J** - The Lothians and Scottish Borders
- **P** - Fife

WEST

- **G** - Greater Glasgow
- **U** - Ayrshire
- **Q** - Lanarkshire
- **L** - Argyll and West Dunbartonshire
- **K** - Renfrewshire and Inverclyde
- **V** - Dumfries and Galloway

Specialist divisions

- Operational Support Division
- Specialist Crime Division
- Licensing and Violence Reduction Division
- Contact, Command and Control Division
- Criminal Justice Division
- Custody Division

Figure 9.1 **Police Scotland's 14 policing divisions and specialist services**
Source: Police Scotland

Fact file

Police Scotland

- Reform of the Scottish police force began in 2012 when the Scottish Parliament approved plans for a single police service under the Police and Fire Reform (Scotland) Act 2012. This service was to be called Police Scotland.
- Police Scotland is a merger of eight former Scottish police authorities and includes the Scottish Police College, the Scottish Crime and Drug Enforcement Agency and the Scottish Police Services Authority.
- The Scottish Government believes the new force, which was established in April 2013, improves frontline services, reduces costs and provides a more equal service across Scotland.
- Police Scotland is led by Chief Constable Sir Stephen House, former Chief Constable of Strathclyde Police.
- The Chief Constable is supported by a command team of Deputy Chief Constables, Assistant Chief Constables and Directors.
- The Police Scotland budget in 2013–14 was £1.1 billion, although budget cuts are required over the next few years.
- There are 17,234 police officers in Scotland and 6701 police support staff.

Interview with Sir Stephen House, Chief Constable of Police Scotland

Figure 9.2 Sir Stephen House

Can you outline your role as Chief Constable of Police Scotland?

As the head of Police Scotland I provide overall strategic and operational direction to the over 17,000 police officers and more than 6,500 police staff who work together to deliver the best possible policing service for the people of Scotland. I ensure that Police Scotland works collaboratively with a wide range of partner organisations to tackle the policing priorities identified by the public and through our own evidence-based analysis of crime.

What do you see as the police's main role in society?

Police Scotland's role and purpose is to improve the safety and well-being of people, places and communities across Scotland. Our focus is on Keeping People Safe, which is at the heart of everything that we do. Our policing priorities – Violence, Disorder and Antisocial Behaviour; Road Safety and Road Crime; Protecting Vulnerable People; and Serious and Organised Crime and Counter Terrorism, as set out in our Annual Police Plan – are aligned to the strategic police priorities set by the Scottish Government and the strategic objectives outlined by the Scottish Police Authority. They are also informed by the local policing plans set at local authority and multi-member ward levels.

What do you consider to be the most effective method of policing?

A national police service that is delivered locally and responsively. By working with all our communities, and by listening and responding to community concerns, we can increase public confidence in our service and help us to achieve our overarching focus of keeping people safe. Through our 14 local policing divisions, each headed by a local police commander, we ensure that local policing in each area is responsive, accountable and tailored to meet local needs. Each division encompasses response officers, community officers, local crime investigation, road policing, public protection and local intelligence. All 14 local policing divisions are supported by a Specialist Crime Division (SCD) and Operational Support Division (OSD). The SCD is a dedicated command which provides equal access to national specialist investigative and intelligence functions in seven key areas: major crime; public protection; divisional crime; organised crime; counter-terrorism; intelligence; and safer communities. The OSD encompasses national support services which divisions can call on for assistance. In addition to an Emergencies Planning Department, additional support services include: road traffic units, the mounted and dog branches, air and marine support, specialist search teams, firearms and public order resources.

What are your views on a fully armed police service?

I do not support the routine arming of all police officers. The deployment of a small number of specialist, authorised armed officers – currently there are 275 – where necessary and proportionate, is assessed as the most appropriate way to maximise public safety and minimise risk to police officers. These officers are available 24 hours a day to protect the public across the country and are available to respond to incidents in which the deployment of armed police officers is assessed as appropriate.

⇨

In what ways is Police Scotland benefiting as a single national police service?

The transition from eight legacy forces to a single force has been a success with little noticeable difference for the public. Public confidence in policing remains high and surveys show high rates of public satisfaction: in 2013–14 82 per cent expressed satisfaction with the service they received. We are more accountable than ever before with the public inputting to our policing priorities at a local, regional and national level. Over 30,000 people took part in this year's survey helping us identify what matters most to our communities. We have met our first year savings target, reducing our budget by £63.9 million. We have made it easier to contact the police with the new non-emergency number (101) and over 1.6 million calls have been received in the first 12 months. And over half a million people are now engaging with the service through social media channels – an increase of over 90 per cent since April last year.

What is the most rewarding part of being a police officer?

For me Keeping People Safe is why I joined the police in the first place. To know that on a daily basis, whether as a beat Constable when I joined the police, or as Chief Constable now, the positive impact I can make to people's lives makes everything I do worthwhile. Every day, being a police officer is a highly rewarding job and I can honestly say that I have loved every minute of my police service, regardless of the challenges I faced along the way.

Show your understanding

1 Outline the role of the police in society.
2 Take down notes on the new Scottish Police service.
3 Outline the arguments for and against a single Scottish police force.
4 Outline the role of the Chief Constable of Police Scotland.

Methods of policing and government policies

Police Scotland uses a variety of methods and tactics to ensure society is as safe as possible. The different regions of Scotland have very different needs and challenges. For example, knife crime and drugs are more of an issue in the Greater Glasgow region than in Dumfries and Galloway. Different areas present challenges that require a certain style of policing that best suits the needs of the community. The police also work hard on crime prevention to tackle the root causes of crime.

Crime prevention

There is strong public consensus that one of the most important functions of the police is preventing crime before it happens. Effective policing is not just about enforcement; tackling the causes of crime is more cost effective and leads to greater social benefits over a longer period of time. The police work hard to divert potential offenders from committing crime in the first place. Much of this work involves the police and associated agencies working with young people and offenders to influence standards, thinking and attitudes. The aim is to prevent potential offenders turning to crime. This method of multi-agency crime prevention is increasing and has positive results. For example, the Violence Reduction Unit (VRU) is a nationwide body that works to specifically reduce incidences of violent crime in Scotland. The VRU works with a whole host of partners, from the police and justice services to education, health and community groups to try to find the best way to make Scotland a safer place to be. In 2010 the VRU had great success with a community initiative to reduce violence in Glasgow's east end, cutting gang crime by over 50 per cent and engaging many youths who felt isolated from society and caught up in gang culture.

Case study: Knife crime prevention

Knife crime in Scotland is a major problem. In Glasgow in particular there is a 'blade culture' where many young people routinely carry knives. This has led to newspaper headlines over the last decade describing Glasgow as the 'knife capital of Europe and the most violent city in Britain'. However, in more recent years statistics show that rates of knife crimes in Scotland are decreasing. Crimes of handling an offensive weapon (including knives) have dropped dramatically in Scotland, falling by 67 per cent in Glasgow and 60 per cent in Scotland since 2006–07. In achieving such a remarkable drop in knife crime rates, both the police and the Scottish Government have intensified crime prevention efforts. The Scottish Government has included provisions in the Criminal Justice Bill to increase the maximum sentences for offences involving handling offensive weapons and knife possession from four years to five years. Furthermore, the No Knives, Better Lives initiative is a collaboration between the Scottish Government and YouthLink Scotland that works to educate young people about the dangers of carrying a knife and the devastating personal consequences it can

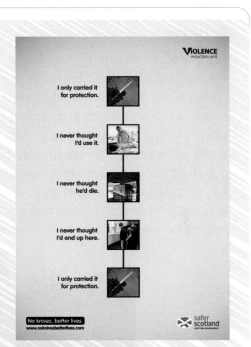

Figure 9.3 The No Knives, Better Lives campaign

have on their future. A range of innovative tactics such as hard-hitting talks in schools, targeted advertising in areas where young people are known to congregate and youth work interventions have worked together with tough enforcement on the streets to tackle the issue of knife carrying and knife crime.

Case study: Government legislation and crime prevention

The Government may take legislative action to tackle crime if a certain type of criminal activity is perceived to be endemic. This was the case with the Offensive Behaviour at Football and Threatening Communications (Scotland) Act 2012. The Scottish Government and the police believed that the actions of some football fans in Scotland required control. The Act criminalises behaviour that is threatening, hateful or otherwise offensive at a regulated football match including offensive singing or chanting. It also criminalises the communication of threats of serious violence and threats intended to incite religious hatred, whether sent through the post or posted on the internet (such as on Facebook). The Act only criminalises behaviour likely to lead to public disorder which expresses or

⇨

incites hatred, is threatening or is otherwise offensive to a reasonable person. It created two distinct offences, punishable through a range of penalties including up to a maximum of five years in prison and an unlimited fine. The Act has allowed the police in Scotland to arrest those guilty of singing sectarian or offensive songs or acting in an aggressive manner.

Criticisms

Many football fans around Scotland believe the Act has needlessly criminalised supporters and that the police already had plenty of powers under existing laws to deal with any issues arising at a football match. Many people are charged randomly under the legislation by a single police officer wielding a handheld camera aimed at groups of supporters whom he/she has already decided will be possible offenders. The length of sentence that is available to impose on those arrested under the Act has been criticised for being disproportionate. Football supporters can end up in jail and with a criminal record for a single chant or phrase which would not be prosecuted at any other sporting event or venue. The Act has been successful in achieving the unity of fans in condemning the legislation with banners appearing at Celtic, Rangers and Motherwell games. Fans believe the Act has put a strain on the relationship and respect between supporters and the police.

Figure 9.4 The Fans Against Criminalisation group is concerned that legislation passed by MSPs has created problems for ordinary supporters

Show your understanding

1. Why do the police focus on crime prevention?
2. How do the police prevent crime?
3. Outline the issue of knife crime in Scotland and the successes of the police in reducing knife crime.
4. What is the Offensive Behaviour at Football and Threatening Communications Act and what criticisms have been made of it?

Community policing

The term 'community policing' covers a variety of different models of practice. In terms of the public experience of community policing, the common elements of the strategy tend to be police 'on the beat', the police attending community meetings and officers who are assigned to a specific area or town who have the responsibility for building relations with the public in that area. Community policing also takes a problem-solving approach to local issues, often in partnership with other public services, which attempts to get to the root of local problems rather than simply responding to crime by arresting individual offenders. Community policing is part of the service the police offer in Scotland, but it is still predominantly response-oriented – that is, based on answering 101 or 999 calls. Police Scotland recognises the significant successes and public popularity of community policing with Chief Constable Sir Stephen House stating: 'Over the next few years, Police Scotland will be putting more officers into the community and providing a visible policing presence on streets.'

Community policing can bring considerable social benefits. These include reductions in crime, disorder and anti-social behaviour, increasing feelings of safety among members of the public and improvements in police–community relations. If a community police team becomes familiar with the local residents of a neighbourhood and builds relationships with those who live there, evidence suggests crime rates will fall considerably.

However, community policing is not always successful and can be hard to manage and maintain. Community policing requires the extensive interaction and involvement of the public, who may have disdain for or negative opinion of the police. Community police who are investigating a crime may come up against silence from members of the public even though they have worked hard to build up links and relations with the local population. This is reflected in evidence from the 2013 Scottish Crime and Justice Survey (see Figure 9.5), which shows that in the 15 per cent most deprived areas higher proportions of the public thought that community relations were poor with the police in their local area (37 per cent compared to 19 per cent of those living in the rest of Scotland), and that the local police were not dealing with the things that mattered to people in their community (33 per cent compared to 23 per cent of those in the rest of Scotland). Community policing is therefore a long-term strategy that requires a degree of commitment from those involved and a consistent approach to staffing.

As an extension to community policing, 55 police officers have been working with 65 secondary schools across Scotland as 'campus cops'. This involves developing strong links with young people and their communities and changing the perceptions of the police by young people. Officers are assigned to schools where they build up relationships with pupils and staff, providing advice on topics ranging from bullying to drugs. The officers, also known as School Link Officers and School Liaison Officers in other parts of Scotland, also improve police intelligence on areas around schools, for example identifying individuals who have been selling drugs or who are involved in gang-related violence.

Stop and search

Stop and search powers enable the police to dispel or confirm suspicions about individuals and detect, for example, those suspected of carrying weapons, stolen goods or illegal drugs. In practice, the law requires the execution of

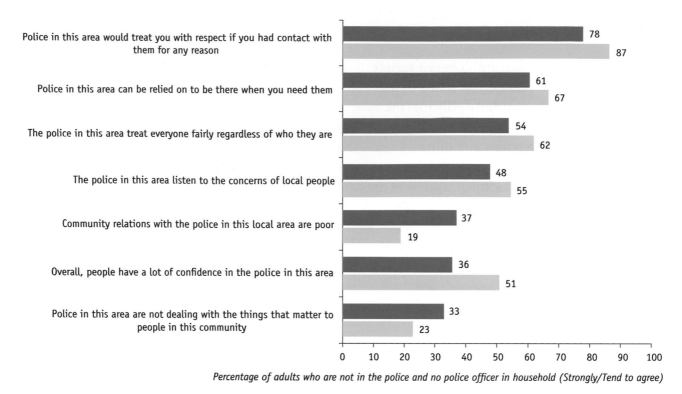

Percentage of adults who are not in the police and no police officer in household (Strongly/Tend to agree)

■ 15% most deprived   ■ Rest of Scotland

Figure 9.5 Agreements with statements about the police in the local area by area of deprivation
Source: Scottish Crime and Justice Survey, 2013

Figure 9.6

such powers to be based on fact, information and/or intelligence and not on the subjective whim of individual officers. Stop and search is generally supported by the public, but people often feel victimised if they are personally stopped and searched themselves. There is almost constant controversy over the use of stop and search. In English cities the police have been criticised for stopping a disproportionate number of black and Asian people. In 2013, black people were six times more likely to be stopped than white people. This has led to ethnic minority youths in areas such as inner-city London feeling discriminated against by the police and alienated from society.

In Scotland the stop and search method is used even more frequently by the police. People in Scotland are four times more likely to be stopped and searched than those in England, and twice as likely as those in London. From April 2013 to April 2014, there were 537,434 stop and searches in Scotland (an average of

1445 a day), with young people more likely to be targeted than older adults. Human rights groups argue that targeting specific groups such as youths in Scotland is having a similar negative effect on community relations as in England. However, Justice Secretary Kenny MacAskill argues that stop and search methodology is about being proactive, trying to prevent crime happening in the first place, and it is reasonable and proportionate. Mr MacAskill does not feel that it is discriminatory and states that it is quite clear and self-evident that crime is disproportionately perpetrated by young people, so they will be stopped more often. Statistical evidence suggests there has been a big fall in violent crime in Glasgow

since stop and search became a more prominent part of policing over the last year, so it is a policy that will continue to be adopted by the police.

Intensive enforcement

Commonly referred to as a 'zero tolerance' approach to policing, intensive forms of law enforcement are often associated with tough methods of crime-fighting. Zero tolerance was first used in the 1990s to tackle urban crime in New York City by the New York Police Department. Zero tolerance policing means that people are arrested for minor offences, with the idea being that if the police stamp out

Case study: The Scottish Crime Campus and the National Crime Agency

The Scottish Crime Campus (SCC) strengthens collaboration between agencies and their fight against organised crime and terrorism. Staff from five organisations including the police, the National Crime Agency, forensics, customs and the prosecution service work together at the SCC in Gartcosh in North Lanarkshire. In the new campus there is advanced technology such as a state-of-the-art forensic laboratory and sophisticated crime mapping systems that allow a multi-agency approach to tackling serious crime.

Figure 9.7 The new Scottish Crime Campus building is designed to reflect the connecting strands of DNA

The National Crime Agency (NCA), which is one of the partners at the SCC, is a UK-wide body that has been billed as 'Britain's FBI'. The role of the NCA is to target organised crime and other major offending that cuts across regional and international borders. The agency is responsible for tackling crimes such as drug and people trafficking, and complex international fraud including cyber crime. The NCA has more than 4000 officers and works with each of the regional police forces in the UK and similar organisations abroad. Unlike some of its international counterparts such as the FBI, the NCA does not have responsibility for combating terrorism. That remains at Scotland Yard, where the Metropolitan Police oversees a number of regional teams comprising police and MI5 officers.

low level offending and show a tough approach, serious crime will become less likely. This policy was very successful in New York, with serious crime decreasing by up to 50 per cent. In the UK, however, zero tolerance is based more on single issues and the idea that responding immediately and consequentially to crime such as street drinking and knife crime will avert a downward spiral of disorder.

Over the festive period of 2013, Police Scotland adopted a zero tolerance approach to knives, with anyone caught carrying a knife automatically charged and facing a court appearance. This resulted in the number of knife crime offences in Scotland reported by the police to the prosecution service dropping by 28 per cent. After the English riots of 2011 (see pages 102 and 116), David Cameron spoke of adopting a zero tolerance policing approach to heal 'broken Britain'. However, zero tolerance policing on a grand scale is at odds with the UK's traditional approach of policing based on a 'service and consent' model rather than the 'crime control' model familiar in the USA. When Sir Robert Peel founded the first police service in the 1820s, he said that police should 'use physical force to the extent necessary to secure observance of the law or to restore order only when the exercise of persuasion, advice and warning is found to be insufficient'. Notably he said that officers must at all times 'maintain a relationship with the public that gives reality to the historic tradition that the police are the public and the public are the police'. It was this idea which led to the unarmed British 'bobby' patrolling his beat, rather than a heavily armed cop storming around neighbourhoods crime-fighting. In our consensual system, the police work *with* a community rather than *against* it, and this is a highly valued part of our justice model.

Show your understanding

1 Explain the term 'community policing' and describe its advantages and disadvantages.
2 Explain some of the findings from the Scottish Crime Survey shown in Figure 9.5.
3 Describe the work of a 'campus cop'.
4 Outline the controversies over stop and search.
5 Explain the term 'zero tolerance' and give some examples.
6 Why does the zero tolerance approach contrast with traditional British policing methods?
7 Describe the work of the SCC and the NCA.

Armed policing

Dunblane, the Cumbria shootings and the brutal murder of drummer Lee Rigby, among other tragic events, have often led to media outcry for two things: the return of the death penalty and the full-scale arming of our police service. British police services have never been like their American colleagues, patrolling the beat with a pistol on their hip, trained and ready to shoot if required. The average British police officer goes about his or her duty unarmed, carrying a baton and handcuffs. Sometimes an officer may carry CS spray and/or a Taser (stun gun), but most of the time they do not. It appears the police themselves are happy with this position, with a recent police survey showing that 82 per cent of officers are against routine arming. If every officer has a gun, there is a higher chance of the police killing an innocent person. This was the case in 2005 when the police shot and killed Jean Charles de Menezes on the London underground after he was accidentally mistaken for a terrorist fugitive.

However, it has been suggested that in modern society, with associated threats from gang violence, knife crime, drugs and terrorism, the traditional unarmed police officer is vulnerable and less effective at protecting the public. Aside from the UK and Ireland, all major police forces in Europe routinely carry firearms, as do those in the USA, Canada and Australia, leaving many questioning whether it is time for the UK to follow suit. Nevertheless, the various police services around Britain believe they have the correct balance of an unarmed police service supported by specialist firearm officers ready to respond when necessary. Police Scotland caused controversy in 2014 when it emerged that specialist armed officers were carrying weapons when out on routine patrol, a shift in practice from tradition. One alternative to armed policing is the routine use of Tasers (see the case study).

Added Value idea

Research whether the police should be routinely armed or not, then carry out a further investigation into whether they should carry Tasers.

Hundreds of police carry weapons in Scotland

Police officers across Scotland are regularly carrying handguns while on routine patrol. Police Scotland said its specialist firearms officers had been authorised to carry weapons while on duty by Chief Constable Sir Stephen House. The revelation led to anger from politicians and human rights campaigners, who said the force should have consulted parliament before the move. Armed response vehicle (ARV) crews are now dealing with everything from missing persons to road accidents.

The change in policy comes despite figures showing gun crime in Scotland is at its lowest level since 1980. Earlier this month, concerns were raised about policing in the Highlands – one of the safest areas of the UK – after it emerged armed police are on routine patrol. Chief Superintendent Elaine Ferguson, divisional commander specialist services, said: 'ARV crews have been deployed under a standing authority from the chief constable to carry handguns and less lethal weapons while on routine patrol.' She said ARV officers supported routine policing duties including dealing with anti-social behaviour and road crime and public reassurance patrols. Chief Supt Ferguson added: 'In addition to responding to over 1300 incidents across the force in 2013–14 in their specialist role, there have been numerous examples where these officers have been instrumental in supporting local communities. For example, in searching for vulnerable missing persons, providing specialist first aid skills or engaging with vulnerable or potentially suicidal persons. Police Scotland are committed to ensuring that all communities have more equal access to specialist support.' Police Scotland said armed officers were carrying handguns in patrol vehicles, not on foot. Such officers are normally armed with a Glock pistol.

Labour's shadow justice spokesman Graeme Pearson, a former police officer and director general of the Scottish Crime and Drug Enforcement Agency, said the issue needed to be debated in the Scottish Parliament. He said: 'The public needs to be asked if it is something that they want. What happens if a gun goes off when the officer is routinely armed? That sort of thing has happened in the US with tragic consequences.'

John Scott QC, chairman of the human rights group Justice Scotland, added: 'The chief constable should not have done this without consulting parliament. To have armed police officers on the street routinely is quite wrong. I am concerned there could also be an increase of illicit firearms on the street in response. What happens if the gun falls into the wrong hands?'

A spokeswoman for Justice Secretary Kenny MacAskill said decisions over where and when to deploy resources were a matter for Police Scotland.

Source: By Chris Marshall, adapted from the Scotsman, *19 May 2014*

Case study: The use of Tasers

A Taser or stun gun uses compressed air to fire two darts that trail electric cables back to the handset. When the darts strike, a five-second 50,000-volt charge is released down the cable, causing the suspect's muscles to contract uncontrollably.

Figure 9.8 Police officers are trained to use Tasers

A police officer's job is often dangerous and fraught with risk. An officer's day may take them into contact with criminals who may be armed and volatile. Using a Taser, the officer can disarm a criminal from a safe distance and render the suspect immobile for a period of time to allow arrest. Although Tasers inflict a certain amount of pain and discomfort, they are unlikely to kill or seriously harm the individual, although deaths from the use of Tasers have occurred.

The use of stun guns by the police in the UK has risen in recent years. Police in England and Wales used Tasers on more than 10,000 occasions for the first time in 2013, an increase of 27 per cent from 2012. Any use of a Taser in Scotland is followed up by the Police Investigations and Review Commissioner, who assess if its use was justified.

Table 9.1 Arguments in favour of and against the use of Tasers

In favour of Tasers	Against Tasers
Police officers who are issued with Tasers go on a three-day training course and must justify their use	If the police were routinely armed with Tasers, the police–public relationship could be damaged and the country would become harder to police
Tasers are an appropriate response to a criminal who is brandishing a weapon	Tasers can be dangerous, and their use changes the nature of British policing
In some situations where violence is threatened, a police officer requires a Taser to protect him/herself and the public	Not all officers are trained in the use of Tasers
If Tasers were carried by all police officers, this would serve as a deterrent to potential violent criminals	There have been cases of fatalities on account of the use of Tasers by the police
Tasers are generally safe and very rarely cause lasting health issues or fatalities	Amnesty International believes that 'Tasers are potentially lethal weapons, which should only be used in serious, life-threatening circumstances and by the highest trained officers'

Figure 9.9 In Scotland, only 1 per cent of police officers are from ethnic minorities

Issues within the police

As the police are funded mainly by the government and because they are expected to uphold the laws of society, they are subjected to a level of scrutiny and accountability that no other profession experiences. In a democratic society, elected officials serve to keep the police accountable and to ensure they reflect the will of the people. As the police enforce the law, it is imperative they reflect a model of professionalism, fairness, consistency and equality within themselves and when dealing with the public. Some specific examples of challenges within the police are as follows.

Inequality

The police should aim to mirror society in that there should be a gender and ethnic minority balance in staffing. Women are an integral part of a police force, not simply because they make it more representative, but because their presence alone punctuates the macho culture that is sometimes associated with police work. At the very least, a police service should be able to relate to the communities it polices; it should be fair and inclusive. In 2013 there were 35,471 female officers out of 129,956 officers in the 43 forces of England and Wales, representing 27.3 per cent of the total. The proportion of women in the more senior ranks

of chief inspector and above was 18.0 per cent compared with 29.7 per cent of women at constable rank. The situation is similar in Scotland, with women accounting for 28 per cent of officers and around 20 per cent of all promoted posts. These statistics may seem poor reading, but they are a huge improvement on a decade or two ago where in Scotland the number of women in promoted posts stood at only 8 per cent (less than one in ten).

Perhaps even more controversial is the issue of the police being representative of ethnic minorities. After the death of black teenager Stephen Lawrence in 1993, the police in England came under criticism for a culture of 'institutionalised racism'. Police forces throughout the UK had a long, hard look at their attitude towards the ethnic minority population and began to work to heal relations and represent the ethnic minority population within the police service. In 2013 there were 6555 ethnic minority police officers in the 43 forces of England and Wales, accounting for 5 per cent of all officers (see Figure 9.10). This is particularly poor when 14 per cent of the population are from ethnic minority backgrounds. In London, the scene of the outbreak of the riots in 2011, the ethnic minority population is 40 per cent. The relationship between the police and ethnic minority residents in the city is tense, with much of the population feeling discriminated against. In Scotland, only 1 per cent of police officers are from an ethnic minority background, which is of concern given that in 2014 the ethnic minority population stood at over 4 per cent.

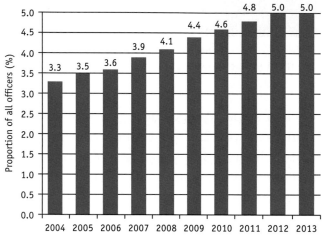

Figure 9.10 **Percentage of police officers in England and Wales from ethnic minorities, 2004–13**

ICT task

Visit **www.semperscotland.org.uk** to research the role of ethnic minority police officers in Scotland in more depth.

Response to major incidents

After the riots in England of summer 2011 (see pages 102 and 116), the response of the police to the carnage that ensued was heavily scrutinised by the public, the media and politicians. The Home Affairs Select Committee's report on the police response to the riots found the operation to police the disorder in many towns and cities, and especially in London, was 'flawed'. Forces were not quick enough in flooding the streets with officers, there was no system to give businesses in areas affected by the riots early and

consistent advice on what to do, and the arrangements for lending officers from one force to another was to be reviewed. It was also suggested in the report that the perception that the police had 'lost control' of the streets was the most important reason why the violence and looting spread to other towns and cities.

As well as politicians, the media scrutinised the police's response in detail. Many newspapers reported that during the riots there were areas that the police had lost complete control of and there was a serious breakdown of law and order where people took advantage of what they perceived to be a lawless situation. Front-page splashes with pictures of rioters looting while the police looked on helplessly fuelled the public image that the police effort had failed.

Figure 9.11 **A tabloid newspaper reports on the riots**

Added Value idea

Research a controversial police incident such as the death of Mark Duggan, Ian Tomlinson or Jean Charles de Menezes. Were the actions and tactics of the police adequate and/or justified?

Budget cuts and desk closures

In 2013–14 Police Scotland met its target to reduce its budget by £64 million. These budget savings will continue over the following years as the Government reduces Police Scotland's annual budget, which currently stands at £1.1 billion. In February 2014, the Scottish Government announced the closure of 70 front-desk police stations in a bid to find more savings. Police stations across the country, including Craigie Street in Glasgow and Edinburgh's Balerno, along with Ullapool and Benbecula in the Highlands and Islands, will see an end to front-counter services for the public. The change will also see hundreds of hours lost in public-counter opening hours from the current set-up. Stations such as Kilbirnie and Largs in Ayrshire will go from an 8 a.m. to 7 p.m. seven-day front-desk operation to 9 a.m. to 5 p.m. Monday to Friday. It has been argued that through the desk closures the police have turned their backs on local communities. The closure of these public counters in police stations could have an impact on long-established links between police and the local community. People value being able to report issues directly at their local police station. Now people will have no option but to make a phone call to an operations centre.

Show your understanding

1 Why is it important to have equality in the police?
2 To what extent have the various police forces in the UK achieved equality in their staffing?
3 Outline the criticisms levelled at the police regarding their response to the English riots.
4 What budget constraints are Police Scotland facing and what actions are being taken?

20-mark question

To what extent have the police been successful in tackling crime?

Structure this essay by referring to each method of policing and analyse the successes and failures of each. Include up-to-date statistics, quotes and examples from this chapter.

12-mark question

- Analyse government policies to reduce crime, *or*
- Evaluate the effectiveness of police methods in tackling crime.

10 The penal system – responses to crime

Aims of the system

In a civilised society, citizens expect to be protected from those who break the law. Victims of crime expect that the criminal will be punished. The traditional form of punishment is prison. Criminals are denied their liberty, and in the past, for the most serious crime of murder, the state had the right to execute them. Capital punishment is no longer used in the UK, but is still permitted in some US states such as Texas.

The purpose of the UK penal system is to protect, punish, deter and rehabilitate. In order to consider the effectiveness of prisons or alternatives to prison, we should ask the following questions:

- Do they protect citizens?
- Do they provide appropriate punishment?
- Do they deter the individual from committing a crime?
- Do they rehabilitate the criminal and provide the support to prevent reoffending?

It can be argued that if over 90,000 UK criminals are locked up at any one time, UK citizens can sleep safely in their beds as they are protected.

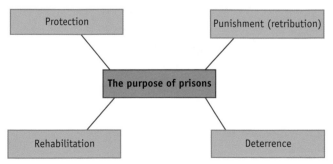

Figure 10.1 **The purpose of prisons**

However, this is perhaps a short-term security as many prisoners reoffend when they are released.

Punishment is clearly a strong argument for a custodial sentence. The criminal is denied liberty and separated from family and friends. The popular press and the Conservative Party (at least until 2010) strongly believe in the effectiveness of prison. The media are full of indignant stories of how prisoners are being pampered with access to televisions in their rooms and a holiday-camp prison environment. However, if rehabilitation is a key purpose of prisons, surely they should provide conditions and opportunities to enable prisoners to change their ways? Rehabilitation aims to look at the reasons behind offenders' actions and how to resolve these, and therefore prevent them reoffending. Surely prison *is* the punishment – with offenders denied liberty and access to family and friends – rather than prison being *for* punishment. It is counter-productive to make prisons harsh, violent and lonely places as this is likely to lead to reoffending: the 'revolving door' of crime. Many people come in and out of jail, never being deterred or reformed – and becoming worse each time. Some three-quarters of short-term prisoners are likely to reoffend.

Overcrowding in prisons

Chronic overcrowding stretches prison resources and has unsatisfactory consequences in terms of hygiene and tension between prison officers and prisoners. It limits the number of prisoners who can take part in educational and offending behaviour programmes because there is no space for them.

The pressures of overcrowding mean staff have less time for vulnerable prisoners. Linda Purves in *The Times* stated: 'Prison can deter and restrain and protect the public; but it can also do great things for resentful, uncontrolled people. The catch, however, is that it can't do this if it's overcrowded.'

Overcrowding can create violent and chaotic conditions and makes it difficult for prison officers to control the abuse of drugs in jails and acts of violence between prisoners. The Howard League for Penal Reform found that in 2012 more than 100 violent incidents were recorded within prisons in England and Wales.

Overcrowding can make conditions unbearable, especially in prisons dating from Victorian times. This can impact on the mental health of prisoners and lead to an increase in self-harm and suicide attempts (see page 141).

Figure 10.2 This mixed-gender prison in Grampian houses all of the region's prisoners in a jail in their own area so that family links are maintained

Fact file

Prison overcrowding

- In 2013 of the 82 prison establishments in England and Wales over 65 per cent of them were overcrowded.
- Prison should provide the opportunity for offenders to improve their employability, to tackle their drug addiction and to maintain their family links.
- A 2011 National Audit Office report concluded that 'prison overcrowding disrupts work to prevent reoffending'.
- In 2009 the number of Scottish prisoners passed 8000 for the first time.
- HMP Peterhead closed in December 2013, followed by HMP Aberdeen in January 2014. A new community-facing jail, HMP Grampian (Figure 10.2), opened in March 2014. This mixed-gender prison houses all of the region's prisoners.

Are short prison sentences effective?

Three-quarters of people given a custodial sentence of less than six months will reoffend within two years. This stark statistic clearly challenges the effectiveness of a short prison sentence for non-violent crimes. Scotland's Justice Secretary Kenny MacAskill has stated that a sentence of six months or less is 'not a sufficient length of time to rehabilitate the offender'.

The Scottish prison population

The total number of prisoners held in Scottish prisons was 8191 in June 2014 (see Table 10.1). Many prisoners have a background of poor mental health and drug addiction, as shown in Figure 10.3 and the Factfile on page 140.

Table 10.1 Scottish prison population, June 2014

Category	Numbers
Untried male adults	1090
Untried female adults	69
Untried male young offenders	109
Untried female young offenders	3
Sentenced male adults	5577
Sentenced female adults	315
Sentenced male young offenders	317
Sentenced female young offenders	19
Recalled life prisoners	76
Convicted prisoners awaiting sentencing	227
Prisoners awaiting deportation	7
Under 16s	0
Civil prisoners	0
All Scotland total in custody	7809
Home Detention Curfew	382
Total	8191
(The total number of prisoners in England and Wales is 85,500)	

Source: Scottish Prison Service

Fact file

Statistics profile of prisoners in 2013

- Unemployment was 13 times higher for prisoners before admission compared with the general population.
- Around 70 per cent had histories of poor mental health and/or drug problems.
- Over 25 per cent of prisoners had been taken into care as a child compared to 2 per cent of the population.
- One-quarter of young male offenders in prison were young fathers.
- Half the prison population came from home addresses in 155 of the 1222 local government wards in Scotland.

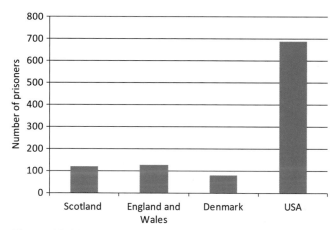

Figure 10.4 Imprisonment rate per 100,000 of population, selected countries

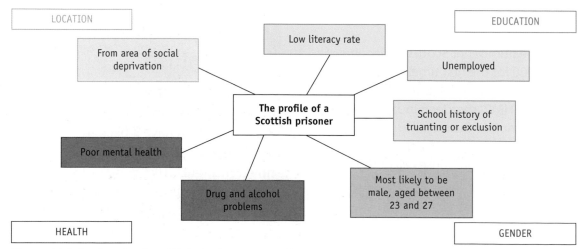

Figure 10.3 Profile of a Scottish prisoner

Suicides

Official Scottish Prison Service (SPS) figures published in January 2014 reveal that in total 28 prisoners committed suicide between 2010 and 2013, and there were 61 attempted suicides. Table 10.2 indicates a positive decline in the number of suicides in custody. However, figures published in February 2014 by the Scottish Government highlight that two in three women in prison are on suicide watch. A spokesperson for Prison Fellowship stated: 'The situation is desperate. We think that most people with mental illnesses should not be there.' Scotland's largest jail, HMP Barlinnie in Glasgow, has the highest number of male prisoners on suicide watch, with 40 per cent of its 1210 inmates on a care plan.

A Scottish Government spokesperson stated: 'SPS staff are trained to identify those at risk of suicide and prison staff continue to work with the health service to ensure that vulnerable people are given the help that they need.'

Table 10.2 Prisoners who have committed suicide in Scottish prisons, 2010–13

Year	Number
2010–11	13
2011–12	8
2012–13	7

The politics of prisons

The traditional view of the political parties until 1997 was that the Conservatives were the party of law and order and of harsh measures against offenders. In contrast, Labour was regarded as more sympathetic to the causes of crime. However, Tony Blair's Labour Government adopted the famous slogan: 'tough on crime, tough on the causes of crime'. One outcome of this policy was the massive increase in the UK prison population across the UK. In England and Wales it increased from 84,887 in 1997 to 96,000 by 2010. The paradox was that, according to the official crime figures, crime was falling, yet the prison population was increasing.

When the Conservatives came to power in 2010 and formed a Coalition Government with the Liberal Democrats, they dismayed many of their supporters by stating that prisons were not the only solution to crime and that greater emphasis should be placed on alternatives to prison. Faced with massive cuts to the welfare budget because of the banking crisis of 2008, the era of building more and more prisons had ended. The prison budget faced significant cuts.

In Scotland, the SNP Government had already stated that prisons were not the solution to crime for many short-term prisoners and that alternatives should be explored. Many in the judiciary supported such a response. In January 2014 Lord Carloway, one of Scotland's most senior judges, argued that the penal system should concentrate more on rehabilitation and less on retribution and this would be in the interest of society. A focus on individuals and programmes to modify their behaviour would be more effective than short custodial sentences. However, Conservative MSP John Lamont criticised the judge for his soft approach. He argued that the public 'would rather the interests of victims were prioritised over the rights of convicts'. (See pages 145–8 for alternative to prisons and rehabilitation models.)

Figure 10.5 Lord Carloway

'What ought to be considered is a move away from this type of approach designed to stigmatise the offender to a model in which the sentences are far more tailored to the individual offender and more inclusive in taking account of the needs of the community.' (*Lord Carloway, the Lord Justice Clerk*)

Show your understanding

1 Outline the four functions of the penal system.
2 Why is there conflict between the view that punishment, not rehabilitation, should be the main purpose of the UK penal system?
3 Why does overcrowding in prisons make rehabilitation more difficult?
4 Create a profile of a Scottish prisoner and say to what extent it can be explained as a result of social exclusion.
5 To what extent do the political parties and the judiciary favour alternatives to prison for short-term offenders?

Female prisoners

The UK prison system caters for over 90,000 prisoners, with only about 4600 females. However, the percentage of women prisoners has almost doubled since 2000. In 2000 the average daily female prison population in Scotland was 210, but by 2012 this had risen to 416. The average length of custodial sentences in the same period had gone up from 228 days to 273 days.

The vast majority of women are in prison for non-violent offences and are not a danger to the public. However, violent crime by women has soared since the early 2000s, fuelled by the hard-drinking 'ladette' culture.

Fact file

Scottish female prison statistics in 2014

- The number of female prisoners has risen from 3.5 per cent of the prison population in the 1980s to 5.7 per cent in 2014.
- 80 per cent of women in HMP Cornton Vale have mental health issues.
- Women are ten times more likely to self-harm in prison than men.
- 71 per cent of women in HMP Corton Vale have used drugs before being sent to prison.
- Two-thirds of women in prison have children, but only 39 per cent of female prisoners in Scotland receive visits from them.
- 71 per cent of women in prison have no qualifications compared to 15 per cent of the general population.
- Since 2008, 32 babies have been born while their mother was in HMP Cornton Vale.
- Some 16,500 children each year in Scotland are directly affected by parental imprisonment. Fifty per cent of looked-after children go on to receive custodial sentences.

The Commission on Women Offenders, chaired by the Right Hon Dame Elish Angiolini, operated independently of the Scottish Government. Its report, published in 2012, looked into the treatment of women prisoners. It called for courts to consider alternatives to remand – the number of women in prison on remand in Scotland has doubled since 2000 – and for fewer women to be sent to prison. Its report found that only 30 per cent of those sent to HMP Cornton Vale on remand received a custodial sentence. The Commission also discovered that there was an 80 per cent reoffending rate for prisoners sentenced to six months or less, and 75 per cent of women receive such short terms. The Commission's recommendations were accepted by the Scottish Government.

Let us have sex equality in our policy on prisons

Okay, someone has to say it. If Cornton Vale prison for women offenders is going to be torn down, as advised by the widely-praised Angiolini Report, how can all the others remain open? If it is wrong to lock up women for relatively trivial offences, aren't we going to have to apply the same reasoning to male offenders? The argument in the report is that most women prisoners have mental health problems, chaotic lifestyles, low self-esteem and a history of addiction. But doesn't that apply to the vast majority of all prisoners? According to the Scottish Association for Mental Health, 90 per cent of male prisoners have mental health problems too. There's a lot more of them too, since women are only 6 per cent of the prison population.

True, the number of women prisoners has doubled in a decade and it makes little sense for most of them to be there. But this is because imprisoning people has become a national obsession. Britain locks up more prisoners than any country in Europe. Scottish jails are bursting at the seams, even as crime falls, largely because voters are so keen on putting people in jail.

The tragedy is the number of young men in prison on remand or for non-payment of fines who become ensnared in a criminal subculture from which they never escape. This really has very little to do with gender and a lot to do with the psychology of incarceration. Which is why I'm troubled by some of the implications of the Angiolini Report. Can you say prison is the right punishment for men but the wrong one for women? Does that not write gender inequality into the very criminal justice system? Can you really apply one law for men and another for women?

There is an unspoken assumption that criminal behaviour is more excusable among women because they have been oppressed by men and, being carers, are not inherently bad persons. It is argued that the prison experience is worse for females. 'For many women in Cornton Vale there's a complete lack of hope for the future,' said the former Lord Advocate yesterday. 'They've lost their children, they've lost their council house because they've been in prison for more than a month, they're isolated and their problems are not tackled.' Again, I can't see that the prison experience is much less damaging for men, the vast majority of whom lose hope, lose their homes and families and end up reoffending or becoming alcoholic.

Source: By Iain Macwhirter, adapted from the Herald, *19 April 2012*

Extracts from the Commission on Women Offenders report

1 The female prison population in Scotland has doubled in the past ten years. Many women in the criminal justice system are frequent reoffenders with complex needs that relate to their social circumstances, previous histories of abuse, and mental health and addiction problems.

2 Short-term prison sentences have little or no impact on reoffending, with 70 per cent of women offenders who received a prison sentence of three months or less reconvicted of an offence within two years. Prison is more expensive than community disposals. The average cost of a community payback order is around £2400, which is approximately half the cost of a three-month prison sentence.

3 Women are more likely than men to:
   a) be of lower risk to public safety and be in prison for dishonesty offences
   b) be remanded in custody
   c) have higher rates of mental health and drugs problems
   d) have histories of physical and sexual abuse, and victimisation
   e) have dependent children.

4 HMP Cornton Vale is not fit for purpose. Overcrowding has caused significant problems for the management and staff, and has inhibited opportunities to rehabilitate women and reduce their reoffending on release. The mental health needs of women are not being addressed adequately. There are high levels of self-harm and there is lack of constructive and meaningful activity.

Alternatives to prosecution

1 Fiscal Work Orders (unpaid work orders of between 10 and 50 hours – 'fine on time') are rolled out across Scotland for offenders as an alternative to prosecution.

2 New powers are given to the police to divert female offenders from prosecution by issuing a conditional caution, directing women offenders to attend community justice centres so that appropriate services can be delivered.

Alternatives to remand

1 The Scottish Government examines further the potential of using electronic monitoring as a condition of bail.

2 *Prison.*
   HMP Cornton Vale is replaced with a smaller specialist prison for those female offenders serving a statutory defined long-term sentence and those who present a significant risk to the public.

3 The new national prison for women offenders should include:
   a) meaningful and consistent work to take place and enable all women prisoners to build skills for release and improve self-esteem and mental health
   b) a separate unit for young women
   c) a medical centre and purpose-built mother and baby unit
   d) a family-friendly visitor centre with an outside play area for children.

Community reintegration

Community reintegration support is available for all female offenders, during and after their custodial sentence. Offenders are met at the gate on release from prison by their key worker or appointed mentor.

Figure 10.6 **The number of female prisoners in the UK has doubled in the last 12 years**

ICT task

Read the full report by the Commission on Women Offenders at **www.scotland. gov.uk/Resource/0039/00391828.pdf** and Iain Macwhirter's full article at **www.heraldscotland.com/comment/ columnists/let-us-have-sex-equality-in- our-policy-on-prisons.17349655**.

Research activities

Investigate the issue of female prisoners and organise a debate on the motion: 'Women prisoners should be treated differently from male prisoners.'

Alternatives to prison

The minority SNP Government of 2007–11 was convinced that short-term prison sentences were ineffective. They did not achieve rehabilitation but were part of the 'revolving door' of crime. Alternative measures would reduce the pressures on prisons, free up the courts to deal with more serious crime while still punishing criminals and providing swifter justice for victims. Home Detention Curfews, community payback orders and disposal orders are used as alternatives to prison sentences.

The number of crimes dealt with out of court rose by 20 per cent between 2006 and 2011. Although monetary penalties are used as a popular alternative to prisons, their overall use has been in decline over recent years. In the 1980s, over 80 per cent of court sentences imposed in Scotland were fines; by 2011, this figure had fallen to 55 per cent. In contrast, community payback orders (probation, community service and other orders) have increased in the same period from 3 per cent to 15 per cent.

Home Detention Curfews

Electronic monitoring or tagging has been used to enforce Home Detention Curfews (HDCs) since their introduction in 2006. This alternative to prison was originally used for low-risk prisoners serving less than four years, although, controversially, since 2008 it is now available for longer-term prisoners. Offenders are still counted as part of the prison population, as shown in Table 10.1. This method is seen as an opportunity to reduce prison overcrowding and prison costs. Sending someone to prison for a year costs at least £30,000, whereas tagging an offender costs about £2000.

The fact that the service is run by the private sector has been criticised. Serco, the private company that runs the service in England and Wales, overcharged the UK Government by tens of millions of pounds and even billed for tags that were not used. In Scotland, the security service is provided by G4S – the company that failed to provide sufficient security at the 2012 London Olympics. The contract in Scotland is worth £13 million over five years.

Electronic tagging

Electronic tagging is the use of an electronic device that is attached to the criminal's ankle, allowing their whereabouts to be monitored. The device locates itself using a global positioning system (GPS) and reports its position back to a control centre. The current ankle device used in Scotland and the rest of the UK consists of a black band with a grey 'heart'. Each ankle device has a serial number and a telephone number imprinted on it. A box in the person's house alerts the private companies that monitor the scheme, currently G4S and Serco, if the offender goes outside.

Her Majesty's Inspectorate of Probation and probation union Napo reports

These two 2012 reports on the use of electronic tagging highlighted defects in its use. Here are some of their findings:

- The inspectors who examined 80 cases where tags had been fitted as part of community orders discovered that more than half broke the terms in some way, with just over 20 per cent committing minor violations and 37 per cent guilty of serious breaches. In 2012, a 15-year-old boy who stabbed an architect to death had been subject to a curfew order.

- Electronic tags often failed to work if offenders were in metal baths or simply lived in remote areas. In 2011 Christopher Lowcock tricked staff into fitting a tag on his false leg.
- In many cases, the security company was not informed about a new case until after 3 p.m., so the offender would spend his or her first night under curfew without being monitored. Sometimes the criminal was not at home when staff went to fit the tag or the company was given the wrong address.
- An offender under order to stay at home for 12 hours a day could go out for 11 hours and 59 minutes but still only receive a mild warning.

Sobriety bracelets and other forms of electronic tagging

Police Scotland is proposing that electronic monitoring should be considered for those convicted of a criminal act fuelled by alcohol. This technology is used in the USA and is referred to as 'sobriety bracelets' or 'tags' (Figure 10.7). The bracelet sets off alarms if alcohol is detected in the sweat of those who wear them. It is argued that giving a short custodial sentence to those with alcohol problems or guilty of binge-drinking is an expensive waste of time as the individual on release will turn back to their previous habits. The bracelet offers an incentive to the individual

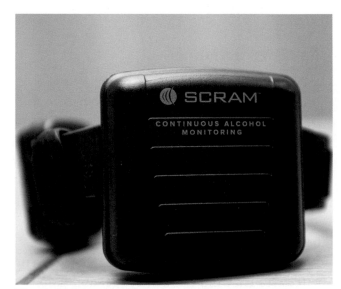

Figure 10.7 A sobriety tag

to give up alcohol and is a way to counter peer pressure, especially if the offender is young. Karyn McCluskey of the police's national Violence Reduction Unit believes that, with the support of social workers and others, this technology can work. She stated that 'Offenders can use it as a tool to justify abstinence to their peers.' Supporters also argue that sobriety bracelets could reduce domestic violence as the violent partner often commits the assault when drunk.

However, the Scottish Association of Social Workers (SASW) is concerned with civil liberty issues and wishes any such scheme to be voluntary. It stated that 'Imposition could be counter-productive and create additional breach offences – GPS with lower risk prisoners would be inappropriate, largely ineffective, cost prohibitive and ethically unjustifiable.'

GPS technology could also be used to monitor the movement of high risk offenders. This satellite monitoring would be able to track the movements of sex offenders, placing restriction orders on the individual's movements. It could also be used as evidence to convict if the high risk offender commits a crime.

Community payback orders

A court can order between 80 and 300 hours of supervised work, which must be completed within six months of the date of sentence. Offenders can carry out these community payback orders (CPOs) in their free time if they are in full- or part-time work. Offenders are also encouraged to tackle any addiction issues. In 2010 over 1700 UK offenders were placed on CPOs involving drug treatment. Some of the advantages and disadvantages of CPOs are given in Table 10.3.

Table 10.3 Advantages and disadvantages of community payback orders

Advantages	Disadvantages
Allow offenders to remain with family, possibly preventing the break-up of the family and children being put into care	CPOs have an image problem – the public and media perception is that they are a soft option that fails to punish the prisoner
Enable the offender to make restitution for their crime by improving the community	Problem of enforcement and monitoring of the offender. Lack of staff and transport can lead to limited action by offenders
Offender avoids the stigma of imprisonment and the possibility of falling into bad company and the criminal culture in prison	Failure of the offender to carry out or complete the order. It is time-consuming and costly for the offender to be taken before the courts for failure to comply with the CPO
Far less costly to implement than a short prison sentence	Only one-third of CPOs are completed

CPOs: What do offenders have to do?

- Carry out unpaid manual work in the community.
- Be subject to periods of supervision.
- Be subject to specific conduct requirements to address reoffending.
- Pay compensation to the victims.
- Participate in alcohol, drug or mental health treatments.
- Have their conduct and behaviour monitored by justice teams.
- Identify employability and training opportunities.

Fiscal disposal orders

The Scottish Court Service (SCS) and the police can issue fiscal disposal orders as an alternative to a court case, the two main types of which are fines and compensation. These combine elements of retribution (based on the seriousness of the crime), deterrence (showing the offender that crime does not pay) and reparation (paying the victim or society back for harm done). In recent years, the Scottish Government has encouraged the use of disposal orders to reduce the number of short-term prisoners and to provide part of the savings required as a result of a decrease in the block grant given by the UK Government to the Scottish Government. This extension of fiscal fines has been criticised as it allows criminals to evade court for offences such as assault and vandalism. Table 10.4 outlines a number of arguments in favour of and against fiscal disposal orders.

In April 2013 Scottish courts were given new powers to crack down on fine dodgers. Fine enforcement officers now have access to information held by the Department for Work and Pensions (DWP) and other UK Government databases. Cliff Binning of the Scottish Court Service (SCS) stated: 'Having access to this information will help us to speed up the process of fine collection and make it more efficient. As an example, we will be able to track a defaulter who moves from benefit into work through DWP information, and accessing DVLA [Driver and Vehicle Licensing Agency] records will let us clamp cars belonging to fine defaulters to secure quick payment.'

Non-payment is a serious flaw in the system and undermines public confidence in the use of fines. Many offenders escape punishment at least in the short term, which reduces the effectiveness of fines as a deterrent and as an instrument to reduce crime. This view is supported by the Scottish Conservative Party. The late David McLetchie stated in August 2012 that 'Fiscal fines are supposed to be an alternative to prosecution, but when they are simply ignored by so many, the public will conclude that they are not much of an alternative.'

Table 10.4 **Advantages and disadvantages of fiscal disposal orders**

Advantages	Disadvantages
Can be flexible with weekly payments and based on the offender's ability to pay	Many people are unable or unwilling to pay fines and are then sent to prison
Prevent the offender having a criminal record, which could damage their future employment prospects	In 2013 the outstanding backlog of fines not paid was £18.5 million
Provide swifter justice for the victims of crime	They favour the well-off who can afford the fine
Offender avoids falling into bad company and the criminal culture in prison	Victims might feel let down that the offender has simply received 'a slap on the wrist'

Fact file

Financial penalties

- A record 72,840 Crown Office disposal orders were processed in 2012–13, compared to 38,419 in 2008–09. The vast majority (47,819) were covered by a fine.
- In 2012–13, non-court disposals included 12,000 drug offences and 1300 common assaults.
- In 2012–13, the police issued over 68,000 fixed penalties, of which 80 per cent were anti-social behaviour orders (ASBOs).
- On average, 619 warning letters for late non-payment of fines were issued every working day in 2013.
- £18.5 million in outstanding penalties have been accrued between 2010 and 2013. This means that a high number of offenders have avoided any punishment for their crime.

Show your understanding

1 Why is the SNP Government in favour of alternatives to prison?
2 Outline the advantages and disadvantages of the following alternatives to prison:
   a) home detention curfews (HDCs)
   b) community payback orders (CPOs)
   c) fiscal disposal orders.

Case study: Rehabilitation initiatives

The Open Gates project in Glasgow provides the opportunity for prisoners serving life sentences (for murder) to be involved in year-long work placements to prepare them for returning to the community and hopefully the world of work. Pat Clark, founder of Open Gates, states: 'Ultimately I want to do the prison officers out of a job by persuading folks not to reoffend. I know how difficult it is to break the cycle of reoffending but I know it can be done.'

HMP Barlinnie runs a National Top End facility for life prisoners approaching the end of their sentence in which the prisoners work voluntarily for projects such as Open Gates. These schemes include the restoration of a former bakery in Maryhill, Glasgow, or furniture restoration as a transition to the outside world. Prisoners are carefully vetted. Owen Currie, the National Top End manager for Barlinnie, stated: 'Before they go out on placement they go through a two-year risk assessment. At some point the parole board will release them. It's much better that we gradually reintroduce them into society than throwing them in at the deep end. Some have been in for 20 years.' It was announced in March 2014 that the Victorian Barlinnie prison would be replaced with a large new jail. The present prison was designed to home 1000 prisoners, with figures in March 2014 reaching 1347.

Research activity

Are alternatives to prisons such as HDCs and CPOs more effective than prison sentences? Working in pairs, investigate this issue and present your findings to the class.

Youth offenders

Scotland is rightly praised for its Children's Hearings System (see page 95) and its supporters argue that the drop in youth crime can be in part attributed to the holistic and humane approach of this system. The Children's Hearings System works in partnership with the police and justice system. The Police Restorative Warnings to children between 8 and 15 act as an early formal recorded intervention to reduce the likelihood of reoffending among youth offenders. Police involved in this scheme are specially trained in restorative warning methods.

A significant development was the SNP Government's decision to raise the age of criminal prosecution. However, the Criminal Justice and Licensing (Scotland) Act 2010, which raised the age of criminal prosecution from 8 to 12, left the age of criminal responsibility at 8. This means that children who commit a crime can still have a criminal record but will not be prosecuted. Some 40 children aged between 8 and 11 have received criminal records since 2011.

Through government funding North Lanarkshire council has used youth courts to reduce youth crime. Central funding enables specialist social workers to be allocated to vulnerable young people and to liaise with the justice system. However, with the UK Government reducing the block grant allocation to the Scottish Government, this funding will end in 2016.

Case study: Youth crime in Glasgow and Edinburgh

Youth crime in Glasgow and Edinburgh has fallen to a ten-year low, reflecting the national drop in youth crime. The Glasgow figures published in late 2013 show that serious violent offending by under-18s in the city nearly halved in 2012–13. In Edinburgh, 216 young people were referred for an offence in 2012–13, down from 299 the previous year and 921 in 2005–06.

The strategy in Glasgow, according to Sean McKendrick, the senior social worker who chairs Glasgow's Youth Justice Strategy Group, is: 'Our evidence-based approach enables us to divert young people involved in low level offending while targeting our resources at those vulnerable young people and families who need them most.' Third sector organisations such as Urban Fox and Aberlour carry out excellent youth work.

The number of 'storm calls' – when people contact the police to complain about youth behaviour – has fallen significantly. In 2007 the figure was 60,500; by 2013 the figure had fallen to 15,600.

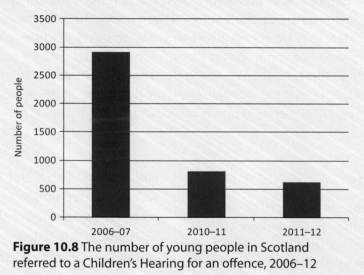

Figure 10.8 The number of young people in Scotland referred to a Children's Hearing for an offence, 2006–12

Show your understanding

1 Read the case study on rehabilitation initiatives. What category of prisoner is involved in these projects and what are the projects' goals?
2 Working in pairs, decide whether you support the raising of the age of criminal prosecution from 8 to 12, and the retention of 8 years old as the age of criminal responsibility. Give reasons.
3 Outline the evidence that supports the view that youth crime is falling.

Interview with Kenny MacAskill, Cabinet Secretary for Justice

Figure 10.9 Kenny MacAskill

In your role as Cabinet Secretary for Justice, what are the main challenges of your job?

As Cabinet Secretary for Justice, my vision is of a justice system that contributes positively to a flourishing Scotland, helping to create an inclusive and respectful society, in which all people and communities live in safety and security, where individual and collective rights are supported, and where disputes are resolved fairly and swiftly. One of the main challenges of my job is to make our vision a reality. We know that this requires all those involved in the justice system to work together effectively.

Fighting crime and making our neighbourhoods safer is an ongoing challenge. If we look at the challenge of protecting young people from crime, either as victims or offenders, we recognise that partnership working is critical to achieving success. The Scottish Government's Whole System Approach to Youth Justice is focused on providing early help and support for those young people most at risk of offending or of graduating to more serious offending. The whole system approach aims to achieve positive outcomes for some of our most vulnerable young people, helping them to fulfil their potential and become valuable contributors to their communities.

By working together to build more consistent approaches to prevent and reduce offending by children and young people, we can support those who offend with early and effective interventions and provide robust solutions for those who present the greatest risk.

We are on the right track, but we must always look at new and innovative approaches – to meet the ongoing challenge of ensuring that people lead productive lives in safe and secure communities, the Scottish Government will continue to work closely with many partners. Together we continue to demonstrate how much can be achieved when decisions about Scotland are taken within Scotland by people committed to delivering the best outcomes for Scotland.

In what way does poverty impact on crime?

Persistent inequalities in society have a crucial bearing on the justice system. We know that inequality leads to a range of negative social outcomes. And evidence has shown that economic inequality is a key driver of crime. This is particularly the case for crimes like theft and burglary, but it's also been linked to violent crimes. The much-cited *Spirit Level* book on inequality by Wilkinson and Pickett (2009) argues that, internationally, greater inequality is associated with higher levels of drug problems, homicides and imprisonment.

Evidence at individual level suggests that inequality can predict offending, and particularly by young people. And custodial rates are highest in our most deprived communities: in the most deprived areas of Scotland, the number of adults in prison is five times higher than in the rest of Scotland.

There are also important links between deprivation and the risk of victimisation from crime. The Scottish Crime and Justice Survey shows that there is a higher risk of being victims of property crime and violent crime for people living in the most deprived communities compared to the rest of Scotland.

⇨

We must always be looking at new and innovative ways of reducing crime in all areas across Scotland. The Building Safer Communities Programme seeks to significantly reduce the number of victims of crime in Scotland by supporting local action that builds on the strengths, skills and resilience of communities across the country. Working closely with communities, Police Scotland and other partners, the programme is helping local areas, particularly those suffering from inequality, to test and develop innovative ways to reduce crime, and share the best practices across Scotland.

Since 2007, in what ways has the Scottish Government attempted to tackle the causes of crime?

Scotland's citizens and communities have the right to live in safety and security and we must ensure our justice system contributes to that right. The best way to achieve that is through appropriate and proportionate penalties and a commitment to prevention. We always need to look at new ways of tackling serious crime. For example, the opening of a dedicated Crime Campus at Gartcosh provides new facilities to allow agencies to work in a joined-up way never seen before in Britain; since 2007, we have developed a multi-agency approach to map and tackle serious organised crime; we are tackling violent crime through a new assets-based approach; and our No Knives, Better Lives initiative has contributed to widespread reductions in knife crime. Maintaining public assurance is also key and our continued commitment to 1000 more police officers will maintain a highly visible, highly accessible police presence in our communities that is engaged with the public on the street.

Policing in Scotland is more local than ever before. There are designated Local Commanders and a police plan for each of our 32 local authorities and, for the first time, a local policing plan for all 353 council wards. Each plan has been developed following consultation with local communities and local partners and more councillors than ever before have the opportunity to have their say on policing in their area.

A key element of our preventative approach to youth justice is to provide young people with access to positive opportunities and facilities within their communities. Since 2008, we have invested or committed over £74 million across Scotland which has provided 1.25 million activities and opportunities for young people.

I believe in a justice system that provides proportionate punishment for those who offend; that keeps serious and dangerous criminals in custody; that provides appropriate support for those seeking to end their offending; and that strengthens society rather than storing up problems for the future. Our focus is on reducing crime across Scotland and recent statistics show us that we are moving in the right direction. However, there is no room for complacency and we will continue to encourage justice agencies to work together to create a Safer and Stronger Scotland for all our communities.

Is too much attention now given to the needs of women prisoners?

When I established the Commission on Women Offenders in 2011, the treatment of women prisoners and the rising prison population was a core part of their investigations. The Commission's report provides a stark reminder of the problems many women prisoners face, and why it is important to pay particular attention to their needs. The report points out that female prisoners have significantly higher rates of poor mental health than the general population; and they are more likely to suffer trauma, including physical and sexual abuse, during their life. 71 per cent of women prisoners reported using drugs in the 12 months before they were imprisoned. 71 per cent have no education qualifications. Only a third of women were imprisoned for violent offences, and three-quarters were serving sentences of six months or less.

I am clear that where a robust community sentence is appropriate, it offers the best opportunity for a woman to pay back to society for her offending, and to have a chance to change her life for the better. But when the courts decide that a custodial sentence is the appropriate punishment, it is right that our prison system is well placed to recognise and respond to the particular needs and problems many women offenders face. This will not only provide the same care and support that we would give to any individual, but also give women prisoners the best chance to rehabilitate themselves, and not to offend again. When that succeeds, it doesn't just help the individual – it also helps to make our families stronger and communities safer in the future.

I was pleased to support the ambitious plans that the Scottish Prison Service has recently put in place for women prisoners in the future. The new female prison in Inverclyde will make rehabilitation and well-being a core part of the prisoners' environment, without compromising on appropriate security or purposeful activity. Having modern prison facilities for women in HMP Edinburgh and HMP Aberdeen will also enable many prisoners to remain closer to their children and families. While these new plans are put in place, SPS [Scottish Prison Service] will continue to improve the facilities at HMP Cornton Vale, and continue to develop specific training and policies in relation to women prisoners.

What are the main purposes of prison?

The Scottish Government is clear that prison remains the right place for serious and dangerous offenders. We have invested considerably in the prison estate and this includes the redevelopment of a number of existing prisons and the building of two new prisons, HMP Low Moss and HMP & YOI Grampian. Through our response to the Commission on Women Offenders we are working to improve outcomes for women offenders at every stage of the criminal justice system. We have a programme of measures in place designed to reduce reoffending and are confident that these measures will be successful in further reducing the reconviction rate (currently at its lowest level in 14 years) and in reducing the demand on prison places. As part of prudent planning the Scottish Government regularly discusses with the Scottish Prison Service their plans for managing prison numbers.

Do you feel community sentencing is more effective than short-term prison sentencing?

The evidence shows that short prison sentences do not work to rehabilitate offenders or to reduce the risk of reoffending. As an alternative to short prison sentences, in 2011 we introduced the community payback order (CPO) to provide a robust and credible alternative to custody. The CPO is our main community penalty and replaced probation orders, community service orders and supervised attendance orders. The CPO is designed to make offenders payback to the community and address the underlying causes of their offending behaviour. Early signs suggest that the CPO is working, with courts in Scotland using the Order to impose community sentences which are more demanding, commence more quickly and have better completion rates.

In 2011 we also introduced a presumption against custodial sentences of three months or less. The presumption provides that a court must not pass a custodial sentence for a term of three months or less unless it considers that no other method of dealing with the offender is appropriate. The presumption is not however a blanket ban, and in any given case the court retains discretion to impose sentences of three months or less.

What action is the Government taking to convince the public that alternatives to prison are appropriate forms of punishment (not soft options)?

We believe reoffending can fall further still, and Phase 2 of our Reducing Reoffending Programme is focused on ensuring that offenders serving sentences in the community, or in short-term custody, build on the support, use the services and make the most of opportunities provided to them so they can move away from offending. Phase 2 includes a consultation on community justice structures, with the aim of ensuring that in the future there will be a more strategic and clearly accountable approach to the commissioning of services intended to reduce reoffending. To supplement this work, the Reducing Reoffending Change Fund will work over three years to support ex-offenders after release, providing practical mentoring services to help them to get their lives back on track and not reoffend. The Programme also includes a project which aims to maximise the use of CPOs as an instrument of rehabilitation and to increase public understanding of the CPO and its use as a robust and effective alternative to prison.

Show your understanding

Read the interview with Kenny MacAskill, Cabinet Secretary for Justice, and answer the following questions.

1 Identify two main challenges facing the Cabinet Secretary for Justice.
2 What evidence does Mr MacAskill provide to support the link between poverty and crime?
3 Identify three courses of action that the Government has taken to tackle the causes of crime.
4 What action has the Government taken to address the needs of women?
5 What action has the Government taken to ensure that community sentencing is effective?

Assessment

Welcome to the new Curriculum for Excellence (CfE) Higher Modern Studies!

The Higher award is made up of internally and externally graded assessments. To achieve the award you need to pass the internal assessment for each of the following units:

- Democracy in Scotland and the United Kingdom
- Social Issues in the United Kingdom
- International Issues.

The Added Value unit for CfE Higher Modern Studies is an externally-assessed course assessment. This consists of two components:

- question paper
- assignment.

To gain the course award, all units and course assessment must be passed. The marks awarded for the question paper and the assignment are added together and an overall mark indicates pass or fail. The course award is graded A to D.

The question paper

The question paper is worth a total of 60 marks, with 20 marks for each unit of the course. Essay questions are allocated 44 marks in total and source-based questions 16 marks in total. The duration of the exam is 2 hours and 15 minutes.

Essay questions/extended response

Essay questions are allocated either 12 or 20 marks. Examples of the style of question are given below.

> **Evaluate** the effectiveness of parliamentary representatives in holding the government to account. (**12 marks**)
>
> **Analyse** the different lifestyle choices that may result in poor health. (**12 marks**)
>
> **To what extent** does a world power you have studied have influence in international relations? (**20 marks**)
>
> International organisations have been successful in resolving a significant world issue. **Discuss** with reference to a world issue you have studied. (**20 marks**)

Source-based questions

These questions are allocated 8 marks each and appear in any two of the three sections of the exam. There will be no choice of source-based questions – for example, in the specimen paper, the source-based question in the Social Issues in the UK unit is on social exclusion, and as such there is no Crime and the Law source-based question.

There are two types of source-based questions:

- one that asks 'to what extent' something is accurate or true, and
- one that asks you to 'draw conclusions' about a topic.

Both of these questions require you to draw on data that is provided in the form of sources, extracting information that is relevant to the question being asked, and to justify your answer using evidence from these sources.

For an example of some source-based questions, have a look at SQA's Specimen Question Paper on the (CfE) Higher Modern Studies page of their website: http://www.sqa.org.uk/sqa/47924.html.

The assignment

The assignment is worth 30 marks out of a total of 90 marks for the course, and contributes 33 per cent of the total marks for the course. The assignment task is to research a Modern Studies issue with alternative views. You will use your two one-sided A4 sheets (Modern Studies research evidence) to support you in presenting the findings of your research. The duration of the write-up is 1 hour and 30 minutes.

The assignment applies research and decision-making skills in the context of a Modern Studies issue. You can choose a political, social or international issue. The information collected

should display knowledge and understanding of the topic or issue chosen. SQA recommends that you should devote about 8 hours for the research stage, including preparation time for the production of evidence.

The results of the research will be written up under controlled assessment conditions and must be completed within 1 hour and 30 minutes. Your Modern Studies research evidence recorded on up to two single-sided sheets of A4 will consist of materials collected during the research stage of the assignment. The allocation of marks is based on the following success criteria.

1 Identifying and demonstrating knowledge and understanding of the issue about which a decision is to be made, including alternative courses of action

You should choose a decision about which there are alternative views, for example:

To recommend or reject the introduction of free prescriptions in England

or

To recommend or reject the abolition of the not-proven verdict in Scottish courts

You should agree an issue to research with your teacher. It has to relate to one or more of the issues that you have studied in your course:

- Democracy in Scotland and the United Kingdom
- Social Issues in the United Kingdom
- International Issues.

2 Analysing and synthesising information from a range of sources including use of specified resources

You will research a wide range of sources to widen your knowledge and understanding of the issue and to provide contrasting views on your chosen issue. By linking information from a variety of sources and viewpoints, you will be able to enrich and synthesise the arguments that are developed in your report. Remember it is important to provide balance in your report and to consider the arguments against your final decision/recommendation.

3 Evaluating the usefulness and reliability of a range of sources of information

You will comment on the background and nature of the source. Does it provide only one point of view, are its findings up to date and are its comments still relevant today? For example, in deciding whether to recommend free prescriptions in England, you might refer to the website of a pressure group such as **www.prescriptionchargescoalition.org.uk** in favour of free prescriptions and comment on its usefulness and reliability (see pages 159–60).

4 Communicating information using the conventions of a report

Remember you are *not* writing an essay. Your report style should include:

- a title
- a formal style that refers to evidence rather than personal opinion
- section headings breaking up the information to present evidence and contrasting arguments in a clear and logical structure
- references to the evidence you have used, especially the research evidence referred to in your A4 sheets
- a statement of the decision you have reached based on the evidence provided.

5 Reaching a decision, supported by evidence, about the issue

Your decision should be based on your research evidence and your own background knowledge of the issue.

Possible Social Issues titles for your assignment

- Should free prescriptions be available to all UK citizens?
- Should the UK 'bedroom tax' be abolished?
- Should the winter fuel allowance for the elderly be means-tested?
- Should the 'not-proven' verdict be abolished?
- Should all Scottish police officers be issued with Tasers?
- Should all Scottish prisoners have the right to vote?

Research methods

In Modern Studies we look at a range of political, social and international issues that affect everyone's lives. Many of these issues are based on evidence gathered by research carried out by a whole series of people and organisations – from the government to charities.

Figure 11.1 **Gathering evidence by research**

How do I carry out a piece of research?

When researching a topic in Modern Studies, it is important to consider where you will get your information from. In the twenty-first century, you have access to huge amounts of information at your fingertips on the internet. However, you need to be conscious of its accuracy and its likelihood of containing bias and exaggeration.

Where do I gather information from?

The information gathered from research can be broken down into two parts – primary information and secondary information – and both provide qualitative and quantitative information.

Primary information

Primary information is evidence that you have gathered by yourself and is unique to your personal research. The ways in which you gather primary evidence can vary greatly. Here are some examples:

- surveys/questionnaires
- interviews
- emails
- letters
- focus groups
- field studies.

Secondary information

Secondary information is evidence that you have gathered from research carried out by others.

You should use it to help support your personal (primary) research. There are vast amounts of secondary information available. Here are some examples:

- newspapers, magazines and books
- official statistics
- internet search engines and websites
- television and radio programmes
- mobile phone apps
- social media such as Twitter
- library research.

Qualitative and quantitative research

Qualitative research is more focused on how people feel, what their thoughts are and why they make certain choices or decisions. Focus group meetings or one-to-one interviews are typical forms of qualitative research. On the other hand, quantitative research largely uses methods such as questionnaires and surveys with set questions and tick-box answers. It can collate a large amount of data that can be analysed easily and conclusions formulated. Table 11.1 compares both types of research.

If you accessed the Prescription Charges Coalition's website at **www.prescriptionchargescoalition.org. uk** in a decision-making exercise on free prescriptions in England, it would have provided both qualitative and quantitative research evidence, as shown in the extract on pages 159–60 from its 2013 report *Paying the Price: Prescription Charges and People with Long-term Conditions.*

Table 11.1 **Qualitative and quantitative research**

	Qualitative research	**Quantitative research**
Objective/ purpose	To gain an understanding of underlying reasons and motivations To provide insights into the setting of a problem, generating ideas and/or a hypothesis for later quantitative research To cover prevalent trends in thought and opinion	To quantify data and generalise results from a sample to the population of interest To measure the incidence of various views and opinions in a chosen sample Sometimes followed by qualitative research which is used to explore some findings further
Sample	Usually a small number of non-representative cases. Respondents selected to fulfil a given quota	Usually a large number of cases representing the population of interest. Randomly selected respondents
Data collection	Unstructured or semi-structured techniques, e.g. individual depth interviews or group discussions	Structured techniques such as online questionnaires, on-street or telephone interviews
Data analysis	Non-statistical	Statistical data is usually in the form of tabulations (tabs). Findings are conclusive and usually descriptive in nature
Outcome	Exploratory and/or investigative. Findings are not conclusive and cannot be used to make generalisations about the population of interest. Develop an understanding and sound base for further decision-making	Used to recommend a final course of action

Source: www.snapsurveys.com/qualitative-quantitative-research

Executive summary

The Prescription Charges Coalition brings together more than 20 organisations concerned with the detrimental impact that prescription charges are having on people in England with long-term conditions. The findings of our survey of over 3700 people with long-term conditions illustrate the effect that charges for medicines have on health outcomes and quality of life and the knock-on impact on society as a whole in terms of employment, welfare and additional costs to the NHS.

Key findings

- 73 per cent of our total survey respondents are paying for their prescriptions.
- 64 per cent of respondents require more than 13 prescription items a year.
- 35 per cent of respondents who pay for each prescription have not collected at least one item due to the cost, with three-quarters of this group reporting that their health got worse as a result. 10 per cent said that they ended up in hospital as a direct consequence of not taking their medication.

⇨

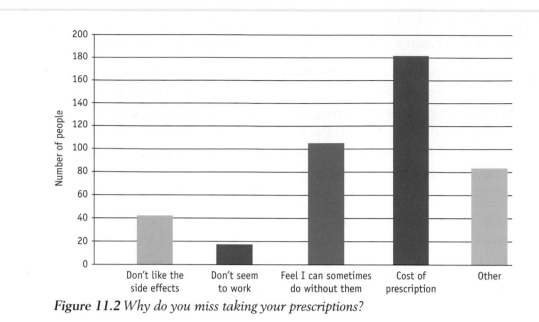

Figure 11.2 Why do you miss taking your prescriptions?

- 29 per cent of respondents who paid for their prescriptions and did not have a Prescription Prepayment Certificate (PPC) reported not taking their medicine as prescribed either occasionally or often. Over half of these gave the cost of the prescription as the main reason for not taking their medicine as prescribed.
- 30 per cent of our survey respondents who did not have a Prescription Prepayment Certificate felt it was unaffordable.

Methodology

The survey ran online for 12 weeks from 8 August to 31 October. It was advertised through the websites, Facebook pages and newsletters of organisations representing people with long-term conditions. As respondents were self-selecting, it is not a representative sample. However, there was a normal distribution across all age groups and a wide range of long-term conditions were represented. 3748 individuals responded to the survey. Of these, 1316 were discounted as they did not live in England, did not have a long-term condition or were exempt from paying charges. This left a sample size of 2432 respondents who provided both quantitative and qualitative responses to the questions.

Results

Although there is a perception that most people do not pay for their prescriptions, 73 per cent of our total survey respondents do in fact pay for their prescriptions, with only 27 per cent exempt.

People with long-term conditions often rely on medication to manage their condition and some have multiple conditions and therefore require a number of medicines on a regular and ongoing basis. Some have fluctuating conditions and may require more medicines at some periods than others, which provides a different set of challenges for them.

Our survey showed that people with long-term conditions generally required prescriptions monthly or more frequently and spent over £100 a year on prescribed medicines.

Qualitative responses illustrate that people who could benefit from a PPC may not find out about this for some time after they have been diagnosed with a condition and incurred considerable expenditure.

- 'This month I cannot pay for a prepayment certificate – and I will not be able to get my medicines at all. I take 15 different tablets and inhalers.'

⇨

- 'I have spent over £200 in the past year due to constant changes in medication. Sometimes I try medication and the side effects are so bad I am advised to stop taking them and prescribed something else – two prescription charges and medication I cannot take [wasted].'
- 'I have to wait till I get paid till I can get my prescription so if I run out of my medication I have to do with out and I'm not supposed to stop taking it without first speaking to my dr. I don't work full time but have been told I earn too much to get help.'

Source: Adapted from Paying the Price: Prescription Charges and People with Long-term Conditions, *Prescription Charges Coalition,* *www.prescriptionchargescoalition.org.uk*

Activities

In pairs, discuss the following questions regarding the extract from the Prescription Charges Coalition's report.

a) What is the nature of the extract and how up to date is it?
b) How balanced and reliable is this information? Does it contain bias or exaggeration?
c) What useful information have we got from this source to help us research our decision-making tasks?